Generation
Ageless

Generation
Ageless

How Baby Boomers

Are Changing the Way

We Live Today . . .

And They're Just

Getting Started

J. Walker Smith and Ann Clurman

Collins
An Imprint of HarperCollinsPublishers

HarperCollins books may be purchased for educational, business, or sales promotional use. For information, please write: Special Markets Department, HarperCollins Publishers, 10 East 53rd Street, New York, NY 10022.

FIRST EDITION

Designed by Nicola Ferguson

Printed on acid-free paper

Library of Congress Cataloging-in-Publication Data

Smith, J. Walker.
    Generation ageless : how baby boomers are changing the way we live today—and they're just getting started / J. Walker Smith and Ann Clurman. — 1st ed.
        p.   cm.
    Includes bibliographical references and index.
    ISBN 978-0-06-112898-1
    1. Baby boom generation—United States.   2. Baby boom generation—United States—Attitudes.   3. Baby boom generation—Retirement—United States.   4. Baby boom generation—United States—Economic conditions.   I. Clurman, Ann.   II. Title.

    HN 59.2.S583 2007
    303.3' 86440973090511—dc22   2007022877

07   08   09   10   11   WBC/RRD   10   9   8   7   6   5   4   3   2   1

Dedications

For my parents,
among the finest of their generation,
with deepest love and thanks
from this Boomer for everything
—J. Walker Smith

For Ari,
whose remarkable insight and great humor
keep this Boomer on track
—Ann Clurman

Acknowledgments

From Walker and Ann:

This book owes much to many people.

First and foremost, our thanks to Mike Hail, who championed this book and stood by us steadfastly as we labored to finish. Mike, we appreciate your support and constancy more than we can say.

No thanks could do justice to the help and insights we get every day from David Bersoff and Holly Moore. You guys make us smarter and keep us honest.

Special thanks to Cristian Blumm, our Alaska-bound colleague, who dug up nearly all the last-minute statistics we needed, and to Amy Pleasant, whose first project at Yankelovich was background research for this book. Special thanks as well to Sarah Catlett, John Page, Chris Hloros, Pete Rose, Mary-Kay Harrity, and Sonya Suarez-Hammond, each of whom provided us with ideas, data, and help when we needed it most. Thanks to Bonnie Burke, who sorted through the data to pull the appendix together. Many thanks to Kathleen Grebe, who gave our charts a tremendous form and look.

The data analysis for this book owes everything to Sudipta Dasmohapatra, who counseled us on the best ways to make sense of it all, and to Mike Morgan, who helped us see how to approach this topic.

We are nurtured and inspired by the collegial, intellectual atmosphere at Yankelovich that is sustained by our senior partners—Kevin Brown, Steve Bodhaine, Mark Graham, Gayle Davey, Mary Ellen Cunningham, Hal Quinley, Jim Cain, Larry Eppard, Emily Ross, Tia Burns, Steve Lerner,

Scott Van Manen, Archie Purcell, John Struck, and Bruce Schnitzer. Thanks to Taffy Fitzmaurice, who keeps us well within our rights. We were helped out of several mid-project computer crises by George Kircher, Stewart Pearce, and Charlie Lambeth. We were saved from many other potential disruptions by Simon Kaplan and Vinny Abbruscato.

Thanks to everyone at our PR firm, Bliss, Gouverneur & Associates, for their continuing support and hard work, especially John Bliss, Samantha Long, Lisa Karel, and Rebecca Neufeld.

Thanks as well to everyone at HarperCollins. We were aided greatly by Ethan Friedman's expert editing and Angie Lee's marketing prowess.

Thanks to all of our wonderful clients for giving us the chance to tackle interesting and important assignments. We would be nowhere without you.

Last but not least, thanks to all of our other Yankelovich colleagues, past and present, who created and nurtured the legacy of thought and insight from which we have borrowed liberally in this book. We hope that our work does justice to all that we owe to you.

From Walker:

Joy, thank you for what's soon to be four decades of love and dedication. Fred was there with me through every part of this book, as you know, in body and in spirit, nuzzling tight and close, always at hand to help in his own gentle way. Like you, he is in every word.

Marjorie and Dorothy, sisters extraordinaire, thank you for always being there for me no matter what. Don and John, you guys keep us sane.

Jeff, Max, Steve (N.C.), Steve (S.C.), Jim, Cathy, Scott, Bobby, Bill, John, David, Harvey, Stratto, Bronco, thanks from one Boomer to another. You, too, Rob.

Bill Bishop, your ideas and perspective gave me a much-needed sounding board that made me smarter about many things. Carol Coletta, the opportunities you have kindly extended to me have made my thinking better. Brian Hankin, your friendship and goodwill have been of enormous help to me. Carolyn Neal, your unshakable confidence in me is something I prize. Sandra Kulli, your zeal, passion, and goodwill are infectious. Ken Bernhardt, your support and insights are always valuable and much appreciated. Greg Fuson, I appreciate the venues and opportunities to learn you have made available to me.

Roy Carlisle, I can't thank you enough for your generosity and friendship. I wish I could match your speed and resilience, but trying is exactly what I need.

My very special thanks to my longtime colleague Ann Clurman, my Boomer co-author for the third time and a true intellectual inspiration to me for more years than I dare say.

From Ann:

Love to Nancy, Denise, Delia, Babi, Kerry, Stephen, Raquel, and Neil—soulmates in different ways and each a treasure.

Billy, Michelle, Athena, and Renee—thanks for listening patiently when I need to spill.

Jen, you are simply the best.

Much love to Judy and Bruce.

Lynn and David—bless you both.

And Walker—thank you so much.

Contents

Introduction

Going the Distance

The tagline for the 2006 release of *Rocky Balboa*, the sixth installment in the Rocky movie franchise, says it all for Baby Boomers nowadays: "It ain't over 'til it's over."

The original *Rocky*, in 1976, made a mega-star of then thirty-year-old Baby Boomer Sylvester Stallone. Depicting a small-time boxer who gets by as a debt collector for a loan shark in Philadelphia, the movie follows Rocky Balboa as he trains for a long-shot, once-in-a-lifetime fight for the heavyweight title. But Rocky is realistic. All he wants is to go the distance, which, against all odds, he is able to do. Now, thirty years and four sequels later, the sixty-year-old Stallone plays an aging Rocky who comes out of retirement for an exhibition fight against the heavyweight champ.

In describing the moral of this film, Stallone was quoted in a *New York Times* article as saying that while many of his Boomer peers are now feeling pressure to "step aside for the next generation . . . [t]his film is about how we still have something to say."[1] This is the Boomer attitude in a nutshell. Boomers will fight to make sure they continue to matter and have their say. They intend to go the distance.

The notion that Boomers are going to keep at it no matter how old they get runs counter to our expectations of old people. Yet this is the reality for aging Boomers. They have no intention of giving up on life's possibilities. Boomers don't intend to age; they want to be ageless. It is this *continuing, emphatic engagement with life* that is the future of Boomers and the subject of this book.

Mattering

Without question, over the next ten to fifteen years Boomers will change the ways in which they live and work. But Boomers are not pondering their endgame; they're thinking about new possibilities. They want to keep going, not let go. In particular, they mean to have a pivotal influence on the way things unfold in the future, however old they are. This will require a new way of thinking about the aging U.S. population. Boomers are ready to reinvent themselves in order to continue to matter.

As Boomers look ahead, two things are uppermost in their minds: endurance and impact. To continue to have a say that matters, they must first continue to be around, and then they must make a difference. So, the future for aging Boomers is a matter of having both a presence and an influence. Or to put it in the way that best reflects the edge they give to it, it's a matter of *immortality and morality.*

These are not entirely new ideas to Boomers; this generation has long been concerned with both. But these two ideas are gaining salience and traction with Boomers as other concerns lose relevance and sway. This dual focus on immortality and morality will steer them as they plot their course to go the distance.

This book is about the impact and implications of immortality and morality for the future of aging Baby Boomers, and thus for the future of the American consumer marketplace and American society as a whole.

A New Self

Boomers may be aging, but they do not see themselves as getting old, no matter how many candles get crammed onto their birthday cakes with each advancing year. Of course, it's not as if Baby Boomers literally believe they can live forever, even though they act like it sometimes. Rather, they believe they will live longer and better than generations before them, so they intend to use this additional time to remake the world into a better place. To put it simply, Boomers are Generation Ageless.

To ready themselves for the future, aging Boomers are reconsidering and reinventing their sense of self. Despite the physical challenges and limitations of aging, they are rejecting a view of themselves as old people. Instead, they are planning for an old age in which they are no less active, involved, and important than they are today. Boomers want midlife to continue forevermore, or at least for many decades more. Aging Boomers want to be *middle age–less*.

The opportunities made possible by an ageless midlife will afford Baby Boomers the unique luxury of a second shot at changing the world for the better. Moral priorities are growing among them, with interests running the gamut from social causes to spiritual revivals to personal charity. Boomers have planted these flags before, of course, but now, with more time, more money, and with fewer distractions or diversions, they are planting them again with greater urgency. A sense of a righteous self is on the rise.

This dual focus on ageless endurance and the righteous self defines the generational character with which Baby Boomers will meet the future. Immortality and morality are the two things to know about this generation in the decades to come.

Starting Points

Talking about the character of an entire generation of people is, admittedly, somewhat abstract. After all, a group of people 78 million strong born from 1946 to 1964 includes many types of persons and personalities. Can there be a single character to such a diverse group? Well, yes. Take a look at Figure I-1.

Yankelovich, Inc. began studying consumer values and lifestyles in 1958 with the founding of our research firm by our renowned namesake, Daniel Yankelovich. Since that time, Yankelovich has made a continuous study of the attitudes that motivate people—Boomers especially—and the ways people make important decisions in their lives, buying decisions in particular.

Would you like a return to more traditional standards?	Boomers 1977	Xers 1997	Boomers 1997
Family life	56%	73%	76%
Parental responsibility	47%	70%	75%
Schools	40%	58%	62%
Social relationships	23%	41%	44%
Sexual relationships	20%	46%	46%
Work	19%	33%	41%
Homemaking	16%	35%	42%

Source: Yankelovich MONITOR

Figure I-1: Comparing Cohorts

Yankelovich research is one of the most comprehensive and detailed sources for understanding the evolution of lifestyle values and consumer motivations during the late twentieth century.

In the late 1970s, Yankelovich research showed that Baby Boomers were very unlikely to favor a return to traditional standards in almost every area surveyed. Only for "family life" did a slight majority of them prefer a return to traditional standards. Obviously, not all Boomers felt this way, but the character of the generation as a whole was pretty clear.

The baby-bust Generation X (GenX) that followed Baby Boomers, born from 1965 to 1978, had a different view. At roughly the same age that Boomers were when we interviewed them in the late 1970s—the oldest Boomers in 1977 were thirty-one; the oldest GenXers in 1997 were thirty-two—GenXers were more likely in every instance to favor a return to traditional standards.

GenX did not get started with the same mix of values as Baby Boomers. However, as also shown in Figure I-1, Baby Boomers and GenXers felt the same way in the late 1990s. But this doesn't mean that these two generations are the same. While they are in agreement as contemporaries, each generation got started in a unique way. This difference in *starting points* is the essence of what is meant by generational character.

There are many things about being a certain age, of course, that are the same irrespective of generation. These are the needs and necessities of life stage. But just as many things are the same, so, too, are many things not the same. These are the different generational experiences. Age is a combination of life stage and generation. Our focus at Yankelovich is on the generational component.

A generational cohort is a sociological concept referring to a group of people who grew up and came of age together. The theory is that shared experiences during formative years have a common and lasting effect on the values and lifestyle decisions of a group of people.[2] Generally speaking, this notion makes intuitive sense, but the specifics for any particular generation are always a bit more complicated.

Generations are groups of people, so naturally they show a diversity of attitudes and values. And attitudes change over time. Thus, in talking about generational cohorts, what's meant by common and lasting effects is something more nuanced than the ordinary sense of these terms.

Notwithstanding the natural diversity of opinions within a group, a generational cohort will show a distinctive mix of certain attitudes and values. This aggregate pattern defines the nature of what it's like to be a part of that group. Certain ideas are more or less likely to be expressed. Certain preferences are more or less likely to be in evidence. Certain norms are more or less likely to prevail. Even those who don't share the opinions of the majority must come to terms with the broader context in which their beliefs and behaviors are not the rule.

The character of a generation sets the tone for what it's like to live and work in those times. To truly understand a group of people, the nature of this experience cannot be ignored. All Boomers didn't spread a blanket in the rain and mud to get high and listen to music at Woodstock, but the tenor of life for all Boomers has been deeply affected by that spirit of self-expression. Some Boomers embraced this spirit; others did not. But all had to react to it one way or another, and thus all were influenced in some manner by this aspect of the Boomer generational experience.

As people age, values and preferences that were once strongly held will change or be replaced by new beliefs. Time and later experiences will soften or even amplify the power of those early impressions. What's lasting and unchanged, though, is a generation's starting point. Every member of a cohort grows up in the same overarching environment and thus shares a common starting point. And starting points matter.

What's new and exciting for one generation will be old hat to the next. What one generation has to pioneer will be taken for granted by future generations. What a younger generation experiences while coming of age will be the experiences of maturity for an older generation. There is no do-over for an older generation. In Figure I-1, Boomers and GenXers looked the same in 1997. But only GenXers went through their twenties and then their thirties with those values. Boomers had other opposite values in their twenties and thirties, and so were a generation with a different character at those ages.

Studying Generations

At Yankelovich, we study generational cohorts in terms of starting points. Shared experiences are important in establishing the starting points for generations. Grouping people on the basis of birth years turns out to provide a fruitful perspective for studying the cohort of people born during the post–World War II fertility boom from 1946 to 1964, the group we know as Baby Boomers. Figure I-2 illustrates our approach to understanding generations.

The societal dynamics prevailing when a generation is coming of age create the context of the times. The economy and technology are most important. Demographics come next. Pop culture and politics, while also important, are typically the least so of these elements.

The prevailing social environment created by these dynamics is the starting point that imbues a generation with a particular set of values from which it begins to understand its place, its opportunities, and its potential. Within this context, a generation learns what's possible, what's valuable, and what it takes to get things done.

"Values" is a loaded word, by the way. Vigorous debates about how to define, measure, and analyze values are never-ending and not infrequently rancorous. At Yankelovich, we avoid getting into these definitional quarrels

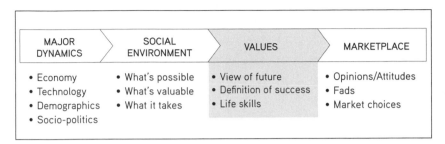

Figure I-2: Generational Framework

by taking a more pragmatic approach. We look at three judgments people make on the basis of what they see in the world around them, the various combinations of which comprise the lifestyle values we measure and track across generations.

First, we look at people's expectations about the future. Do they believe the future will be better or worse than today? What's in the offing? Second, we look at people's definition(s) of success. Who do they want to be? What do they place value on? Finally, we look at the life skills people think they will need in order to be successful in the way(s) they prefer given the kind of future they expect. Altogether, these opinions comprise the values that drive the decisions people make, the fads they follow, and the things they choose to buy in the consumer marketplace. After all, people don't buy just because they can. People shop in ways that reflect and satisfy the kinds of lifestyles they value and want to achieve.

For example, available technologies affect a generation's sense of empowerment. Think of today's generation of teenagers, who have never known a world in which they were not a click away from accessing, even customizing, virtually everything ever written, recorded, filmed, invented, or produced. It is a different experience of possibility, and it is a unique generational starting point.

Now, it's not as if Boomers don't have the same fingertip computer power as today's teenagers. Mobile computers and the Internet are not generationally exclusive, and in many cases Boomers are just as proficient with these technologies as teens and young adults. But Boomers can't go back and be teenagers with these new ways of thinking. As teenagers, they held values appropriate to their times, which are not the values of teenagers today. Boomers approach today's technologies the way they have approached every aspect of their lives—with a distinctive generational character.

Boomers in the Making

Lots of things went on during the 1960s and 1970s that were experienced by different Boomers at different ages, and therefore in different ways. When the Beatles first arrived in the United States at New York's Kennedy International Airport on February 7, 1964, the oldest Boomers were eighteen and the tail end of the Boomer cohort had yet to be born. In 1969, when Neil Armstrong took the first small step on the moon and the largest antiwar demonstration in U.S. history took place in Washington, D.C., the oldest Boomers were twenty-three, the youngest were just shy of five. When President Nixon resigned the presidency on August 8, 1974, the oldest Boomers were twenty-eight; the youngest were not yet ten. When hostages were taken in Iran on November 4, 1979, the oldest Boomers were thirty-three; the youngest were almost fifteen.

This stretch of time between the oldest and youngest Boomers is big, which leads directly to the question of whether people separated by so many years can be part of the same generational cohort. It's a good question, but it betrays a misunderstanding about generational influences and shared formative experiences.

There is a perception among some that the social upheaval of the 1960s is the defining experience of Baby Boomers and that anyone who came of age before or after that decade is not a Boomer. For example, this seems to be the reason that trailing Boomer and Illinois senator Barack Obama (born 1961) speaks of himself as a leader from a new generation. He came of age in the mid- to late 1970s, so he claims no formative connection with those who stood as young people on opposing sides of the barricades during the 1960s.

Without question, the social upheaval of the 1960s was a searing experience for many. Boomers of different ages relate to that time in different ways. If this experience were all that mattered, then it would be correct to look at leading and trailing Boomers as being from different generations. But it is not.

Other dynamics were at work that all Boomers encountered in similar ways, irrespective of age and timing. In fact, these other dynamics—economic prosperity, in particular—are more important for understanding this generation. The formative experiences that Boomers share are responsible for the generational character of the cohort. Other experiences are important, but not for understanding Boomers as a generation. The formative experiences that are overarching are deeper and more profound than marches on Washington; indeed, they account for the very nature of what those protestors were seeking to accomplish.

The Psychology of Affluence

First and foremost, Baby Boomers grew up during a time of economic plenty. After decades of worry, parsimony, and for many, utter hardship, people could finally indulge themselves and, more important, their Boomer children. During the quarter-century after the end of World War II, the U.S. economy was booming and America was flexing its muscle on all fronts, domestic and international.

Suddenly and happily, the parents of Boomers were thrust into a world of accessible prosperity. The GI Bill put a college education and home ownership within reach of millions more than ever before. The Great Depression had pushed home ownership down to 43.6 percent of Americans in 1940, the lowest level of the twentieth century. A decade later, the 1950 U.S. Census found that for the first time ever more than half of Americans, 55.0 percent, owned a home. In 1960, it was 61.9 percent.[3] Rapidly growing prosperity was the context of life for all.

Brown University historian James Patterson emphatically declared in his acclaimed volume of the Oxford University Press series on the history of America that "[e]conomic growth was indeed the most decisive force in the shaping of attitudes and expectations in the postwar era."[4] This prosperity did not abate until the first oil crisis in 1973, and even then people did not fully come to terms with it until after the second one, in 1979.

All Boomers came of age with expectations of unlimited potential fueled by a prosperity of "unimaginable heights," to repeat Patterson's phrase. Even though leading Boomers had a head start on trailing Boomers, who struggled with economic setbacks that leading Boomers did not face at the same age, all Boomers grew up with a view of possibilities and promise deeply rooted in a quarter century–plus of unprecedented economic boom times. The story of Boomers throughout their lives has been that of reconciling these formative expectations with adult realities, mostly by seeking ways to avoid accepting limits. The economy, not protests, is the central dynamic shaping the shared generational character of Baby Boomers.

The starting point for Boomers was their shared expectations about the future, rooted in the robust economic growth of their formative years. They took for granted a world of unbridled economic optimism, unprecedented abundance, and wide-ranging prosperity. This economic context was the defining shared cohort experience for Boomers, and it imbued them with a common and lasting approach to life. During the 1960s and 1970s the culture was bracing and vibrant, but these cultural phenomena, while prominent in the memories of aging Baby Boomers, were surface reflections of a deeper current.

Boomers grew up with a presumption of economic security, and thus a sense that the future could be taken for granted and would assuredly turn out to be a brighter place than yesterday or today. A growing economy meant plenty of room at the top for anyone willing to work. But even those with lesser ambitions would be secure in a future with more than enough to go around.

Atomic power was going to produce unlimited energy for pennies, if not for free. Robots would do the chores. The American breadbasket was going to feed the world. Everyone would be able to go to college. Cancer would be conquered just like polio. Social scientists launched the discipline of leisure studies to research what people would do with the extra time that prosperity and technology were going to bring. Life would assuredly turn into some version of the 1964 World's Fair—a vision of the future Boomers inherited from their parents, one of streamlined cities populated by people in space-age outfits getting around by hovercraft or monorail.

Prosperity poured into American households: nylon, Styrofoam, vinyl flooring, appliances galore, instant cameras, plastic toys, color TVs, TV dinners and frozen foods. Big, roomy cars owned the highways, and new models tempting consumers to trade in or trade up rolled off assembly lines working overtime shifts.

This formative experience has been described as the Psychology of

---

Marketing Thought-Starter: Intangibles

Psychologically freed from worries about basic material needs, Boomers have always put more time, energy, and thought into nonmaterial pursuits. Boomers never worried to the degree that their parents had about securing a comfortable material life, so they went in search of the meaning of life instead.

The standard marketing advice is to emphasize experiences with Boomers. Boomers take material things for granted, so create value through experiences. This is good advice . . . as far as it goes.

The dichotomy of relevance is not material things versus experiences; it's tangibles versus intangibles. Boomers like stuff. They buy as much stuff as they can afford and will always do so. What they are seeking from the stuff they buy, though, is an intangible benefit.

Think of a simple example like price. As a tangible attribute, a good price means cheap. The tangible benefit is that it saves money. As an intangible attribute, though, a good price means good value, for which the intangible benefit is smart choice. Boomers don't want to be cheap; they want to be smart. Intangibles have more pull.

Experiences are one sort of intangible, but don't overlook the others: smarts, vitality, energy, authenticity, relationships, security, achievement, excitement, self-esteem, social recognition, and joy, to mention just a few.

Boomers want something more than things per se. They definitely value experiences, but more broadly, they are looking for intangibles.

Affluence, the experience of growing up in a world of presumptive prosperity. Coming of age from the mid-1950s to the late 1970s, Baby Boomers
shared a confidence that progress and prosperity would never stop. Whatever problems Boomers saw or encountered along the way—and there
were plenty—they believed would be easily remedied on the march to
this better future.

Boomers didn't have to aspire to the American Dream; they felt they
were born into it. The presumption of prosperity freed them from the psychological burden of worrying about basic survival and allowed them
to pursue other, more self-absorbed, self-focused things like fulfillment,
enlightenment, and meaning. This was different from the experience of
their parents, who felt a greater need to make sacrifices in order to get by.
Boomers no longer worried about getting by, so they felt no corresponding
need to sacrifice their own interests and desires nor any need to accept conformity or limitations. Instead, they championed a new notion: that of an
unfettered, indulgent, absorbed, celebratory self.

The New Values

Daniel Yankelovich, the renowned founder and namesake of our firm,
wrote about this at the time as the replacement of self-sacrifice by self-
fulfillment as the driving force in American society, and thus in the consumer marketplace as well. As Boomers grew up, limitless horizons
stretched out around them. So, why stifle personal expression and fulfillment when there was no economic need to do so and so much out there to
experience?

The new values weren't sex, drugs, and rock'n'roll, but the far-reaching
lifestyle consequences arising from the impact of the Psychology of Affluence. Virtually all Boomers reflect this in some way. At Yankelovich, we
tracked this at the time as a threefold shift in outlook toward a greater emphasis on self, less structured lifestyles, and more enriching personal
environments. People differed in the degree to which they emphasized
one or more of these three elements, but everyone began to exhibit this

new approach to life. Cutting across class and ideology, these were the so-called New Values tracked by Yankelovich during the late 1960s and 1970s, values rooted in new views about the future and success and practiced with new life skills.

The value changes characteristic of Baby Boomers were only peripherally related to campus protests and the counterculture. As Dan Yankelovich has pointed out on many occasions, our firm's research at the time found only about one-quarter of college students involved in any of this. For the populace as a whole, the percentage was minuscule (only about 2 percent).[5] Marilyn Quayle, wife of the vice president, was absolutely correct when she said in a speech at the 1992 Republican National Convention that "not everyone joined the counterculture, not everyone demonstrated, dropped out, took drugs, joined in the sexual revolution or dodged the draft." While true, this is not to say that *all* Boomers don't share the New Values of self-fulfillment and a common generational character. The Psychology of Affluence influenced all Boomers, Republicans and Democrats alike.

In fact, it is worth remembering that with but a few exceptions the protests of the 1960s were about guaranteeing the bright promise of that era, not about rejecting the American Dream. In his book on the year 1968, journalist Jules Witcover quotes Eugene McCarthy speechwriter Jeremy Larner to the effect that the young volunteers working in McCarthy's presidential primary campaigns, despite their opposition to the Vietnam War and the draft, "still believed" that America could be great if it would just "live up" to American "principles."[6] Larner called them "American optimists at heart," a similar observation to that of emeritus Harvard political scientist Samuel Huntington—of recent "clash of civilizations" fame—who viewed the protesters of the 1960s, counterculture notwithstanding, as "Puritans" demanding that institutions live up to American ideals.[7]

The rule-breaking endemic to that era was about overturning barriers to the self, not about overthrowing the system. The self was not to be hemmed in, so Boomers became rule-breakers *par excellence.* Life was all about the new—indeed, almost the moral—superiority of novelty. Newness was a good in and of itself, of which youth was the epitome. Boomers forced marketers to emphasize new brands.

Boomers saw only promise and potential as they looked ahead. There were plenty of things to set right, such as civil rights and Vietnam, but they were confident that problems could be easily remedied on the road to tomorrow. After all, there was plenty to go around, so no need to restrict opportunities for anybody. There were no limits to the successes awaiting them.

At least until 1979, that is.

Fending Off Limits

The American economy was tripped up in 1973 by the OPEC oil embargo imposed as a result of the Yom Kippur War between Israel and the Arab countries of Egypt and Syria. This crisis both set off and intensified a toxic series of economic tribulations that plagued the nation through the mid-1980s (and beyond in some cases): raging inflation, high unemployment, soaring interest rates, a sluggish stock market, and declining productivity. The ensuing economic decline was so unusual that the term *stagflation*, coined by British prime minister Iain McLeod in 1965, became part of the popular vernacular. But even as WIN buttons—Whip Inflation Now—became ubiquitous and gas lines stretched around the block, people still believed that America's prospects remained undiminished. Muscle and determination would prevail, just as it had since America's entry into World War II. Those presumptions were finally undone in 1979.

The year 1979 was the turning point, the year when the external conditions of the world at large changed dramatically. No more hopeful promise of a future filled with unbounded abundance and economic security. Gas lines reappeared as oil prices skyrocketed. Sirens sounded at the Three Mile Island nuclear power plant. Chrysler, facing bankruptcy, came to Congress for a bailout. Radical students seized the American Embassy in Iran, taking fifty-two people hostage. The Soviets invaded Afghanistan. The U.S. space station Skylab fell from the sky. Inflation, interest rates, and unemployment continued to soar at double-digit levels. It was a year in which Francis Ford Coppola captured the prevailing mood in the title of his 1979 hit movie, *Apocalypse Now.*

President Jimmy Carter spoke to this mood in a nationally televised address on July 15, 1979, when he delivered his infamous "national malaise" speech, declaring that America faced a "crisis of spirit" that could be met only by facing up to a future of limits. Much of the tone taken in this speech was based on polling completed by advisor Pat Caddell that showed for the first time, more Americans believed the future would be worse than the present than believed it would be better.[8] Pessimism had taken hold.

This crisis of confidence had been building for years. All the events of the 1960s and early to mid-1970s—the Bay of Pigs, the assassination of President John F. Kennedy, race riots, Charles Manson, the Kent State shootings, the My Lai massacre, the Pentagon Papers, Attica, the Munich Olympics, Watergate, Patty Hearst, Jim Jones, and Love Canal, just to mention the biggest headlines—fed an undercurrent of suspicion and paranoia in which lunatic conspiracy theories often passed for hard fact. Indeed, the year 1968 was felt at the time to be a hair's breadth away from cataclysmic. The 1973 oil embargo, persistent inflation, and declining productivity were already sapping the strength of the economy. Trust in public institutions and authorities had dropped substantially.

Still, optimism had not yet slipped away. America had put a man on the moon. Important civil rights legislation had been passed despite withering opposition. The Fourth Estate of the press had proven to be an effective watchdog over presidential excesses in Watergate. Important strides had been taken in environmental protection, consumer product safety, women's rights, and aid to the poor. Problems looked programmatic, not systemic. With the right programs, they could be solved. There was nothing wrong with the system itself.

But the confluence of crises in 1979, especially the oil crisis early in the year, drained away the last vestiges of optimism about an unlimited future. Problems now looked intractable. The frayed ends Boomers had been ignoring for years seemed to unravel completely. The system appeared to be failing. If limits were the unavoidable condition of life ahead, Boomers realized they could either downsize their expectations and learn to live with less or gear up to be more aggressive about securing what they wanted and let others learn to live with limits. By and large, Boomers chose the latter.

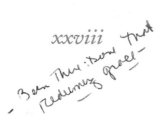

The New Realism

The 1970s drew to a baleful close. Yet Boomers refused to give up the out-sized expectations they had internalized through the Psychology of Afflu-ence. Instead, they redirected their focus on self from self-expression to self-indulgence.

After 1979, Boomers realized they could no longer take the future for granted. In our research at Yankelovich, we tracked this as the emergence of a harder-edged approach to life we called the New Realism. It was not an abandonment of the New Values, but the adoption of a new style that could ensure the promise of those values even in an era of limits.

As the 1980s dawned, the gap between formative expectations and adult realities led to a single-minded Boomer focus on not losing. Yuppies crept out from behind the long hair and tie-dye. If Boomers couldn't make the world a better place, they would simply enjoy it as much as they could while they were able to do so. The result was cutthroat competition through con-sumption. The new philosophy: "He who dies with the most toys wins."

This New Realism kicked into overdrive as the economy began to acceler-ate again in the mid-1980s, with a burst of opportunities for the smartest and the shrewdest. The end of the Reagan recession put more money into the hands of Boomers who had learned to aggressively take care of their own self-interests. Conspicuous consumption became the new self-indulgent version of self-expression. Boomers turned luxury into an everyday experience.

It was during this period that GenX began to come of age. Their starting point was different from that of Boomers. GenX grew up with the presump-tion of limits, hearing repeatedly that they would be the first generation in American history not to live as well as their parents. So this generation was shaped by formative experiences unlike those of Baby Boomers. While Boomers struggled with the same realities as GenX, they did so at a later age, with a perspective rooted in a very different starting point.

Both the 1980s and 1990s closed out with economic hiccups that frus-trated Boomers. In the new millennium, the shock of 9/11 and three ensu-ing years of scandals dropped public trust to record lows. Global terrorism has made the intangible satisfactions that were always important to Boomers an even greater priority.

Through it all, though, Boomers have refused to give up their fundamental belief in a future that affords them the generational luxury of focusing on self-discovery, self-development, and self-fulfillment. Sacrifice of self has never been part of their generational character.

Today, Boomers feel that their refusal to give in to limits has been vindicated, at least in part. The stock market has risen to levels once thought impossible, as have home values. Medical breakthroughs have made eighty-plus-year-olds the fastest-growing demographic group. Inflation, unemployment, and interest rates are at or near record lows. The Internet has opened up information and access to everything.

Accepting limits means compromising. Boomers don't accept limits, so it's no surprise that they have long been confrontational, polarizing, and uncompromising. And they see no reason to start compromising now. Their take-no-prisoners style looks to be working, albeit with the occasional setback every now and then.

Boomers face up to challenges and limits not by abandoning their focus on self but by changing the kind of self on which they focus. Predicting what's next means anticipating the ways in which Boomers will focus on self in the future.

As aging Boomers look ahead, the limits they see next are those related to physical age. But Boomers don't accept these limits now any more than they have accepted limits of any sort. They think in terms of immortality.

The self-fulfillment that they want for themselves in the (extra) years to come continues to be tinged by the indulgence that is a corollary to fending off limits. But it reflects as well the principles and causes that Boomers now have the time, money, and passion to pursue. They are interested in morality, too.

Boomers fight for everything they want. They will fight for immortality and morality no less than anything else that has ever concerned them. Boomers are going to have their say by staying the course through their aging years. In the process, they will reinvent everything they encounter. That means a world to come in which Boomers will matter no less, and perhaps more, than ever before.

Marketing Thought-Starter:
Nth-Degree Luxury and Service

The refusal of Boomers to compromise directly affects what they want from the consumer marketplace. They bring the same moralistic sense that things must be done "the right way" to every sphere of their lives. Boomers want the Nth degree of everything, particularly things of two sorts.

First, they demand quality and touches of luxury. No matter the price, everything must be above average. Finishes and details are the best ways to deliver this to them. Special touches, even the smallest, offer the biggest value. Boomer luxury entails none of the traditional scarcity. Luxury is not just for the elite; it is for every sophisticated palate.

Second, Boomers insist upon high levels of customer service. They want something beyond the hyperboles of recent decades—excellence, delight, and the like. Boomers have come to expect continuous improvement in the quality of both products and customer service. What comes next must provide customized solutions supported by a relentlessly personal touch. And not at a premium price; rather, as a mandatory cost of entry even to be included in the Boomer consideration set.

Immortality

The first half of this book is about the Boomer desire for immortality. Youthfulness has long been the most celebrated aspect of Baby Boomers. The fertility boom that produced them was a twentieth-century demographic anomaly. By sheer numbers alone, young Boomers created skyrocketing demand in successive sectors of the economy. Throughout their lives, they have been told that their youthfulness was their most powerful attribute, so Boomers have nurtured and cherished it. Their midlife has had a distinctively youthful flavor to it. Their old age will have it as well.

Being old yet living youthfully means taking a fresh approach to old age. Boomers won't fade away; they want to continue to matter just as they always have. Indeed, they have a new agenda to champion. They do not intend to be

Matures (Born before 1946)	Baby Boomers (Born 1946-1964)	Xers (Born 1965-1978)	Echo Boomers (Born 1979-1990)
Converse	Adidas	Nike	Sketchers
Peyton Place	*Dallas*	*Melrose Place*	*Dawson's Creek*
This Is Your Life	*Candid Camera*	*America's Funniest Home Videos*	*Punk'd*
Orange Juice	The Juice Runs	The Juice Walks	The Juice Writes
George and Gracie	Cheech and Chong	*Beavis and Butthead*	*Dumb and Dumber*
The Vanderbilts	The Louds	The Bundys	The Osbournes

Figure I-3: Generational Culture

sidelined. They will look to push past the traditional limits of old age and everything associated with it. They want to be ageless in their ability to impact the world. They want to be middle age–less.

Boomers will refashion retirement. They will redefine work. They will experiment with remedies to keep them vigorous and engaged. They will nullify age.

However old they become, Boomers want to continue to matter. It is a mistake to plan for Boomers as if they are decelerating. Not only does such planning run counter to their generational character, it fails to take account of the emerging marketplace of consumer control that demands a youthful sensibility at all ages. This world of self-invention is one in which youthful possibility is essential. Constant learning and continual self-discovery are the keys to success in a marketplace in which closure and dependency are no longer valued or rewarded. Boomers are ready to meet this challenge.

There are a lot of myths and misconceptions about how to approach aging Boomers. This book puts them to rest. Mortality is a limit that Boomers intend to test, and, in typical Boomer fashion, they see no sense in pushing limits without being prepared to go all the way. For Boomers, it's not about eking out a little more time; it's about amassing as much time as they can get, and more. Immortality is what Boomers want.

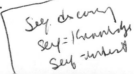

Morality

The second half of this book is about the moral agenda that Boomers will spend their immortality promoting. Their hopes, dreams, and aspirations for the next stage of their lives are grounded in a sense of self that revolves around moral causes and principles.

Of course, no single agenda has ever commanded the devotion of all Baby Boomers. All Boomers share the same starting point and embody the same generational character, but they do so in diverse ways that reflect more particular interests and commitments. This will be true in the future, too.

The development of this moral focus is a natural progression in the abiding Baby Boomer focus on self, as illustrated in Figure I-4.

Three broad eras of self define the evolution of the Boomer cohort. In the first era, the expressive self dominated, accompanied by the righteous self. In the next era, the righteous self dropped away and the indulgent self dominated, complemented by the expressive self. As we look to the future, the righteous self is becoming dominant, with the expressive self losing force and the indulgent self continuing as a secondary element.

The expressive self was dominant when Boomers were young. This was the heyday of economic optimism, when self-sacrifice was being cast aside in favor of unfettered self-expression. Perceived abundance contributed to an implicit belief that more could be done for others with little or no sacri-

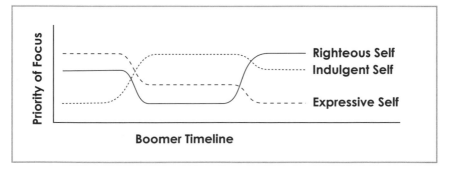

Figure I-4: Boomer Focus on Self

Sef Actul. Act Rig/
Sey Fnd.
Sey G H

fice. This added to the general support for various social causes. Indulgence
had not yet taken hold.

As the 1980s arrived, the indulgent self became dominant. Egoism,
selfishness, and exclusivity became more prevalent. Self-expression remained important, but less so than before.

As Boomers move past midlife, the expressive self is losing relevance.
It is the sense of self most tied to puerile pursuits, so it's no surprise that it
has less staying power. Indulgence remains strong, though. Boomers
have developed sophisticated tastes, interests, and palates that they will
carry forward. They will be a highly discriminating generation of older
people.

But the righteous self, not the indulgent self, will be dominant among
aging Boomers. Boomers are going to repurpose their lives. Every personal
concern is likely to be framed as a moral issue. More than that, though,
Boomers will be committing themselves to new agendas. In a way, this, too,
is a sort of indulgence, one that they will be better able to permit themselves
given the life stage into which they are headed next.

Re Frame Life

Boomers have always had a pronounced sense of moral certainty. In their
earliest years, they were convinced that the system was perfectible if they
could only root out evil. They took on the mission of pushing and prodding
the system closer to perfection. This is the puritanical sensibility that Samuel Huntington identified. Every fight was a clash of moral principles—good
versus evil, the Dark Side versus the Force, with us or against us. As emeritus
Loyola University psychology professor Eugene Cullen Kennedy has put it,
Boomers "do not negotiate, they expect their needs to be met" once they "put
their demands on the table."[9]

This moral sensibility is restrengthening. The righteous self will set the
agenda for the ways in which Boomers indulge and express themselves in
the years ahead.

To better understand the future agenda of Boomers, Yankelovich fielded
a special research study among them that is different from the typical
Boomer study about retirement or health. While these are important issues, they offer few insights into the hopes, dreams, and aspirations inspir-
ing Boomers as they contemplate the impact they want to have and the

legacy they want to establish. This is what the Yankelovich Boomer Dreams study is all about.

Baby Boomers are gearing up for the next stage of their lives. They will have to defy expectations and reinvent the rules in order to get what they want. But they've done it before and, old geezers or not, their numbers will make it impossible to ignore them in the future. Ageless Boomers want to stay involved and pursue their passions. They are seeking immortality and morality. They won't take no for an answer.

Immortality

one
Ka-Boom!

*N*obody saw them coming, this explosion of people known as Baby Boomers. Seventy-eight million strong, they were beyond imagination. The biggest generation in American history took America by surprise.

Throughout the first half of the twentieth century, birth rates were dropping and population growth was slowing. During the 1930s, government demographers worried aloud that the U.S. population would plateau around 148 million and maybe even decline by century's end, a prospect that was doubly alarming in the context of the political and economic turmoil darkening the globe during that time.

Demand is the fundamental, necessary platform for growth and innovation, so extrapolation of these declining population trends into the future augured shrinking business prospects and an attenuating marketplace. This dismal view of the future was unhappy and unwelcome, but the trend lines offered no evidence to expect anything else.

The Baby Boom changed these trend lines. Immediately following the end of World War II, the birth rate soared. The boom had begun and it wouldn't subside for nearly two decades. Without notice or warning, in defiance of all trends and expectations, Baby Boomers exploded onto the American scene, and in the process changed everything. Demographers' fears were quickly put to rest. By the end of 1949, a mere four years into the Baby Boom, the U.S. population had soared well past 148 million.

Although a surprise at the time, there is no ignoring Baby Boomers now. Every other generation gets defined by and measured against them.

Everything associated with them is interminably scrutinized, usually yielding yet another Boomer cliché. But trite though they may be at times, Baby Boomers are anything but trivial. From infancy to maturity, they have been the driving economic force in the American economy, and thus the world, for the past sixty years. Even as they age, they will continue to dominate the marketplace.

Baby Boomers, more than any other demographic group, will shape the future of the marketplace. They are in control and will remain so for decades to come. For Boomers, getting older does not mean resigning oneself to a deceleration into death. They will continue to be actively involved in their lifestyles, spending lots of money and searching for more new things to try.

The essential thing to know about Boomers is simple yet profoundly important: *Do not count them out because they are aging. They are going to continue to matter.*

There is no group now or ever before with the power of Baby Boomers to move markets and spark change. Baby Boomers are a generational phenomenon unlike any other.

Boomers have always wanted to be the catalyst for change. Their huge numbers and eager ambitions made this easy to do in years past. But now that they are aging, the question arises as to whether Boomers will continue to matter, and if so, in what way. Numbers notwithstanding, ask skeptics, is it possible for aging Baby Boomers to continue to matter? Indeed, will they even want to in the first place?

Resoundingly, Boomers answer both questions in the affirmative. They have no intention of retiring from the scene. Baby Boomers stand at the threshold of a future that will give them unprecedented opportunities to remain vital, vigorous, and valuable in virtually undiminished proportions. The sustained, active engagement of aging Baby Boomers will be possible as never before, not to mention a lot more necessary.

Yet they still seem to catch marketers by surprise. Their vigorous, relentless engagement with their lifestyles and the marketplace has always meant a style of consumerism that can't be predicted by extrapolation from the past. Baby Boomers have never wanted to follow tradition or model themselves on those before them. They have been determined to do things differently and to invent for themselves a superior approach. They have thrived with a generational sense of spirited youthfulness that, more often than not, has meant a willingness to and enthusiasm for breaking the rules. This Boomer brio will not diminish with age.

Marketers shouldn't expect Baby Boomers to turn into "old" people just because they are now aging into their senior years. Boomers have an undying commitment to growth, exploration, and possibility that cannot be mapped by plotting a trend line based on the physical declines of old age or life-stage progressions into retirement. Boomers will age, but they won't get old. And in this nullification of age as it is typically understood and envisioned, they will continue to take America by surprise.

Exploding onto the Scene

Defining the Baby Boom has long been a popular quarrel among pundits and trend watchers. But it's a debate in vain, because the Boom defines itself unambiguously. *Above all else*, the Baby Boom is a population phenomenon. It's all about numbers.

Two demographic charts show this clearly. The first, Figure 1-1, shows annual fertility rates from 1909 to 2006. Annual fertility rates are the actual number of live births per thousand women of childbearing age (defined by demographers as ages fifteen to forty-four). The trend seen here is one of long-term decline. From nearly 127 births per thousand in 1909, there was a steady drop until the end of World War II. Births per thousand fell below one hundred in 1927 and did not exceed that level again until 1946, the first year of the Baby Boom.

During the war years of 1940 to 1945, there was an inkling of change as births per thousand began to inch upward. But this turnaround was small in comparison to what came next and offered no hint of the huge surge just around the corner. From 1946 to 1964, births per thousand were always above one hundred, peaking in 1957 at nearly 123. In 1965, births per thousand dropped below one hundred again, eventually bottoming out at much lower levels in the mid- to high sixties.

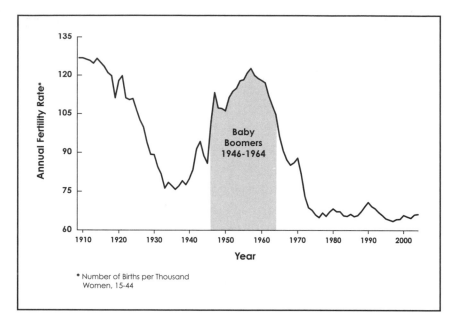

Figure 1-1: Annual Fertility Rates

The conclusion from Figure 1-1 is unequivocal: The Boom was a distinctive anomaly in U.S. population trends that began and ended at specific points in time. The Baby Boom of 1946 to 1964 was a dramatic yet temporary reversal of a long-term decline in annual fertility rates. It was a long, unbroken stretch of more than one hundred births per thousand women of childbearing age, a level not seen since then. The 16-point jump from 1945 to 1946 was far and away the largest over this period; the 8.4-point drop from 1964 to 1965 was exceeded by a mere fraction only three other times during the twentieth century, only one of which—from 1971 to 1972—came later.

The same clear-cut generational boundaries are seen no matter how U.S. population trends are examined. Consider the total number of births each year as shown in Figure 1-2. Not only does this confirm the boundaries of this generational cohort; it reveals the impact of the sheer size of the Baby Boom.

Total births dropped significantly during the 1930s from a steady number of about 2.8 to 2.9 million per year in the prior decades. They began to climb again during the war years, even exceeding 3 million in 1943. But in 1946,

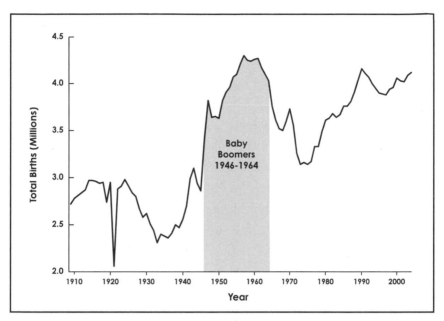

Figure 1-2: Total Births

total births jumped dramatically to just over 3.4 million, a record number at that time. The numbers climbed to just over 4 million in 1954, reaching an all-time record of 4.3 million in 1957. Total births didn't fall below 4 million again until 1965. Total births during every year of the Baby Boom exceeded those of every earlier year in the century.

Boom Numbers

By every measure, the Boom was an extraordinary population phenomenon. It began in 1946 with radical jumps in the fertility rate and in the total number of births. The Baby Boom ended in 1964 with drops no less dramatic and definitive than the jumps had been in 1946. In 1965, births per thousand and total births were robust but far below the sustained high levels seen during the period from 1946 to 1964.

After 1964, total births did not exceed 4 million again until 1989, one-quarter of a century later. Unlike the Baby Boom, though, the higher total number of births in 1989 was not due to higher fertility rates. There were 4 million–plus births that year because there were so many more women having children, not because individual women were having more children.

In 1964, there were roughly 38.5 million women of childbearing age. By contrast, in 1989 there were about 58.4 million. It took half as many women in 1989 as it did in 1964 to reach the same number of births! And the reason there were so many more women in 1989 was the Baby Boom that had occurred twenty-five to forty-three years earlier. In other words, the sheer numbers of Boomer women more than made up for a substantial deficit in fertility rates, a prime example of the ways in which Boomer numbers have dominated American life.

The Baby Boom was huge. Boomer numbers were unprecedented and unexpected. No hyperbole is too great to describe it, but perhaps the most common characterization of Baby Boomers is the best: the pig in the python.

In 1965, the year after the end of the Boom, nearly 36 percent of the U.S. population was under eighteen years of age. By comparison, only 18 percent of the population is that young today. In relative terms, young Boomers were a much more influential and overshadowing social and marketplace force than young people today, notwithstanding the incessant media hype about today's younger generation.

Because of the Baby Boom, in less than two decades the U.S. population ballooned to an extent seen in previous American history only during periods of massive immigration and a much smaller total population. As Boomers came of age, they found crowds of their young peers everywhere they looked.

Boomer numbers continue to dominate. The U.S. Census Bureau projected in 2004 that the number of those age fifty-five and older would grow a little over 45 percent between 2005 and 2020, while that of those twenty-five to forty-four years of age would grow only 5.6 percent. By 2030, those sixty-five and older are projected to account for almost 20 percent of the total population, compared to 12.4 percent in 2005.

Everything Boomers have done has mattered a lot simply because of their numbers. Even a moderate percentage of Boomers has made for big markets. A large percentage has made for gargantuan, record-setting markets. No wonder so many growth records—in the stock market and real estate, for example—have been set during the ascendancy of Baby Boomers.

If the Boomers living in New York City alone were a city of their own, they would be the fourth-largest city in the United States, coming in behind only New York City (even without these Boomers), Los Angeles, and Chicago.

If Boomers were a nation unto themselves, they would be the sixteenth most populous country in the world, just behind Egypt and ahead of countries including France, the United Kingdom, Italy, Iran, Turkey, Spain, and Canada. The $2 trillion–plus in buying power controlled by Baby Boomers[2]

Marketing Thought-Starter:
Boomers Create Shortages

Boomer numbers always create shortages of resources, supplies, and services. Tracking Boomers in terms of what they need and what they want will point the way to growth opportunities. Figure out what's going to be in demand and then figure that for a shortage. Gear up to satisfy the demand that will be unmet.

On March 14, 2007, *USA Today* led with a headline announcing that aging Boomers were going to generate more demand for cancer doctors than there would be physicians to meet the demand.[3] Citing an analysis then just published in the *Journal of Oncology*,[4] the article notes that the total number of cancers will swell from 11.7 million in 2005 to 18.2 million by 2020, an increase directly linked to the growing number of people over sixty-five, which is to say aging Boomers. This need will be underserved. By 2020, it is projected that there will be four thousand fewer cancer specialists than needed.

Although other research shows rates declining for some types of cancer, the sheer size of Boomer numbers will remain overwhelming. Even with lower rates, Boomers are so numerous that a huge increase in the absolute numbers of cancer cases will come about anyway, an increase that will overwhelm the capacity of the health-care system.

This particular shortage illustrates the impact of Boomer numbers: A shortage always occurs, which creates opportunities for smart marketers who can develop innovative ways to meet the surging demand.

would make them one of the largest economies in the world—far smaller than the GDPs of the United States, China, Japan, and India, but bigger than those of the United Kingdom, France, Italy, Russia, Brazil, Canada, South Korea, Mexico, and Spain, among many others, and not too much smaller than the GDP of Germany.

In a reanalysis of data from the Consumer Expenditure Survey conducted by the U.S. Department of Labor, AARP calculated that in 2001 consumers forty-five–plus—Baby Boomers and older—accounted for 52 percent of total consumer spending, including majority shares of spending for food, housing, health care, transportation, personal insurance, and pensions.[5] The increase in spending among consumers age forty-five and older from 1984 to 2001 exceeded the average for all consumers by 2 percentage points (8 percent versus 6 percent), a consequence of the "aging of the Boomers." As one example, in 2002, women fifty-five to sixty-four years of age spent more than any other age group on women's apparel and 34 percent more than the average, followed by women forty-five to fifty-four years old, who spent 25 percent more than the average.[6]

According to some estimates, by 2010, the projected $2.6 trillion of spending by consumers over forty will dwarf the spending of consumers under forty by $1 trillion.[7]

The power of Boomers is in their numbers. Boomers may be aging but their numbers are undiminished and thus their importance, both today and tomorrow, is undiminished, too. It is the size and pattern of their numbers that defines the start and the end of the Baby Boom, and the experience of numbers is a Boomer hallmark.

A Paradox of Numbers

Every Baby Boomer has some personal memory connected with numbers. One of the authors of this book recalls sitting down in the mid-1970s to calculate the costs and benefits of applying to law school. Numbers made acceptance chancier than ever. Lots of peers had the same idea—many more than in years past, so the competition to get in was tougher. Yet the benefits of a law degree became less secure and less sure even as the degree itself grew harder to get. Many more lawyers were hitting the streets, numbers that made it a buyer's market for the law firms doing the hiring. Exclusivity no longer guaranteed value—a degree that was more exclusive than ever had simultaneously become less valuable than ever, too—a paradox of Boomer numbers.

Many Boomers faced similar quandaries. On the whole, they were better educated than generations before them. Yet because of their numbers, highly educated Boomers struggled to find jobs commensurate with their training. As *Newsweek,* one of many resolute chroniclers of Boomers throughout their lives, noted in 1981, a "new class" had arisen of "underemployed" college-educated youth. The forecast reported by the magazine was that by 1990, one-quarter of college-educated Boomers would work in jobs for which they were overeducated. Boomers were so numerous, this article said, that they had "depressed" their own salaries, an intra-generational competition that this article predicted would plague them throughout their careers. Indeed, the size of the generation was such that notwithstanding an improvement in the unemployment rate for twenty-five- to thirty-four-year-olds from 1975 to the time of that article, there were still 200,000 more young people looking for work than there were in 1975.[8] In these ways and more, their numbers have always presented Boomers with the paradox that things could be better and worse for them at the same time.

Matures (Born before 1946)	Baby Boomers (Born 1946-1964)	Xers (Born 1965-1978)	Echo Boomers (Born 1979-1990)
Dr. Spock	Dr. Strangelove	Dr. Kevorkian	Dr. Phil
Milk and cookies	Milk and Oreos	Milk and Snackwells	Kidsmilk (and no carbs)
Blackouts	Black Power	Black linguini	Black nail polish
Auntie Em	M&Ms	REM	Eminem
Blacklist	Enemies list	*Schindler's List*	Buddy list
Singin' in the Rain	"Dancing in the Street"	Surfin' the 'Net	IM'ing my friends

Figure 1-3: Generational Culture

One of the things that certainly got better because of Boomer numbers was demand in the marketplace. *Newsweek* weighed in on this subject a mere two years into the Boom in a 1948 cover story entitled "The Boom in Babies: What It Means to America." After fretting for years about the prospect of declining markets, businesses were now awash in a rising tide that would lift all boats. Already, the Baby Boom was creating welcome yet unanticipated and often exponential growth in demand for baby food, infant clothing, children's books and recordings, toys, and juvenile furniture. The longer-term future for agriculture, housing, construction, and manufacturing looked even brighter.[9]

As they came of age, Boomers drove huge expansions of demand for education, housing, home furnishings, appliances, transportation, clothing, restaurants (especially fast food), entertainment, consumer electronics, leisure, and financial services, just to mention the obvious. CNN, *USA Today*, Nike, Microsoft, Apple, Home Depot, Charles Schwab, and McDonald's went from start-ups to world-beaters by riding the Boomer wave. The Ford Mustang, the Honda Civic, the Toyota Corolla, the Dodge Caravan, the Mazda Miata, and the Ford Explorer found the road to success by following Boomers. Because of this generation, entire categories went from niche to big-time markets, including skiing, adventure travel, running shoes, rock'n'roll music, yoga, organics, mutual funds, and athletic clubs.

As Boomers continue to age, their numbers will create scarcity in new areas that in turn will create new opportunities for growth. A big area of worry is a critical worsening of the current shortage of home-based caregivers. Opportunities will grow for technologies and smart homes that can provide those services as well as for new companies offering more traditional home-based care. A related area is the provision of support services to keep aging Boomers active and self-sufficient, such as specialized exercise programs, city transportation services, shopping services, and the like.[10]

The downside of all this demand is that it challenges businesses to expand fast enough to keep up. And when they can't, as has happened periodically in many categories including housing, prices skyrocket. Even more problematic is the diversion of capital and manpower into less productive investments. As economist Jeff Madrick observed in his post-dot-com crash book, *Why Economies Grow: The Forces That Shape Prosperity and How to Get Them Working Again* (New York: Basic Books, 2002), one important reason for the slowdown in productivity growth during the latter half of the twentieth century was the burgeoning demand for labor-intensive services for which productivity improvements are harder to realize, such as housing, education, health care, elder care, child care, financial services, and consulting. The growth in demand for these services is rooted in the maturation of the massive Baby Boomer generation.

Baby Boomers are present in such large numbers that there is nothing uncomplicated or straightforward about their impact on society and the marketplace except, perhaps, that their numbers mean they matter a lot. For better and for worse, numbers define Baby Boomers and their power as a generation. Thus, it is essential to know what's on their minds, because whenever Boomers decide to do something, they do so in big numbers, the consequences of which are often paradoxical and always far-reaching.

Marketing Thought-Starter: Niches Are Mass Markets

The most opportune paradox of Boomer numbers is that Boomer niches are the equivalents of mass markets. Subsets of Boomers are often large enough to provide sufficient mass to realize efficiencies of production, distribution, marketing, and customer service. Boomer niches offer scale.

Differences of tastes and preferences among Boomers do not automatically necessitate more expensive micro-marketing tactics. Marketers should look for niches, but go after these niches with mega-brands and scalable strategies.

(continued)

(continued)

The 2006 Yankelovich MONITOR shows many rich niche opportunities for mass success. For example, look at the new things taken up by empty-nest Boomers:

Things have done since last child left home:		*Business Opportunity Area:*
Give children financial support	63%	(Financial planning)
Cook less often	59%	(Meal solutions/gourmet cooking)
Live healthier	57%	(Exercise/diets/health foods)
Enjoy life more	55%	(Entertainment/risk-taking/home)
Put money aside for retirement	54%	(Investments/financial planning)
Go out to eat more often	53%	(Restaurants/entertainment)
Discover more about self	52%	(Arts/education/seminars)
Make new friends	51%	(Clubs/Web sites/churches)
See decrease in stress	50%	(Spas/alternative medicine)
Reconnect with spouse	46%	(Romance/travel/home/gifts)
Read more	46%	(Books/magazines/education)
Splurge on a vacation or something always wanted but couldn't afford	41%	(Luxuries/travel/decorating/gifts)
Convert kids' bedrooms	38%	(Home improvement/decorating)
Pay more attention to how look	34%	(Cosmetics/fashion/surgery)
Take up new hobby	31%	(All hobbies)
More community/charity work	30%	(Nonprofits/social causes)
Get a pet	27%	(Pet products)
More time with parents	26%	(Home health care/gifts)
Move to smaller home	22%	(Real estate/travel/health care)

Things have done since last child left home:		Business Opportunity Area:
Be less conservative with investments	18%	(Financial planning)
Buy smaller, sportier car	15%	(Autos/travel/restaurants)
Go back to school	11%	(Education/seminars/books)

As an example of how Boomer niches translate into markets with scale, look at one item in this list: getting a pet. Twenty-seven percent of empty-nest Boomers is 6.2 million people. (It's 27 percent of the 29.4 percent of Boomers who fit our definition of empty nesters—no children under twenty-five living at home or away at school.) Assume that this works out to roughly 3 million pets (converting people into households and correcting for respondent misstatement). And assume for argument's sake that the pets are limited to dogs and cats. The average annual amount spent per household on a dog is $1,571; for a cat it's $919.[11] Some households have multiple pets, so it's a smaller amount per pet. To make it simple, use $1,000 per pet for both dogs and cats. Do the multiplication and the result is $3 *billion*. That's equal to 7.8 percent of the $38.4 billion in total pet-product sales in 2006. This Boomer niche has more than enough scale. The marketing rule-of-thumb that 10 percent of sales should be reinvested in advertising yields a figure greater than the combined $235 million spent on advertising in 2005 by PetSmart, Petco, and PetMed Express.[12]

Yankelovich MONITOR data shows that another 10 percent of empty-nest Boomers are planning to get a pet in the next year. This niche is big business.

In the Catbird's Seat

Boomers have been the vanguard of change over their lifetimes, but not always by pioneering new ideas. Oftentimes it's simply that they put their numbers behind the ideas of others, ideas that then came to shape their life experiences and the direction of America as a whole. But now that is going to change. Baby Boomers are in charge.

During most of their lives, Boomers have shared power with others and taken much of their inspiration from prior generations. No longer. Boomers now run everything. Their passions will have to be of their own making from here on out. And Boomers are ready to do so.

From John F. Kennedy's (b. 1917) election to the presidency in November 1960 to President George H. W. Bush's (b. 1924) last day in office in January 1993, the generation preceding Baby Boomers led America. (At Yankelovich, we refer to this group as the Mature Generation.) In fact, all seven of these Presidents were from the World War II end of Matures. The Korean War group of Matures, those born in the 1930s, never saw one of their own elected President.

Bill Clinton (b. 1946) was the first Boomer President. He won election and reelection against two Mature-generation opponents. The election in 2000 was the first in which two Boomers competed to win, Al Gore (b. 1948) and George W. Bush (b. 1946).

The Congressional Research Service reports that the 109th Congress elected in the midterm elections of 2006 installed what is "likely" the oldest Congress in American history, with an average age across both houses of fifty-six, right in the thick of the Boomer cohort.[13]

Boomer Chief Justice John Roberts (b. 1955) heads the U.S. Supreme Court. Fellow Justices include Boomers Clarence Thomas (b. 1948) and Samuel Alito (b. 1950).

In 2006, over three-quarters of the companies in the Fortune 500 had a Boomer CEO. Two of the three network news anchors are now Boomers: Brian Williams (b. 1959) on NBC, who took over for Tom Brokaw (b. 1940), and Katie Couric (b. 1957) on CBS, who took over for Dan Rather (b. 1931). Boomers Bob Woodruff (b. 1961) and Elizabeth Vargas (b. 1962) succeeded Peter Jennings (b. 1938) as co-anchors of ABC's *World News Tonight* until Woodruff was injured by an explosion while reporting from Iraq, at which point Charles Gibson (b. 1943) became the anchor. Boomers have a dominant presence on daytime talk TV as well, including Oprah Winfrey (b. 1954), Ellen DeGeneres (b. 1958), and Montel Williams (b. 1956). Boomers now occupy more than their fair share of the top positions in the arts, sciences, and clergy.

Boomers now control more than their fair share of total wealth as well. Data from the U.S. Census and the Federal Reserve show that as of 2001, those fifty and older controlled $28 trillion, or two-thirds of the nation's wealth,[14] an amount that is steadily inching up as Boomers accumulate more the older they get. The General Accounting Office reported in 2006 that Boomers own one-third of the value of stocks and bonds alone, a share that totals over $7.6 trillion.[15]

Boomers are no longer just a force of numbers. Over the last fifteen years or so, they have come to occupy most of the thought leadership positions in American society. Boomers cannot look to the future by borrowing from the prior generation. That generation is now exiting stage left, so Boomer ideas matter more than ever.

To understand where Boomers are headed, the past is no help. Baby Boomers have a view of their future possibilities that is more expansive than getting old and retiring. They have hopes, dreams, and aspirations about new directions and fresh pursuits. Boomers are not dropping out or downsizing their dreams. They continue to be inspired by big ideas.

With their numbers, interests, and determination, Boomers are driving an agenda that reaches beyond themselves. The entire marketplace will be affected.

There is a concept in the academic study of mass communications called agenda-setting that has a direct parallel here. Many academic researchers argue that the most important role of the media is not to tell people what to think but to tell them what to think about. By bringing certain topics and issues to people's attention, media determine the focus of public debate. Sometimes various media organs may take sides in a debate, but advocacy is not how they influence events. More than anything else, the impact of media comes from the power to focus people's attention on one thing instead of on another. It is the power to make certain issues salient, not the ability to control opinions about an issue. It is through this power of agenda-setting that media matter.[16]

Similarly, the big ideas that motivate aging Boomers will set the agenda for everyone else. It is in this way that Boomers will matter in the future—not so much by determining how various issues will be settled as by getting certain issues onto the table for active debate and consideration. Boomer numbers along with the Boomer resolve to stay engaged make anything in which they are interested important and salient to all. Predicting the future is as simple and as hard as knowing the big ideas motivating Boomers as they look toward the future.

Under Our Microscope

A core part of the Yankelovich business is to survey and track lifestyle and value trends in the consumer marketplace.[17] This has been a special expertise of our firm since the early 1960s, when Yankelovich pioneered the practice and study of generational marketing in a series of breakthrough studies about the role young Baby Boomers were playing in the social change then sweeping through American society. No organization has studied Boomers longer or in more depth than Yankelovich.

Florence Skelly, one of the co-founders of our firm, is the person who came up with and popularized the very term "Baby Boomers" itself.[18] Daniel Yankelovich led a series of nine studies between 1964 and 1974 that constitute the earliest and most definitive body of research about the rapidly changing values of America and of Baby Boomers, too, as Boomers were coming into their own.[19]

The first of these nine studies was conducted in 1964 and reported in 1965 for the Institute for Life Insurance. The results of the next study appeared in a *Fortune* magazine article in January 1968.[20] This was followed by a study that was the basis for a 1969 CBS documentary about Baby Boomers and social change, narrated in part by Walter Cronkite, called "Generations Apart."[21]

On the strength and visibility of the research for CBS, our firm was engaged by the John D. Rockefeller III Fund to complete six more annual studies from 1969 to 1974 tracking the values of Boomers.[22] The results of these tracking studies were published in two books, including *The New*

Morality: A Profile of American Youth in the 70's (New York: McGraw-Hill, 1974), which was excerpted at length in the *New York Times*. These were the first book-length treatments of Baby Boomers. On the basis of these and other insights developed over the next several years, Daniel Yankelovich authored a groundbreaking book about social change in America called *New Rules: Searching for Self-Fulfillment in a World Turned Upside Down* (New York: Random House, 1981).

As Baby Boomers came of age, generational marketing did, too. In 1997, senior Yankelovich consultants and the co-authors of this book, J. Walker Smith and Ann Clurman, published a highly regarded overview of different generations in their book *Rocking the Ages: The Yankelovich Report on Generational Marketing* (New York: HarperBusiness, 1997). New research reported in their book provided an updated understanding of the key elements of the Baby Boomer psyche.

Most of the Yankelovich research about Baby Boomers has focused on the things they want from their lives. People make shopping decisions on the basis of an underlying vision of the good life. This is the foundation guiding them about the sacrifices worth making and the things worth having in order to achieve a life worth living.

Yankelovich has now updated its understanding of the hopes, dreams, and aspirations of Baby Boomers in "Boomer Dreams," the only study of its kind ever completed about aging Baby Boomers. Conducted from June 26 to July 5, 2006 among a nationally representative sample of 1,023 Boomers, the results from this hour-long, in-depth interview are published for the first time in this book.

This study of Boomer dreams for the future covered three broad areas. First, Boomers were asked to score various aspects of their current situation. Second, they were asked to rate their worries and concerns about the future. Finally, Boomers were asked to gauge their commitment to different values and aspirations for the future. What Boomers are looking to achieve in the decades ahead constitutes the agenda of priorities that will shape the marketplace to come. The Yankelovich Boomer Dreams study estimates the significance of each priority by parsing the attitudes and ambitions of Boomers into those true of all and those true of only a few.

Booming Ahead

For decades, Baby Boomers have been chided for being self-centered, self-absorbed, self-confident, and utterly self-centered, even narcissistic. There's no argument here. Guilty as charged. But so what? It's all part of a generational sensibility rooted in numbers and mindset, and there's nothing bad about it per se. Boomers could not have turned out any other way. It's channeling this self-interested energy that's the challenge as well as the opportunity ahead.

The sheer size of the Boomer cohort has kept this generation front and center. From year one of the Boom, they have been the elephant in the room, hulking and looming, a cohort far too big and far too restless to ignore. Indelibly writ large in the public consciousness, Boomers have reveled in the attention like babies at bath time.

Boomer numbers and youthful vigor have made whatever they have pursued or followed the dominant concerns of America. But predicting the concerns and interests that will next dominate the country takes more than simply extrapolating from what Boomers have wanted in the past; it requires a fresh and deeper understanding of what they want next. Boomer numbers will catapult these ambitions to the top of the marketplace agenda for all generations.

two

Not Getting Old

*I*f one thing is true about Baby Boomers, it's their penchant—some would say their extravagant obsession—for making a federal case out of everything that personally affects them. It's no surprise, then, that in his 2006 State of the Union Address, President Bush used the fact that he was turning sixty later that year as his segue into a discussion of the "unprecedented strains on the federal government" ahead.[1] For Boomers, everything seems to start with what's happening to them.

In Bush's words, his sixtieth birthday was going to be more than unprecedented; it was going to be a "personal crisis." The unprecedented strains on the nation? Just a "national challenge." A very serious challenge, of course, but not a "crisis."

Now, maybe this is reading too much into Bush's remarks, but there is something telling, even if inadvertent, about the stronger language used to characterize his birthday than that used to describe the nation's challenges. It's emblematic of Baby Boomers struggling to come to terms with this personal milestone. It's a struggle that matters to everyone, because how Baby Boomers work this out will shape the next four decades no less than their numbers and attitudes have shaped the last six.

Yet despite all the hand-wringing, Boomers know how to make the most out of their personal situations. After all, Bush's bit of hyperbole was the setup for the best stand-up line of his presidency: "The first of nearly 78 million Baby Boomers turn sixty" in 2006, he noted, "including two of my dad's favorite people"—himself . . . and former President Bill Clinton!

..s Bush and Clinton are in good company. The list of Baby
...ers who turned sixty in 2006 is a cultural who's who: Steven Spielberg.
Cher. Reggie Jackson. Liza Minnelli. Diane Keaton. Sylvester Stallone.
Dolly Parton. Susan Sarandon. Donald Trump. Suzanne Somers. Robert
Reich. Loni Anderson. Linda Ronstadt. Susan Lucci. Susan St. James. Ken
Starr. Oliver Stone. Joe Greene. Tommy Lee Jones. Pat Sajak. Bob Beamon.
Jimmy Buffett. Michael Milken. Robby Krieger. Loudon Wainwright III.
Candice Bergen. Connie Chung. Al Green. Cheech Marin. Naomi Judd.
Richard Carpenter. David Lynch. Patricia Nixon Cox. Larry Csonka. Patty
Duke. Sandy Duncan. Sally Field. (Just to name a few.)

And don't forget about Kathleen Casey-Kirschling, the very first Baby
Boomer, born in Philadelphia an instant into the New Year on January 1,
1946. She was unearthed by Landon Jones, writer, historian, and former editor of *People* and *Money* magazines, as he was researching his groundbreaking 1980 book *Great Expectations: America and the Baby Boom Generation*
(New York: Coward McCann, 1980). Profiled again by Jones in the January
2006 issue of *Smithsonian*, Casey-Kirschling has lived a prototypical Boomer
life. Her father was a veteran and her mother a housewife. As a teenager, she
danced on *American Bandstand.* For a while, she drove a BMW. She married for the first time at twenty, later divorced and then remarried. She
has two children, one fewer than her parents, and five grandchildren. She
and her husband own investment property in Florida as well as a forty-two-
foot trawler they keep in Chesapeake Bay called "First Boomer."[2]

Stories about Baby Boomers turning sixty began appearing in late 2005
and made the front page of the *Wall Street Journal* as well as the covers
of *Newsweek*, *Business Week*, *American Heritage*, and *Parade.* During
2006, NBC and ABC aired continuing features about aging Boomers on
their evening news shows. *Newsweek* and MSNBC featured regular stories
about Boomers throughout 2006.

This explosion of media attention happens every time Baby Boomers
pass an age milestone—any excuse to ponder yet again the pig in the
python.

Roughly eight thousand Baby Boomers turned sixty every day in 2006.
This number will grow to more than ten thousand per day as the middle of

Marketing Thought-Starter: Celebrating Boomers

It is pretty well recognized that Boomers should not be addressed as "old people" or "seniors." This language does not resonate with Boomers and usually alienates them. On the other hand, they are responsive to marketing that uses an active, lively, youthful tone. This is longstanding marketing advice about aging Boomers, but Boomers are looking for more.

Boomers want to be celebrated. They like to be reminded that they are special, important, and unique. They crave the notice and the applause. The intensive media focus on their generation has conditioned them to expect accolades and acclaim. They revel in the attention, even when it's unflattering.

Since the first year of the post–World War II fertility boom, Baby Boomers have beguiled America, fascinating, infuriating, exasperating, and charming all observers, including Boomers themselves. The more they are debated and scrutinized, the more they hold center stage and thus the more they matter.

So don't lament their age by offering them fixes for old people who want to stay youthful. Celebrate their age as an enviable time of life. A youthful vocabulary is necessary but not enough. Boomers want plaudits, too.

the Boom reaches that threshold. This matters more than previous milestones, because sixty is a different kind of threshold. President Bush fretted about it so much that his misgivings became national news, including a front-page story in the *New York Times*.[3] He should take heart, though. A 2006 AARP survey of Baby Boomers born in 1946 found a plurality of 37 percent rating turning sixty as "more significant" than turning fifty.[4]

Every generation eventually reaches this turning point, but it matters more to Baby Boomers because reaching it is forcing them to confront a reality they have long ignored and denied: getting old. And it's not only leading-edge Boomers who are being forced to face up to this. The pervasive, unremitting media fixation on the topic of Boomers turning sixty has brought this subject to the attention of all Boomers. What's happening to a few Boomers has become the occasion for all Boomers to gaze into the future and picture themselves as ... *gasp!* ... old people.

Youthfulness

Four decades of Yankelovich research has found one thing about Boomers over and over again—an unwavering determination to *not get old*. To date, this repudiation of anything to do with getting old has been expressed primarily as a tireless, ongoing celebration of youthfulness. Their parents celebrated victory; the generation that followed them (Generation X) celebrated savvy. For Boomers, it's been all about youthfulness.

Youthfulness has been the most celebrated characteristic of this generation. Throughout their lives, Baby Boomers have been regaled with paeans to their youthful vigor and potential. Over and over, they were told that youth would lead the way, so unsurprisingly, they came to value their youthfulness as their most powerful and meaningful characteristic.

As Baby Boomers grew up, everything tied to their youthful generation mushroomed. First, baby products took off. Then school enrollments skyrock-

	Matures	Baby Boomers	Xers	Echo Boomers
Defining focus	Duty	Youthfulness	Savvy	Authenticity
Future	Rainy day to work for	"Now" is more important	Unpredictable but manageable	Working for my big break
Navigating	Right & Wrong	Good vs. Evil	Paradox	Shades of gray
What "new" needs to be	Revolutionary	Novel	Interesting	Genuine
Managing money	Save	Spend	Hedge	Control
Networking	Country club	Woodstock	At work	MySpace.com
War	World War II	Vietnam	Gulf War	War on Terrorism

Figure 2-1: Generational Essence

eted. Then active recreation exploded. Then travel went sky high. Then the stock market soared. Then real estate values surged. The interests and priorities of Baby Boomers became the concerns of America as a whole. Both lauded and reviled, Boomers and their youthful approach to life held center stage.

Youthfulness still holds sway as our shared understanding of Baby Boomers. The October 24, 2005 *Business Week* lead story on aging Boomers was promoted on the cover with a drawing of two older Boomers on a sailboard (with a C-note for a sail). The October 2005 *American Heritage* cover for its story on the "Boomer Century" used a picture of two children in a 1950s suburban setting. The December 11, 2005 *Parade* cover proclaiming that "Life Begins at 60" featured a picture of an active older woman wading through breaking surf. Youthful vigor is the consistent theme in all of this cover art.

Many things have been posited as characteristic of this generation: individualistic, spiritual, organic, experiential, experimental, adventurous, discriminating, extravagant, vigorous, self-righteous, rebellious, skeptical, questioning, searching, self-absorbed, self-seeking. To a greater or lesser extent, all of these things are true of Baby Boomers, but an underlying mindset of youthfulness accounts for all of them.

Baby Boomers have brought a youthful sensibility to every situation and to every stage of their lives. In the years ahead, the challenge for Boomers—and for marketers and policymakers who want to win their allegiance—will be negotiating the intersection of the emerging physical reality of aging with the enduring psychological dynamic of youthfulness.

Not Getting Old

Youthfulness is a multifaceted attitude about life. Not teenage immaturity or angst, but a lifestyle involving an intense, critical questioning of established ways of doing things and a desire for fresh, exhilarating experiences. It is about always looking at things anew, with fresh eyes and fresh energy and with a willingness to try something different.

Youthfulness is a sensibility that defines itself as much by what it is *not* as by what it is. It is not acting, thinking, or being old. For Boomers, being old involves closure; youthfulness involves continuous exploration and re-invention. Being old involves deceleration and frailty; youthfulness involves energy and robustness. Being old involves convention and tradition; youthfulness involves transformation and innovation. Boomers have not matured into midlife reconciled with being old; instead, they have endeavored to stay youthful at every age. Or to put it another way, the youthful mindset of Boomers has always been about not getting old.

Generally speaking, youth is thought to be a time of exploration and self-discovery. For Boomers, though, this journey of self-discovery is life-long, not merely a time of life.

For marketers, connecting with this sense of youthfulness means more than populating ads with young-looking actors. It means leveraging the multifaceted hooks associated with the various dimensions of youthfulness. Figure 2-2 shows the manifold ways in which this dynamic shows up in the texture and character of life for this generation.

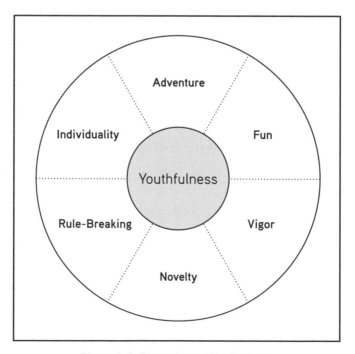

Figure 2-2: Dimensions of Youthfulness

Throughout their lives, youthfulness has meant a style of life for Baby Boomers that is adventurous and fun, lived with vigor and energy, devoted to novelty and experimentation, and committed to going one's own way instead of being bound by a bunch of old rules. It means not getting old by staying youthful in one or more of these several ways.

Not getting old means constantly questioning and experimenting. Not getting old means having renewed vigor and energy for the ongoing adventure and fun of life. Not getting old means refusing to be pigeonholed by age. Not getting old means being open to novel possibilities at each stage of life.

Indeed, limitations from getting older are unlikely to trouble Baby Boomers to the same extent as they did prior generations. While Boomers will have to face up to the realities and costs of age-related infirmities, they will benefit from a better overall quality of life. For one thing, most people overestimate their risks of disease and debility in old age, so Boomers will mature into a period of life that is better than they thought it would be and that is getting better all the time. Today's generation of older Americans enjoys a much longer health expectancy, or years of active old age, than the generation before them—about a decade more. Baby Boomers will enjoy even longer spans of healthy years with continuing declines in chronic disabilities and mortality rates from heart disease and cancer.

Of course, not all Boomers are committed to wellness and fitness. The 2005 Yankelovich Preventive Health Care study found that 38.4 percent of Boomers never exercise and that 31.3 percent, the highest percentage across all generations, report a BMI (Body Mass Index) that would classify them as obese. Other studies have found that obesity, asthma, diabetes, high blood pressure, and certain types of cancer have risen among fifty- and sixty-year-olds in recent years.[5] Some researchers have started to worry aloud that obesity, more stress, less sleep, and fewer support networks put aging Boomers at greater health risks than the previous generation, something reflected already in less positive self-characterizations by Boomers of their health.[6]

Nevertheless, for the most part, Boomers have lived fitter lifestyles than prior generations. They have more education and have worked in less dangerous occupations. They have smoked less and eaten better diets (albeit with plenty of room for improvement on both counts). And they will continue to benefit from advances in medicine and pharmaceuticals and from improvements in the safety of the things they use and the environments within which they work, play, and live. Compared to older people in the past, Boomers will actually have a greater opportunity and ability to live a more youthful old age.

Already, the percentage of those over sixty-five with a substantial, life-altering disability is lower than in the past—only 19.7 percent in 1999 compared to 26.2 percent in 1982. These data were reported by a major U.S. Census Bureau study released in 2006 that was completed on behalf of the National Institute on Aging. Compiling and analyzing data about the health of older people from nearly a dozen federal agencies, these researchers found that older people today are healthier than ever before and will be even healthier in the future. Citing better education and greater prosperity—key correlates of better health—they forecast a growing health expectancy for Boomers as they get older.[7]

Old age with a youthful feel to it will, in turn, cause Boomers to remain more vigorous and engaged as they age, and the impact of this will be to transform the experience of aging for many Boomers into one of not getting old. A decade-long study on aging sponsored by the John D. and Catherine T. MacArthur Foundation found that on average, only one-third of the variance in how people age is genetic. Two-thirds is attributable to environmental and lifestyle factors. The ways in which people choose to live determine the quality and character of how they age. Staying engaged in one's life is a big part of how well one ages.[8] In contrast to prior generations, Baby Boomers bring a lifetime of youthful attitudes and habits to their advancing years that will serve them well as they age.

All Together Now

The commitment to a youthful approach to life is universal among Baby Boomers. It's apparent in everything they do as well as in the results of the Yankelovich Boomer Dreams study. Boomers have many differences, yet their universal agreement about youthfulness and the related dimensions of impact and possibility demonstrate both the value and the validity of looking at everyone born from 1946 to 1964 as part of the Baby Boomer cohort.

All Boomers can be said to share a common value or attitude if 80 percent or more express the same opinion and if that percentage is invariant across Boomer subgroups. These are the foundational beliefs of Boomers, the values and attitudes for which Boomers of all types think alike and in nearly universal proportions.

By this measure, all Boomers, whatever their birth year during the fertility boom, believe in three things:

1. Youthfulness: A belief in an ageless engagement with life that is active, spirited, and exuberant.
2. Impact: A desire to have an enduring influence in making a difference.
3. Possibility: A sense of personal development built upon empowerment and continuous progression.

Each of these beliefs is an important component of the mindset of aging Boomers who want to matter. Youthfulness is particularly important, because it is the primary element that transforms the Boomer experience of aging and their future sense of self.

Figure 2-3 shows the various questions about youthfulness in the Yankelovich Boomer Dreams research.

Boomers see unlimited opportunities in their futures. They don't fret about getting old, nor do they believe that there is little to look forward to in their older years. They believe the future belongs as much to them as to young people and they believe in cross-generational sharing and borrowing. Boomers are carrying this youthful sensibility forward:

- Agreement with "maintain[ing] a youthful spirit" was the attitudinal statement garnering the highest level of agreement for any item in the Boomer Dreams study. This is *the* defining attitude for Boomers.

People should try to maintain a youthful spirit about life	96.6%
Young people can learn a lot from my generation	92.6%
There is no reason why young people and older people can't enjoy the same kinds of things	92.2%
There is no reason that you have to feel less vital and energetic as you get older	89.0%
In the future, older people will be much more active and engaged than older people in the past	88.7%
I like knowing what young people are doing and creating	87.7%
Disagree: There is little for people my age to look forward to besides getting older and coping with old age	85.6%
Disagree: I worry all the time about getting older	84.5%
Disagree: The future belongs to the next generation; my generation won't have much to do with it	83.2%

Top 2 box or bottom 2 box on 4-point scale
Source: Yankelovich Boomer Dreams Study, 2006

Figure 2-3: Youthfulness

- Boomers have no expectations that aging will or should slow them down.
- Boomers see no reason to model their older years after the experiences of prior generations. They believe that they will be more "active and engaged" in their older years than prior generations.
- Aging is not such a declining or gloomy prospect that Boomers are worried about it.
- Boomers intend to have as much to say about the future as the generations to come. They want to teach what they know to the next generation, as well as learn what the next generation has to teach them.

This Boomer spirit is also seen in the shared belief that they can have an impact and make a difference. Figure 2-4 shows the numerous ways in which this interest is expressed.

Tip 3

I am very passionate about the causes I care about	94.8%
The actions of a single individual can make a big difference in life	94.8%
People have a responsibility to leave the world a better place than they found it	94.2%
I think it is important for all of us to look for ways in which we can get involved and improve society	93.7%
I like to keep up with politics and public issues	92.2%
I feel a responsibility to help others out and support the common good	89.9%
The challenges our society faces in the future are formidable and alarming	89.6%
We can solve the social problems we face today if everybody would just do their one small part to help	85.3%

Top 2 box on 4-point scale
Source: Yankelovich Boomer Dreams Study, 2006

Figure 2-4: Making an Impact

Boomers are passionate about what they can do and contribute as individuals to keep up, get involved, and help out. They believe no social problem is beyond solution if everyone does his or her part.

- Boomers feel that "passion" is what they bring to the things that are important to them.
- Boomers evince a strong sense of personal responsibility. They believe individuals can make a difference for a better society and the common good, so everyone should do his or her "one small part to help."
- Boomers believe there is a critical need for passion, personal responsibility, and unending involvement to deal with the future.

In contrast to many of the stereotypes of their generation as selfish and cavalier, Boomers believe in duty and accountability. They recognize that they have obligations for which they are personally responsible, and that they are not merely responsible for themselves but for "leaving the world a better place," "getting involved and improving society," and "supporting the common good." Not only do Boomers believe that they should pitch in and do their part; they feel empowered, not encumbered or deficient.

In fact, all Boomers believe in a number of bedrock values related to morality, private property, duty, independence, thrift, and the social responsibilities of business, as shown in Figure 2-5.

These attitudes cut across the diverse political and religious beliefs of Baby Boomers and belie the stereotype that they are utterly and irredeemably self-absorbed and hedonistic. Boomers of every stripe believe in "living a clean, moral life." They may not acquit themselves on every single moral and social value, but on these, at least, they do.

As Figure 2-6 shows, Boomers believe in technology as a means of enabling them to explore and enjoy life. The "possibilities" opened up by technology are not going to end anytime soon; they are "only going to continue to grow."

Boomers have always believed in the potential of technology. They may

Living a clean, moral life is a very important value	87.4%
Private property is sacred	86.1%
A woman does not have to have a man around to be happy	85.5%
Duty comes before pleasure	85.2%
In every situation, I have a very clear sense of the right and the wrong thing to do	80.6%
I feel the need not to live beyond my means	80.3%
Business is too concerned with profits and not enough with public responsibility	80.2%

Top 2 box on 4-point scale
Source: Yankelovich Boomer Dreams Study, 2006

Figure 2-5: Basic Values and Beliefs

The possibilities afforded to us by technology are only going to continue to grow	96.6%
I know how to use technology to make my life more interesting and more enjoyable	90.2%

Top 2 box on 4-point scale
Source: Yankelovich Boomer Dreams Study, 2006

Figure 2-6: Technology

have a different style and purpose than younger generations when it comes to technology, but they are no less devoted to the mastery and adoption of new technologies. Boomers ushered in the PC era and then funded and facilitated the emergence of the dot-com era. Boomers still matter in the rapidly evolving arena of technology.

Boomers are guarded about government, which is not terribly surprising for a generation weaned on Vietnam and Watergate. Governmental involvement and solutions are viewed with circumspection, as Figure 2-7 shows.

However, these attitudes don't suggest that Boomers see no place for government. More than a statement about government, these attitudes betray the sense of competence that Boomers feel about their own powers and possibilities. Boomers want to challenge and improve themselves and their own capacities for remaining engaged and in charge. They don't want government to take the initiative away from them.

Government is far too involved in our private lives	81.8%
Government isn't the best answer for most of the problems we face	80.5%

Top 2 box on 4-point scale
Source: Yankelovich Boomer Dreams Study, 2006

Figure 2-7: Government

The Boomer sense of personal possibility is a belief that life should be an ongoing journey of self-exploration and self-improvement. Boomers don't want to mature into anything fixed and immutable; they want to stay flexible and adaptable, questioning and curious, discovering and learning. This openness and elasticity is one hallmark of youth, not to mention the essential ingredient for a continuing focus on self. Boomers never want to lose this youthful plasticity of aptitude and form. They want to be as adaptable in the future as they ever were in the past. They want to develop their next self. To this end, they value continuous discovery, experimentation, and re-invention, as Figure 2-8 shows.

Boomers don't believe in closure. They don't believe in limits. Boomers don't believe that age should be a limiting factor on life's possibilities. Rather, they believe that life is "a set of endless opportunities no matter what your age."

The shared beliefs of all Boomers about youthfulness, impact, and possibility constitute the platform on which they will come to terms with everything else, as well as the only context within which generalizations about them can be properly made. But there are pitfalls from misreading or over-interpreting the Boomer focus on youthfulness. Youthfulness is an approach to aging, not some clinging to juvenilia or a happy-go-lucky way of life. Boomers simply want an old age with a youthful spirit in which they can continue to matter. They live for the possibilities to come.

I believe life is a set of endless opportunities no matter what your age	87.3%
I am concerned about trying to stay in shape	80.0%
I am concerned about taking care of myself	79.6%
It is important in my personal life today to stretch myself and try new things	78.1%

Top 2 box on 4-point scale
Source: Yankelovich Boomer Dreams Study, 2006

Figure 2-8: Self-Improvement

Middle Age–less

Aging tempered by youth is neither old nor young. It is something in between, something in the middle. That is the age Baby Boomers want forever—not an old age in which they fade away, but an older age in which they are endlessly vital, indeed, as vital as they are now in their midlife prime. Boomers see old age as the next opportunity for their youthful lifestyles. Aging with a spirit of youthfulness is the new context of their lives.

Boomers recognize that they are aging, but they do not see themselves as getting old. They are far from the age at which they think old age begins. In 1996, when the first Baby Boomers were turning fifty, Yankelovich conducted a survey asking them, among other things, the age at which they thought that old age begins. The median response was 79.5! It's interesting to note that in 1996, the average life span in the United States was 76.1, so it is not too far a stretch to conclude it is literally true that Baby Boomers think they will die before they get old.

More important, though, is the fact that if Boomers think that old age starts around eighty, then those in their fifties and sixties are in early middle age, not early old age. With the start of old age decades away, Boomers expect to enjoy an extended middle age, not an extended old age. The extra years of energy and vitality that they will have are not being tacked onto the end of their lives. Boomers will be able to enjoy and prolong the middle of their lives. As far as they are concerned, middle age is where they are, where they will be for decades to come, and where they would most like to be forever.

Boomers may be aging, but even so they remain middle-aged. They don't want to live longer as old people; they want to live endlessly as middle-aged people. Boomers want to be *middle age–less*.

Boomers will not abandon their youthful spirit, but neither will they return to juvenile things. Instead, they will employ their sense of youthfulness to remake the experience of aging into one of aging without getting old, heralding a coming era of perpetually middle-aged people, not a generation of active old people.

There is no existing term to describe Boomers who don't want to be young or old but who, instead, want to be youthful even as they age, so no measurement of Boomers using traditional labels or concepts can capture the way they are thinking about their advancing years. A new way of characterizing aging Boomers is needed: middle age–less.

Middle age–less means they are neither old nor young, but in their prime, in the midlife in which they have had the means and the opportunities to fully express and enjoy the youthful spirit they value so much. Not fading from the scene, but ageless, transcending the limitations and stereotypes of old age to be more engaged, more influential, and thus more youthful than ever.

Portrayals of Boomers as old people or as retro-juveniles are both misleading. Boomers don't want to be either one. They know that it is time to move on, but they are no less determined than ever to keep from getting old. Boomers are seeking a new state of maturity. They want to age without ceasing to matter, and they intend to do so by forging a new alloy of old age and youthfulness that is best described as middle age–less.

For some observers, this push toward an endless middle age degrades the dignity and satisfaction of old age. Daniel Callahan, a leading bioethicist and co-founder of The Hastings Center, a bioethics research institute, has warned that "pretending" old age can be lived as an endless middle age

Marketing Thought-Starter: Empty Nesting, Not Retirement, Is Next

Over the last several years, there has been a plethora of media stories about Boomers and retirement, as if this is the next life stage for Boomers. It is not. Their next life stage is empty-nesting. Even if Boomers retire at sixty-five (which is unlikely, as discussed in the next chapter), there are years to go before the majority of them reach that age. Building near-term business strategies around Boomer retirement is premature by decades. The focus should be on Boomers as empty-nesters, spreading their wings for years to come, with retirement a distant prospect over the horizon.

"robs" the elderly of a vital and consequential part of their old age, that of "meaning and significance."9

Yet this is *precisely* the issue for Baby Boomers. As they age, they want to matter in significant and consequential ways no less than they have already. This is why Generation Ageless Boomers are determined to not get old. If getting old means being ignored, dismissed, or disparaged, then Boomers will finesse it in the way they know best—by redefining old age with a youthful spirit in order to be middle age–less.

Boomers have never known an age at which they didn't matter. Due to their numbers, Boomers mattered a lot even during their youngest ages, defying traditional expectations. So continuing to matter during their oldest ages, also in defiance of traditional expectations, is completely in keeping with their generational experience.

Boomers have learned that getting what they want comes from having a youthful spirit, so it is by redefining getting old, not by accepting getting old, that they see the chance to remain connected, engaged, and influential and thus avoid losing relevance and regard. For Boomers, endless middle age is the best way to hold onto the meaning and significance that Callahan and others see as crucial to the well-being and self-esteem of older people.

A Life in Progress

Ignoring Boomers because they are older is risky. Yet advertisers pay a premium only for younger audiences—about 30 percent more per TV ad minute for a prime-time audience of viewers thirty-four to forty-nine versus viewers fifty-five–plus[10]—so in turn, networks and media buyers routinely give short shrift to fifty-plus audiences.

It is presumed that brand choices are fixed for older consumers. Marketing to them is thought to be unproductive if not pointless since they are unlikely to try anything new. It is also assumed that older people without children living at home won't spend as much, because the needs of their households are not as great without children to buy and save for. Finally, it is felt that the shopping interests of older consumers are only about things to fix the ailments of old age.

These notions may have been true of older consumers in the past, but they are not true of middle age–less Boomers. The rules of thumb for buying media presume that age is a good shorthand for motivations and preferences, so aging Boomers get pigeonholed by age. Yet the nullification of anything strictly tied to age better typifies Boomers. To think that they are finished simply because they don't measure up on media targeting criteria is to miss the huge opportunity that middle age–less Boomers continue to represent in the marketplace.

The fact that aging Boomers are less fashion-forward than young people does not mean that they are uninterested in originality and innovation. Boomers are not closed to new experiences or new products that can further their ongoing quest for self-discovery. The AARP reports that contrary to stereotypes, 60 percent of those over forty research and consider a variety of brands before buying.[11] Young people are not the only ones attracted to novelty and experimentation.

Certainly, many products and media are not relevant to older consumers, but Boomers are far from the age at which they believe further self-development is no longer possible. In the Yankelovich Boomer Dreams study, the average age at which Boomers felt that "a person is beyond starting anything new and innovative" in his or her life was 86.6—much older than today's average life span and well past the age at which they think old age begins. For college-educated Boomers, it's even older, at 89.3.

Boomers are not yet done with their lifelong focus on self. They remain unfinished—still evolving, developing, and creating.

This is why the investment firm Ameriprise has named its retirement and financial planning process "Dream > Plan > Track > sm." For Boomers, what comes first is to dream; working through the numbers comes second. This involves more than setting goals. This is envisioning a life in progress, not a life in its final act. "Passion," "satisfaction," and "fulfillment"—the language used by Ameriprise—are the pillars of a good plan. The financial inputs of current age, retirement age, current income, monthly savings, life expectancy, tax shelters, retirement income needs, and the like go into the planning calculus but don't start the planning process.

Ameriprise wants its Boomer clients to begin by answering the ten questions about personal "possibilities" in its *Dream Book*sm. Other firms typically begin with something more mundane, such as an inventory of financial assets. Ameriprise understands that middle age–less Boomers want something in addition to financial security; they want the means to continue their dreams of self-discovery and personal fulfillment. In print ads, Ameriprise crosses out 401(k) in the question "Do you have a 401(k) plan?" and replaces it with the word "dream."

Boomers won't chase fashions and fads, but they will keep evolving in fresh, original ways. Youthfulness, not maturity, is their spirit. Impact, not surrender, is their aim. Possibility, not closure, is their spur. Reengagement, not retirement, is how they envision the future.

Keeping Their Place

Stereotypes and ageism play a part in the societal expectation that getting old necessitates a loss of import. But Boomers, with a lifelong focus on youthfulness as the essence of their lifestyles, do not aspire to becoming respected elders in a more understanding and inclusive society; they want to be forever influential on their own.

Indeed, by remaking what it means to be old, Boomers will add their numbers to yet another revolution of social values. Boomer numbers will make it difficult if not impossible to treat old people as before. The vestiges of ageism and its biased stereotypes are likely to be overwhelmed by the new spirit and fresh voice of millions of Boomers demanding respect and the right to be heard. In the same way that the mass of outspoken and impatient Boomers brought critical weight to environmentalism, the anti–Vietnam War movement, women's rights, gay rights, and even the civil rights movement, so, too, are Boomers likely to be decisive in the cause of greater rights, protections, and guarantees for older people.

By redefining the experience of aging through their example, Boomers will undermine stereotypes and discredit prejudices, particularly as they continue to occupy key positions of power and thought leadership.

Boomers won't be pioneering the fight against ageism, of course. Important legal protections already exist, particularly the Older Americans Act of 1965 and the Age Discrimination in Employment Act of 1967. Yet prejudices persist. They are rooted in views of older people as infirm and past their prime. The result is a chauvinistic approach to interacting with old people that can often be noninclusive, pandering, and demeaning as well as discriminatory in medical care, employment, and social services—exactly the sort of treatment against which youthful-minded, middle age–less Baby Boomers will rebel. To an extent far greater than prior generations, Boomers have the numbers, the votes, the pocketbooks, the verve, the experience, and, at last, the self-interest to make a difference by taking a stand.

As Boomers advance their own generational interests, they will sometimes find themselves squared off against younger generations. Hence many dark scenarios have been advanced about an intergenerational conflict to come. However, none of these projections contemplate Boomers as middle age–less; all are predicated upon their getting old. "Old" Boomers would demand more, offer less, and bring little but needy numbers to the future. Middle age–less Boomers, on the other hand, will continue to be active, engaged contributors. Middle age–less Boomers will pay their way. Middle age–less Boomers will matter no less than ever.

Almost all of the headlines about Boomers bode little but horror stories about their pending retirements. But the fact of the matter is that retirement is not next up for Boomers. And even when it does arrive, they will not settle into it as a deceleration into death. A retiree stereotype is not the best way to divine the future for Boomers who want to continue to matter.

three
Working on Mattering

*O*ur common understanding of the concept of retirement does not apply to Baby Boomers.

Not only is it unclear whether Boomers will be able to afford a retirement like their parents; they don't want it. (So is it really any surprise that
they haven't saved for it?) Yet so many products and services have been ar-
chitected on the expectation that they will retire in this manner that we
have trouble seeing Baby Boomers for what they really are—a generation
with no interest in retirement, at least not as we define it today.

Although the resolve of Baby Boomers is clear, many generation-watchers
miss it because they continue to plot the trajectory of Boomers with an out-
dated mode of reckoning. A word to the wise: *Do not plan around the expectation that Baby Boomers will retire in the manner of the generation before
them.*

The whole notion of retirement as it has come to be understood over the
last seventy years is not a relevant framework within which to think about
what Boomers will mean for the future of the marketplace. Yet we throw the
word "retirement" around as if we take it for granted that retirement as we
know it today is an intrinsic, predestined stage in life going back to time im-
memorial. In fact, the contemporary style of retirement is a relatively recent
phenomenon arising from an unusual confluence of circumstances that are
now changing rapidly.

As late as 1930, when the average life expectancy in the United States
was 59.7, nearly 60 percent of men sixty-five years of age and older were
active participants in the labor force. In other words, they continued to

work for a living. From the middle of the nineteenth century to the end, a period in which the average life span was about forty, two-thirds to three-quarters of men sixty-five and older continued to work. It wasn't until the mid-twentieth century that rising income levels and a growing number of public and private pensions made it possible for the overwhelming majority of men to retire by age sixty-five. Today, with the average life span almost seventy-eight, fewer than 20 percent of men sixty-five and older continue to work.[1]

Life span comparisons can be misleading, because infant and adolescent mortality rates were much higher in the past, thus dragging down the average. In fact, the biggest part of the increase in average life span during the twentieth century was due to declines in infant mortality. So for the comparisons just discussed, it's relevant to add that in 1930, only 5.4 percent of the U.S. population was sixty-five or older versus 12.4 percent in 2000.[2] In other words, differences in infant mortality notwithstanding, men in 1930 were much more likely to work to the very end of their lives than men are today.

Of those in that much smaller percentage who did live to the retirement age of sixty-five in the late 1930s and early 1940s, their average life expectancy at that age was close to another thirteen years. Nowadays, it's five years longer than that,[3] so a comparable retirement age today would be at least seventy. Conceptually, this is an extension of a working middle age in precisely the way that middle age–less Boomers think about their lives in general: more years for their midlife prime, not for their old-age senescence.

For the prior generation, declining costs and more time for leisure made retirement an attractive lifestyle. By and large, medical expenses were affordable or covered, so there was no need to keep working to ensure good health care coverage. And a growing population of young Boomers vying for their jobs pinched off the need and opportunities for them to work longer. As these factors came together, retirement assumed its current incarnation of a life phase built upon a complete and worry-free disengagement from the workaday world.

Consumer marketing of a leisure-only retirement helped sell the concept to a generation of workers under pressure to make room for younger workers, first during the Depression and later as Boomers grew up. This lifestyle eventually became known as the "golden years," a marketing neologism coined by developer Del Webb to promote his Sun City retirement communities. More broadly, though, a retirement filled with leisure was seen as a profound break with the past that was yet another triumph of American economic prosperity. It was a broad social idea that promised a reward to workers for decades of demanding and often unfulfilling labor and reassured them that life after work would continue to have value. It was good for business, too, especially for developers, homebuilders, automobile manufacturers, travel companies, and the like.[4]

Nowadays, to retire means to step aside and let others take the reins. Retirement has come to entail a resignation and a retreat underwritten by the work of younger people who aspire to enjoy for themselves one day the same comforts and support.

It is a specific combination of attitudes and finances that makes this kind of retirement a viable possibility. Older people must be willing to let younger people take charge, and younger people must be able to generate a surplus sufficient to provide for retirees. Neither is the case for Baby Boomers, however. Most especially, Boomers are unwilling to disengage and relinquish control. They don't aspire to nothing more than an eternal vacation.

The worst part of retirement for Boomers is that, generally speaking, you do it when you get old. While Boomers are willing to accept that they are aging, they are unwilling to think of themselves as getting old. So they reject anything associated with getting old, like retirement.

It probably goes without saying that the term "retirement" triggers images of old age, but it's worth hearing a Baby Boomer say it. When Boomer Bill Cowher (b. 1957) announced in early 2007 that he was resigning as head coach of the Pittsburgh Steelers, he made a point of not using the word "retirement." "That [word]," he said, "makes you feel old."[5]

Some media headlines of late have taken a new tone about retirement. The cover of *U.S. News & World Report* on June 12, 2006 proclaimed "Seven

Marketing Thought-Starter:
Retirement Is an Attitude, Not a Life Situation

Retirement is more than the presence or absence of work; it is also an attitude about how one is engaged in life. Traditional retirement carries with it a presumption of deceleration and withdrawal—less involvement with the world at large and more focus on one's particular situation. Declining health often necessitates this.

Aging Boomers are going to stay in the workforce longer, perhaps indefinitely, but even more than that, they are going to stay more tightly engaged. Boomers are not yet ready to give up their influence and impact, and they do not anticipate ever being willing to do so.

Whatever the status of Boomers with respect to work, their attitudes will never be consistent with the traditional idea of retirement. In this way at least, Boomers will never retire. Attitudinally, they won't retire and decelerate; instead, their attitudes will reflect a new sense of involvement and possibility.

For marketers, this will mean an end to the correspondence between material life situation and consumer motivations now taken for granted and built into business strategies and advertising campaigns. For Boomers, retiring from work won't mean retiring from an active, engaged life. Marketers will find new opportunities for connecting with aging consumers as they are forced to remake their approach to a generation that views itself as middle age–less, not old; reinventive, not retiring.

Reasons *Not* to Retire." The entire 2006 Annual Retirement Guide included in that issue—20 percent of the issue's pages—delved into reasons why "working longer could be better for you—and your wallet." For Boomers, there's more to consider than just the prospect of golden years.

Workers believe that work is crucial in their lives. A 2002 AARP survey of workers ages forty-five to seventy-four found nearly universal agreement about the importance of work.[6] Ninety-one percent said that working keeps them healthy and active; 87 percent said it is important to their self-esteem; 84 percent said they would work even if they didn't need to financially;

76 percent said they enjoyed working; 62 said they wouldn't feel as good about themselves if they weren't working. Indeed, 89 percent said that their work makes a useful contribution to society.

Not only is retirement not the right concept for understanding Baby Boomers; the traditional retirement age is not even on the horizon for the vast majority of them. All the to-do about Boomers and retirement is misleading. The very next stage of life for Boomers is not retirement, so approaching them as if they are on the verge of retiring puts the focus on the wrong set of needs, interests, and opportunities. While Boomers won't continue to be engaged in the same pursuits that have absorbed them so far, they will pioneer new ways to channel their enduring desire for engagement. Simply put, Boomers are not going to give up their place at the table.

No Gold Watch

To say that Boomers won't retire so that they can continue to matter is not to say that they will continue to do what they are doing now. Certainly, Boomers will progress, develop, and do different things, and they will change the ways in which they are connected to and involved with the workforce. But these changes won't move them into a state of retirement.

The idea of retirement as we commonly think of it today entails several key elements:

1. *Not working:* Quitting work after reaching a certain age or asset level for a life centered on leisure activities and other nonwork pursuits.
2. *Pensioned:* Living comfortably yet more frugally on a reduced income that is secured through personal savings and/or a guaranteed pension.
3. *Maturity:* Viewing future possibilities with a maturing sensibility and perspective about age, limitations, and legacy.
4. *Surrender:* Stepping aside to allow the next generation to set the societal agenda and hold sway in the marketplace.

5. *Closure:* Settling into a final identity and approach to life that is the culmination of a lifetime of experiences and learning.

Retirement isn't relevant to Baby Boomers because none of these elements will be true of aging Boomer lifestyles. Most Boomers are not thinking in terms of these elements as they contemplate their futures.

Certainly, Boomers think about retirement. They are bombarded with marketing appeals and media headlines admonishing them to save for retirement. Almost everything they read and hear about their generation nowadays is rooted in something to do with retirement. And for many Boomers, retirement is more than just some future abstraction. These Boomers have firsthand experience with the retirement of their parents. A 2005 survey found that 13 million Boomers are caring for their retired, ailing parents.[7] In fact, a fifteen-year study conducted by researchers at the Leonard Davis School of Gerontology at the University of Southern California and published in 2006 found that Boomers exhibit a stronger commitment than the prior generation to caring for their aging parents.[8] When it hits this close to home, they can't help but think about retirement and what the future may hold for them.

When Boomers think about their futures, though, they have something else in mind than what retirement has meant for their parents. In every way, they look at it differently.

	Grandma Was	Grandma Is
Food	"Please...eat, eat! Do you want some more?"	"Do you have the kids on South Beach?"
The market	"How much are bananas?"	"What's the Dow doing?"
Plastic	On the couch	In the wallet
Jewels	"This was my mother's."	"This is my new bling."
The Web	Dust it	Surf it

Figure 3-1: Not the Same "Old" Retirement

> ## Marketing Thought-Starter:
> ## A New Role for Boomers
>
> In rejecting the notion of retirement, Boomers are also refusing to take on the role of "retiree." Having thought of themselves as youthful for so long, they now find themselves psychologically unable to fill those shoes. As we punned in our first book, *Rocking the Ages: The Yankelovich Report on Generational Marketing* (New York: HarperCollins, 1997), Boomers will not retire; they will retread. Retreading is a role they're willing to play. Boomers want to stay mentally and physically active and connected with others. It's okay to relax as long as doing so is taking a break, not dropping out.
>
> The role of retiree puts leisure first. Boomers aren't averse to leisure, but they want a balance of work and leisure, not too much of one or the other. In the 2006 MONITOR survey, 70 percent of Boomers agreed that "having balance between work and personal life" is a sign of success and accomplishment, a data point typically interpreted to mean that Boomers want less work. That interpretation is true enough, but this data point doesn't mean no work at all. It literally means balance.
>
> The role of retiree also involves family, travel, and medical care. Boomers like these, too, but envision them more broadly as relationships, experiences, and vitality. They want a role that preserves possibility, not one that necessitates closure. Not retiring but renewing, resurging, and remaining on the scene.

Nine to Five

Even as they age, Boomers remain highly engaged in their jobs. Aging Boomer employees are not simply punching the clock. A 2003 survey by consulting firm Towers Perrin found that employees age fifty and older are much more motivated than younger employees to "exceed" expectations in their jobs.[9] This kind of employee engagement is crucial to business performance. As a Towers Perrin analysis shows, companies with higher employee engagement outperform their competitors across a range of key financial measures, including revenue growth and cost management.[10]

Companies ignore at their peril the vigor and commitment of their Baby Boomer employees.

The issue is more than work style, however; it's the fact of working at all. Boomers are not going to leave the workforce in a hurry. A survey conducted in late 2006 for the U.S. Department of the Treasury and Federal Reserve Banks found that only 16 percent of Boomers who had not yet retired planned to start collecting Social Security as soon as they become eligible at age sixty-two, compared to 34 percent of those already retired who had done so.[11] Every survey ever conducted on this subject finds the vast majority of Boomers agreeing that they will work either full- or part-time after retirement or work past the traditional age of retirement. In the Yankelovich Boomer Dreams study, 74.6 percent of Boomers said they would work either full- or part-time in retirement.

AARP surveys in 1998 and 2003 found 80 and 79 percent, respectively, of Boomers expecting to work in retirement.[12] In a 2005 Merrill Lynch survey, it was 76 percent of Boomers.[13] In a 1999 Scudder Kemper Investments survey, it was 74 percent of Boomers.[14] In a 2005 survey conducted by the Rutgers University John J. Heldrich Center for Workforce Development, it was 66 percent.[15] In a 2005 survey conducted by Pulte Homes, parent company of Del Webb and its iconic Sun City developments, it was 64 percent (with another 13 percent saying neither retirement nor work, perhaps because for them retirement is not an unambiguously better option).

There is more to Boomers and retirement than working *in* retirement. Boomers will work longer and therefore retire at older ages, too.

Compared to the prior generation, a much bigger percentage of Boomers expect to work *past* the traditional retirement age of sixty-five. In a 1979 survey completed for the National Commission on Social Security, only 9 percent of nonretirees expected that they would retire at an age past sixty-five, and only 15 percent of those already retired reported having retired at an age past sixty-five.[16] In the 2005 Rutgers study, on the other hand, 22 percent of Boomers thought that they would be older than sixty-five before they would be able to retire. Similarly, in the 2005 Pulte survey, 22 percent of Boomers agreed that they would not be retiring "as soon as I thought." In the 2005 Merrill Lynch survey, 13 percent reported an actual or expected retirement age of seventy. Compared to thirty years ago, expectations today are very different.

Obviously, finances play a big part in shaping these expectations, ambitions, and plans. The need for income as a motivation to work in retirement is not unimportant, but, typically, surveys find that enjoyment is a more frequently cited reason than need. The AARP found in both 1998 and 2003 that a larger percentage of Boomers said they would work part-time in retirement mainly for enjoyment than mainly for needed income. The Rutgers University survey found the same pattern.

Marketing Thought-Starter: Work in Place

Not retiring does not mean that Boomers will keep commuting. Boomers will develop new work styles to fit their new personal priorities. Work will come home.

Home is a central point of life for Boomers. In the 2006 MONITOR survey, 65 percent agreed they prefer spending their leisure time around the house rather than out and about. Fifty-one percent, the highest of any generation, said they express themselves by making home improvements. This extends to all home-based activities—48 percent express themselves through do-it-yourself projects, 46 percent by cooking from scratch, 46 percent by gardening, and 37 percent by redecorating.

Boomers will keep working, but they will also be spending more time at home. They will achieve this balance by setting up home offices. The Ladera Ranch subdivision in Orange County, California, is already anticipating this trend with floor plans designed for dual residential and business uses. Some of these homes even have a separate business entrance.

Boomers will look to find the amenities and services they used to have near their offices newly located near their homes. And they will be in search of new venues, virtual and real, for the social connections they will lose by working from home.

Boomers are willing to invest to keep their homes current with their evolving lifestyles. In the 2006 MONITOR survey, Boomers estimated they would spend an average of $4,299 in the coming year on home improvements, far more than any other cohort and almost $1,500 more than they estimated in 2004.

However, it is worth noting that the percentage of Boomers in the AARP surveys saying they would work part-time in retirement mainly for enjoyment dropped from 35 percent in 1998 to 30 percent in 2003, and those mentioning a need for income rose very slightly, from 23 percent to 25 percent. Similarly, the percentage in the Rutgers University survey saying they would work part-time in retirement for interest or enjoyment shrank from 42 percent in 2000 to 27 percent in 2005, while those saying they would work part-time in retirement for the income it provides increased from 10 percent in 2000 to 18 percent in 2005. Money concerns are growing as Boomers get older.

Whatever their finances, though, Boomers want something more from retirement than the golden years prized by the generation before them. They are looking for lifelong rewarding work, not a late-life reward after work. Or as Marc Freedman, founder and CEO of Civic Ventures, a think tank and business incubator focusing on the skills and experience of older people, so aptly put it, Baby Boomers intend to "swap" the traditional retirement dream of "freedom from work" for a new retirement dream of "freedom to work."[17]

Keeping At It

Perhaps the one good thing about Baby Boomers worrying more about retirement income is that their financial concerns will be another reason for them to work longer, thus sparing the economy from the disaster scenarios making headlines about too few workers while also sparing Boomers themselves from the kinds of isolated, inactive lifestyles researchers have found to be associated with less successful aging, even death.

Two economists took advantage of a 1977 change in Social Security payments to investigate the impact of having means enough not to have to work in retirement.[18] The 1977 change reduced payments to people born on or after January 2, 1917. These researchers looked at the mortality rates of people born three months before and after that date. The mortality rate for people over sixty-five was lower for those receiving smaller Social Security payments, because people with lower payments were more likely to be working, probably because they needed the money. Working is exactly the sort of life-style engagement known to be correlated with longevity.

Already, older workers are staying on the job longer. From 2000 to 2005, the percentage of all Americans over age sixty-five still on the job increased from 12.5 percent to 14.5 percent.[19] Labor-force participation rates for sixty-five- to sixty-nine-year olds in particular have been trending up since the early 1990s, and in 2003 were nearly 33 percent for men and 23 percent for women.[20] Even many who formally retire don't quit working; about half continue to work in other jobs.[21] When Baby Boomers reach these ages, they will raise the percentages dramatically. They are doing so already as fifty-somethings. For the twelve months ending in November 2006, the total number of workers fifty-five and older grew 5.6 percent, or more than twice the overall rise in employment.[22]

By working longer, Boomers will ease pressures on governmental programs. Longer working years for Boomers would mean more Social Security contributions, postponement of claims against Social Security and Medicare, and more income tax revenue. That combination would substantially ease the projected strains on these programs and on federal and state budgets. (Some economists estimate that raising the age for Social Security benefits by three years would erase projected deficits in that system for the next seventy-five years.[23]) Additionally, Boomers who work longer would remain highly active consumers for many more years, thus adding to overall economic vitality and growth.

Despite the intentions of Boomers, though, some observers question whether aging Boomers will actually be able to stay engaged at work. A 2006 survey by the Pew Research Center noted that while 77 percent of adults eighteen years of age or older expect to work after retirement, only a small percentage of current retirees actually do so (although, as noted earlier, this percentage has been trending up in recent years). The Pew report mentioned similar findings from a 2006 survey by the Employee Benefits Research Institute that found only 27 percent of current retirees have ever worked during retirement.[24] In a related vein, a 2006 AARP survey found only 54 percent of sixty-year-old leading-edge Boomers are currently working, compared to 74 percent of all Boomers.[25]

These are useful, astute reality checks. Even so, notwithstanding any caveats based on the past and the present, the future will be different. Obviously, we should temper our expectations of even the most work-obsessed Baby Boomers. But the circumstances of work for aging Boomers will create more opportunities and more acute demand for older workers than have been true for prior generations. Extrapolations don't fully reflect these evolving circumstances.

Boomers will face unprecedented pressures to stay involved. The demand for capable older workers is going to grow. This is new to the future retirement situations in which Boomers will find themselves, so it is not unreasonable to put more stock in the stated intentions of Baby Boomers. Labor market demand will create the opportunity for Boomers to do as they say.

Working It Out

Retirement is often triggered by disabilities or job changes that are sudden and unexpected. The determination to remain employed can be defeated in an instant by abruptly deteriorating circumstances. But Boomers will find themselves less exposed to these disruptions, and thus will enjoy expanded prospects for staying on the job. Medical advances will help combat disabilities, while the needs of the workforce and the economy will open up Boomers' prospects.

The biggest difference between the past generation of retirees and the coming generation of aging Boomers is the shift in the age distribution of the labor market. Previous retirees found it harder to stay engaged because the glut of young people behind them left fewer opportunities for them in the job market.

This is not the situation in which Boomers will find themselves. For Boomers, there is no outsized cohort of younger workers breathing down their necks to replace them. Instead, there is a looming labor shortage for which their continued involvement in the workforce is the most important part of the solution.

Demographic extrapolations of a wholesale and absolute retreat of aging Boomers from the workforce project a labor shortfall too substantial for the economy to handle. The Conference Board estimates that 40 percent of the nation's public and private workforce will be at retirement age by 2010, a pressure that won't ease up anytime soon.[26] If all of these retirement-eligible Boomers opt to leave the workforce, the gap in numbers of needed workers will be far too large to fill. Other estimates project a shortfall of over 10 million qualified workers by 2010 and over 18 million by 2020.[27]

The baby-bust generation behind Baby Boomers lacks the numbers to make up this difference. Immigration can supply but a mere fraction of the additional workers needed. Furthermore, productivity levels have declined in recent years and are not expected to improve enough to offset the labor gap.[28]

Beyond numbers is the experience and expertise of Boomers. A 2005 survey sponsored by Ernst & Young, ExecuNet, and The Human Capital Institute found that 63 percent of human resources professionals believe that the retirements of Baby Boomers will lead to a critical brain drain of knowledge and know-how within their organizations.[29]

Companies are going to be in dire need of workers, so Boomers are going to find themselves in high demand, putting them in the driver's seat when it comes to negotiating attractive terms for staying on the job (such as top-notch health-care coverage). Baby Boomers will have to remain active in the workforce for the foreseeable future, at least part-time or in some kind of phased-in retirement.

Even experts who think that the hue and cry about a coming labor shortage is overwrought feel this way because they believe that it can be easily averted by Baby Boomers continuing to work. Management expert Peter Capelli, director of the Wharton School for Human Resources, describes the looming labor shortage as a "popular myth," arguing that greater efficiencies in the utilization of technology and of the existing pool of workers will easily meet future needs.[30]

As Capelli notes, the availability of sufficient labor is a function of multiple factors including worker productivity, overall population growth, the varying needs of different business sectors, the unemployment rate, and the age at which older workers retire. Capelli thinks it is wrong to assume that Boomers will retire at sixty-five. He believes that they will continue to work in some capacity beyond this age and that this will be a significant corrective factor in preventing a labor shortage.

Peter Francese, founder of American Demographics, makes a similar point. He believes that the predicted labor shortage, while a real threat, will not materialize because automation, immigration, offshoring, and the later retirement of Baby Boomers make it "incredibly unlikely" to occur.[31] Francese notes that the continued workforce participation of aging Boomer women is a key yet often overlooked source of future labor. The improved character of the jobs women hold today compared to those held by women in prior generations—in large part the result of greater education among women today—will enable aging Boomer women to work longer. These jobs are less physically demanding and pay higher wages, so these women will be better able, as well as more motivated, to keep working.[32]

Some authorities believe that even with Boomers working longer, a labor shortage cannot be averted. This is not to say that Boomers won't be working longer, just that they will be working longer to make the labor shortage less severe than it would be otherwise. For whatever impact, though, Boomers will be needed in the workforce.

Putting Them to Work

Every labor forecast rests upon a critical assumption about the retirement plans of Baby Boomers. If Boomers can't or won't work past age sixty-five, then projections are grave. If they do work past age sixty-five, then the labor shortage will turn out to be an apocalyptic fiction like Y2K. The question to ask is whether the assumption about quitting work for a life of leisure in the traditional model of retirement is relevant to understanding Baby Boomers. The answer is no.

Over the latter half of the twentieth century, older workers weren't needed past age sixty-five. This will not be the case for Baby Boomers. They will be needed, so innovative incentives to keep them working are likely to proliferate as businesses start to encounter the threats of a Boomer brain drain and labor shortage. Businesses will not allow themselves to be ruined because they can't recruit and retain critical human capital. As a generational cohort, Boomers will have the leverage to demand more suitable work environments as well as needed health-care coverage in return for continuing to work. Companies will make the investments needed to stay competitive, while Boomers will wind up in satisfying situations that enable them to continue to matter.

Already, placement of older workers, especially fifty-plus Boomers, is big business for employment agencies. Manpower has a program called Reinvent Retirement that offers training and flexible job opportunities for older workers. Internet job boards are springing up that specialize in matching older workers with suitable job opportunities, including Alumni InTouch.com, SelectMinds.com, RetiredBrains.com, RetirementJobs .com, RetireeCareers.com, SeniorJobBank.com, Seniors4Hire.com, and YourEncore.com.[33] Job placements for retirees are the fastest-growing part of the business at Kelly Services.[34] A local recruitment firm in the young-entrepreneur hotbed of Silicon Valley reports that its success in placing workers over fifty years of age has doubled year over year, and that three-quarters of its recent placements were of fifty-plus workers.[35]

In 2005, the AARP launched a Featured Employers Program to link partner companies with older employees. Information about openings and training at participating companies is made available on the AARP Web site. This program grew out of a successful cooperative initiative begun in 2004 between AARP and Home Depot to place older workers at the home-improvement chain. Many other companies now work with the AARP as well, including AlliedBarton Security Services, Borders Group, Express Personnel Services, Johns Hopkins Medicine, Kelly Services, Manpower, MetLife, Pitney Bowes, Principal Financial Group, Universal Health Services, and Walgreen's.

Older workers are the greatest underexploited resource in a tightening labor market and an increasingly competitive marketplace.

Money Enough

Some object that when Baby Boomers say they intend to work beyond age sixty-five or work in retirement, they are only rationalizing their failure to save enough to retire. It's easier to justify making no sacrifices to save with a belief that one can work as long as necessary. But the evidence on Boomer financial plans for retirement is not as ominous as it's typically made out to be. It is true that Boomers have saved at much lower rates than the prior generation. But savings are only one part of retirement income. (Besides, to be fair, no generation saves very well anymore. The overall savings rate was negative 0.5 percent in 2005 and negative 1 percent in 2006, the lowest rates since 1933, when it was negative 1.5 percent.[36])

Compared to the prior generation, Baby Boomers have enjoyed higher incomes per person because of fewer children and two-income households, greater run-ups in the worth of their homes and the value of their stock portfolios, and lower inflation and interest rates in their midlife years. The cumulative effect of these economic advantages is that Boomers are in a better position than the prior generation was at the same ages.

In a detailed 1998 review of all previous economic analyses of the retirement prospects of Boomers, the late Daniel Radner, a pioneering economist with the Social Security Administration, concluded that the current economic position of Boomers is higher than that of their parents at the same ages, and that this will also be true when Boomers become elderly.[37] Radner added as a caveat that this will not be so for all Boomers. Some Boomer subgroups will be less well-off, so special attention must be paid to their needs.

More important, Radner emphasized that projections about Boomers are inexact because of uncertainties related to their future savings rates and the ages at which they will quit working. Increases in savings or retirement at later ages could easily erase all hypothesized retirement income gaps, enabling most Boomers to maintain their standard of living.

A similar conclusion was reached by an AARP analysis comparing the financial position of Boomers in 2001 with the prior generation at the same ages in 1983. On every measure—income, net worth, financial assets, and net worth minus home equity—Boomers were better off, and on every measure except for income, substantially so.[38]

Nontraditional approaches to financing retirement are more popular nowadays. Many retirees are turning to the equity in their homes as their retirement plan rather than relying solely upon pensions, savings, or investments. Reverse mortgages enable them to make up the difference.

There is even an emerging belief among many economists that Americans are saving too much for retirement. By their calculations, the amount of money that people need to save for retirement is less than half of that typically recommended by the models used by financial planners.[39] While these conclusions are still being debated, there is at least a growing recognition that the financial plight of Boomers in retirement is likely to be far less severe than the gloomy prospects so often decreed to be the inevitable fate of spendthrift Boomers. (Affordable health care, though, is a different issue, examined in later chapters.)

Boomers are under little if any income pressure to rationalize their interest in working past retirement. The bottom line is that they want to keep working because they want to continue to matter and have an impact to a degree not true of prior generations. Working is both an avenue for continuing to matter and the means for continuing to matter. As long as they can draw breath Boomers want to have a say, and they are willing to work for it.

Meaning It

Work has long been a central part of the Baby Boomer psyche. The idea of meaningful work has had a strong allure for Boomers, who came of age engrossed in a broader search for meaning during an era when traditional rules, mores, and aspirations were under attack. Work for no purpose beyond earning a living was regarded as a dead end. Every activity, it was felt, should be a meaningful experience, work included.

Boomers got an early introduction to this idea from Dustin Hoffman's character, Benjamin Braddock, in the acclaimed 1967 film *The Graduate*. Braddock is a recent college graduate adrift in search of meaning and direction. He fights his father's entreaties to enroll in graduate school and is dismayed by the one-word career advice he gets from a family friend at a party: "Plastics." For Braddock, traditional options were devoid of meaning and fulfillment, not to mention corrupt and degenerate.

Betty Friedan's 1963 clarion call to women in *The Feminine Mystique* advocated a life beyond domestic duties. Careers are essential to authentic lives, she argued, so women must demand an equal opportunity to find meaningful work for themselves. Boomer women took up this gauntlet. Combined with economic pressures on traditional, single-income households, these aspirations pushed the labor-force participation of women ages twenty-five to fifty-four to 75.3 percent in 2005. It was a mere 35.0 percent just after the start of the Baby Boom in 1948.[40]

In the work our firm did in 1973 for the John D. Rockefeller III Fund, eight in ten Boomers, both college educated and non–college educated, agreed that "commitment to a meaningful career is very important." This Boomer focus on meaningful pursuits is seen, too, in the surveys conducted since 1966 of incoming college freshmen by the American Council on Education and the Higher Education Research Institute at UCLA. In the 1960s, when Baby Boomers were flooding college campuses, the most frequently cited goal of a college education, mentioned by roughly 80 percent, was to develop a "meaningful philosophy of life." Less than half said it was to be "well off financially." Today, financial success is the most frequently cited goal, mentioned by three-quarters of incoming freshmen, while finding purpose and meaning in life is mentioned by only about four in ten. The trend lines show that money overtook meaning in the early 1980s after the baby bust behind Baby Boomers came along and filled out the ranks of college students.[41]

The most celebrated cultural icons of the 1960s and 1970s were the celebrities and public figures who eschewed crass commercialism and went their own way to pursue their creative visions. Their work was more about finding meaning than accumulating wealth. Work gave them fulfillment, purpose, and joy. Their eventual financial success was proof that meaningful work was the most rewarding in every way.

These cultural trendsetters included singer-songwriters like Bob Dylan, James Taylor, Jackson Browne, Carly Simon, Jimmy Buffett, Dan Fogelberg,

Jim Croce, Neil Young, and Joni Mitchell. They were also auteur film directors like Federico Fellini, Ingmar Bergman, Francis Ford Coppola, Robert Altman, Woody Allen, Sam Peckinpah, Stanley Kubrick, Steven Spielberg, and George Lucas, as well as independent-minded publishers like Jann Wenner of *Rolling Stone* and Hugh Hefner of *Playboy*. They were iconoclasts of all artistic media, including painter Andy Warhol, photographer Annie Leibovitz, and writers Tom Wolfe and Hunter S. Thompson, both of whom used the fresh voice of the New Journalism to write about the new breed of mavericks then redefining the American scene, like hippie Ken Kesey, test pilot Chuck Yeager, stock-car driver Junior Johnson, and Hell's Angel Sonny Barger.

It was an era in which the rugged American individualist was redefined as an antihero and celebrated in books and movies for refusing to sell out his or her self-defined sense of meaning and morality. These new role models included characters as diverse as Randall Patrick McMurphy in Ken Kesey's 1962 bestselling novel *One Flew Over the Cuckoo's Nest* and the Korean War field surgeons in Robert Altman's 1970 classic *M.A.S.H.* They were the title characters played by Warren Beatty and Faye Dunaway in Arthur Penn's 1967 award-winning film *Bonnie and Clyde* and the enigmatic vigilantes portrayed by Clint Eastwood in Sergio Leone's classic spaghetti westerns. Perhaps most famously, they were the antic train robbers played by Paul Newman and Robert Redford in the 1969 movie *Butch Cassidy and the Sundance Kid*.

The lesson for young, impressionable Boomers was unambiguous: Pursue your life's passion through your work and make no compromises in following your own path.

Work continues to be central for the majority of Boomers. Work has meant a paycheck to Boomers, yet much more, too. In the 2005 Yankelovich MONITOR, only 45 percent of Boomers agreed that they "would be willing to work at a boring job as long as the pay was good," while in the 2006 MONITOR survey 63 percent agreed that "being really good at your job" is a sign of success and accomplishment.

Baby Boomers intend to work in retirement because to quit would mean abandoning one of the principal touchstones of their lives. For Boomers, work has long held out the possibility of more than just a paycheck. Work is supposed to provide meaning that matters.

Marketing Thought-Starter:
Reinvention, Not Retirement

The idea of reinvention better captures the ways in which Boomers envision themselves and the future than the traditional notion of retirement. Reinvention entails four things in particular: perpetual engagement, pay to play, possibility, and purpose.

Perpetual engagement means a sustained, ongoing involvement with both work and life. Work won't be full-time, but it will be ever-present as projects and opportunities cycle in and out. Part-time work will prevail, much of it episodic work that is full-time but only part of the time. In the Yankelovich Boomer Dreams study, of the 74.6 percent saying they would work after retirement, few said they would work full-time—70.1 percent said part-time; only 4.5 percent said full-time.

Pay to play means that Boomers want to earn their keep. Boomers will ante up. They won't be expecting freebies or special privileges. Boomers know that the only way they can legitimately demand to have their say and be a player is if they are contributing and paying their way.

Possibility means that Boomers will be in a constant state of "becoming." Self-discovery and exploration won't stop. Boomers will not give up the quest to know more about themselves and to experiment with new identities and lifestyles. Continuing education and lifelong learning will become more important the older they get.

Purpose means finding and pursuing a mission in life—not necessarily a societal mission, but some pursuit of real value and significance. Too many Boomers have found themselves stuck in jobs going nowhere. They will leave those dead ends behind and connect only with endeavors and activities that offer meaning, worth, and true fulfillment.

Boomers are still searching for the meaning and fulfillment that was the early promise of their lives. Sixty percent in the 2006 MONITOR survey agreed that "if I had the chance to start over in life, I would do things much differently." Their older years will be, in fact, that fresh start. This is the opportunity sought by the 48 percent who "often feel that something is missing" from their lives and by the 64 percent who "feel the need to know [themselves] better" (2006 and 2004 MONITOR surveys, respectively).

Reinvention is more than just the opposite of retirement. It is an entirely new constellation of attitudes and aspirations.

Cycling with a Mission

None of this is to suggest that all Boomers have been happy in their jobs or have found fulfillment through their work. Nor is it to imply that they will continue in retirement with the same jobs they have today. Obviously, lots of Baby Boomers are looking forward to the day when they can leave behind the workaday world they have inhabited for so long. Many of them work in physically or psychologically demanding jobs that they simply won't be able to continue in their older years. Boomers will have to change their involvement in the workforce, but they are reluctant to walk away completely, because doing so would mean not mattering.

Baby Boomers are not of a single mind about work. While the majority intend to work in retirement, one-fifth to one-third, depending on the survey, say they will not. Although relatively much smaller than those who say they will work in retirement, their numbers are large. These Boomers are going to leave the workforce upon retirement from their current jobs. At least in terms of quitting work, their retirements will be more traditional.

For the largest number of Boomers, though, work will continue to be a key part of their lives. These working Boomers will shape the broader context of the future for their entire generation.

Most Boomers working in retirement will change how they work—with different fields, new skills, dream jobs, hobbies turned into jobs, lower-paying jobs, work at home, shifts to greater or lesser responsibilities, consulting, flex-time positions, job sharing, and, most important, part-time work. In the 1979 survey conducted for the National Commission on Social Security, 47.5 percent of nonretirees forty-five to sixty-four years of age said they would work part-time in retirement. In the 2006 Yankelovich Boomer Dreams survey, 70.1 percent of Boomers said they planned on working part-time in retirement. More so than the prior generation, Boomers are focused on part-time work. This is the work style they see as the best way to reinvent retirement, although it is not part-time work as typically defined.

Boomers want the rewards of retirement without relinquishing their hold on mattering in the marketplace. Part-time work provides both. Many Boomers will work part-time in a traditional way, but the largest number will cycle themselves in and out of the workforce with work that is full-time when they're doing it but that they do only part of the time. Cycling is a better way to describe it—periodic or episodic work that is full-time for short periods of time followed by complete disengagement to enjoy interests like travel, family, sports, hobbies, and other adventures. Boomers will cycle in and out of the workforce, thus remaining engaged while dedicating time to other priorities as well.

Larry Cohen, a consultant with SRI Consulting Business Intelligence, has coined the term "revolving-retirement" to characterize the pattern of cycling that will be characteristic of aging, middle age–less Boomers. By this, Cohen means a lifestyle of episodic work and leisure supported by an investment strategy of ongoing wealth accumulation rather than low-risk maintenance and wealth depreciation.[42]

"Rehirement" is another term for characterizing the post-retirement lives of aging Boomers. This term has been popularized by Ken Dychtwald, founder and CEO of the consulting firm Age Wave.[43] As Dychtwald notes, aging Boomers will be engaged with a "cyclic," threefold combination of work, education, and leisure, so rehirement is not simply about a new style of work or "rehiring"; it involves a wholesale reinvention of what aging is all about. Boomers will be fully engaged in all of their priorities through a lifestyle built around cycling.

Economists use the term "bridge jobs" to refer to the kind of work that carries people over from their primary careers to their retirement years. These are transitional jobs, part-time or full-time, usually held for less than ten years and often paying less than what people earned during their peak earning years. "Phased retirement" is another transitional approach in which older workers gradually reduce the number of hours worked in stages until they retire.

Both bridge jobs and phased retirement have the effect of extending the time to retirement, thereby increasing the percentage of older workers active in the workforce.[44] But both presume that retirement in the traditional sense is the ultimate endpoint. For Boomers, the goal is not retirement per se, but a rebalanced lifestyle that also keeps them engaged. Boomers want to change their lifestyles and work styles without ceasing to matter. Bridge jobs and phased retirement may carry them through to a new phase in their lives, but this phase will not entail, as it has before, a complete disengagement from work. Instead, Boomers will reinvent retirement through a work style of cycling, which will offer them the kind of job flexibility that nearly half of white-collar workers say would "prevent" them from retiring.[45]

It is a safe bet that to attract these cycling, middle age–less Boomers, employers will have to offer jobs with less stress, lots of social connection, more control over working conditions and time off, greater flexibility of hours and pace, and, above all else, the chance to earn more than a paycheck. Boomers will look for jobs with a mission, big or small, that offers them a purpose and a calling. The work that they will do in their middle age–less years must make an impact that rewards them with a sense of meaning and fulfillment. The mission will be as important as the money.

When Boomers say they want to work in retirement, they mean it literally and figuratively. They want to work, and they want to matter, too. It's not that Boomers don't want to retire from work so much as they don't want to retire from the scene. If quitting work means quitting life by fading away and losing influence and import, then Boomers won't quit.

The bigger issue is that Boomers want to matter. Working in retirement is one of the chief manifestations of that mindset. When Boomers say they want to continue working, they are saying that they do not want to be relegated to irrelevance by retiring. It's less about working—although work they will—and more about mattering.

In the generational experience of Boomers, work has always been linked to meaning and fulfillment, so to renounce work entirely is essentially to relinquish any claim to further self-development or societal impact. Boomers will do whatever it takes to stay in the game, work included.

Everything Boomers face as they get older will be approached with a determination to stay actively engaged in their lives and the life of the world around them. Resignation and retreat are not on the table. Boomers will not retire from the field.

four

A Life of Self-Invention

*T*oyota launched Scion in June 2003 with a radical announcement to customers: "We relinquish all power to you."

Literally, Scion wants its customers to tell it what to do; in particular, to invent for themselves the cars they want to drive. The company will then assemble and deliver not merely a custom-designed car but a custom*er*-designed car.

This is more than customization. This is self-customization, or to characterize it more precisely—because it is more than just customizing—it is self-invention.[1] And self-invention is the future facing Baby Boomers.

Self-invention is nothing that companies do for customers. Self-invention is customers inventing what they want for themselves.

Scion is not the only company relinquishing control. Self-invention is transforming the character and experience of everything. "Create your own card" is Bank One's proposition. Motorcycle manufacturer Ducati invites customers to provide online feedback about prototype designs. People can personalize Nike footwear, backpacks, and watches at NIKEiD.com. At Dell.com, they can configure a computer that is customized for their needs. The Honda Element, designed for younger buyers, and the Nissan Quest, designed for young mothers, have modular interiors that can be reconfigured at the touch of a latch to fit personal needs and preferences. Ralph Lauren offers the "Create Your Own Collection" on its Web site. Build-A-Bear Workshop enables kids to "pawsonalize" their own stuffed animal. L.L. Bean lets buyers customize tote bags, book packs, and messenger bags. A variety of Web sites enable people to create vanity postage stamps. People can put their pictures on Jones Soda labels and Wheaties boxes, or short messages on M&Ms and Heinz ketchup bottles, or their own labels on Johnny Walker bottles, or personalized wrappers around Hershey's chocolates. Online RSS feeds deliver customized, up-to-date information and content.

Winners on *American Idol* are selected by the votes of viewers. In 2005, Crest toothpaste asked consumers to vote online for the next flavor to be offered. The Gap Casting Call promotion featured six ordinary people chosen by online voting to appear in a 2003 Gap print ad. In 2007, Touchstone books ran a contest called First Chapters, in which members of the social networking site Gather.com nominated five books by first-time authors for consideration by a grand-prize jury that selected one as the winner of a book contract.

Self-invention is a radical transformation of consumer involvement. Consumers are now creating the very options from which choices are made, including the invention of fresh content. Blogs, online reviews, personal Web pages at sites like MySpace and Facebook, bulletin board postings, wiki sites, photo sharing at sites like Flickr and Shutterfly, and other such Internet resources have given people unprecedented abilities to create and distribute content. Commercials aired during the 2007 Super Bowl showcased several consumer-created ads. Dove sponsored a contest in 2007 in which women were invited to create and submit their own TV ads for its products.

This is a cultural scene that is more collaborative, participatory, and empowering than anything seen before. It has captured the popular imagination to such an extent that new catchphrases have been coined to describe it—citizen journalism, blogosphere, smart mobs, Web 2.0, consumer-generated media, peer-to-peer, podcasting, moblogs, and vlogs, just to mention a few.

In some cases, consumers have even begun to displace traditional experts as the sources to consult for critical information and recommendations. In health care, for example, individuals who have personal experience with a disease or a treatment regimen are influencing the decisions of an increasing number of others who view them as more trustworthy authorities than doctors. User reviews and product-comparison Web sites are having a growing impact in the same way across all product categories.

The dynamic of customer control is no less important in the business-to-business arena. National Semiconducter's WEBENCH® is an online tool that enables engineers to simulate and design their own electrical products, which are then assembled and produced according to their specifications. Eli Lilly's Innocentive® Web site matches interested scientists with research and development needs that major companies are willing to contract out for innovative solutions.

Letting Go

Marketers are beginning to come to terms with this new reality. Top-down, push-style traditional marketing cannot be effective in a marketplace in which consumers want to invent for themselves, because if denied that option, consumers have the tools, the smarts, and the willpower to reject and block traditional marketing altogether.

A. G. Lafley, CEO of Procter & Gamble (P&G), one of the most storied marketing powerhouses of all time, is preaching this message. At the 2006 annual conference of the Association of National Advertisers, Lafley stood on the dais of the Ritz-Carlton Orlando to exhort his audience to move more quickly in responding to this new "let-go world" of self-invention in which marketers must allow consumers to take control.[2] Two years earlier, Jim Stengel, the Global Marketing Officer of P&G, made his own headlines at the annual Media Conference of the American Association of Advertising Agencies when he declared traditional marketing "obsolete" and "broken" and insisted that consumers be given more control.[3]

With such dramatic changes afoot, it's no surprise that *Time* magazine anointed "You" as its 2006 Person of the Year.[4] It was an homage to individual people who have seized control over information and creative content.

There is much more to self-invention than the Internet, though. The entire character of contemporary life encourages people to think in terms of self-invention.

Me Making Myself

The most common experience of life nowadays is difference. There is no shared communal norm anymore to which people can look to conform their own attitudes and behaviors. People feel less need to fit in and more permission to be different.

Racial and ethnic diversity are exploding. Predictions are that by mid-century, non-Hispanic Caucasians—white people—will no longer be the majority population in the United States. They'll just be another minority group like everyone else. Already, whites no longer constitute the majority in California, Hawaii, and New Mexico. This will soon be true in Texas as well.

The 2000 Census counted almost 6.8 million multiracial, multi-ethnic people, a group that includes some of the most recognizable names in sports, entertainment, news, and politics: Tiger Woods, Greg Louganis, Derek Jeter, Halle Berry, Vin Diesel, Lisa Bonet, Jessica Alba, Christina Aguilera, Jennifer Lopez, Benjamin Bratt, Lenny Kravitz, Nia Peeples, Mariah Carey, Norah Jones, Ben Harper, Alicia Keys, Soledad O'Brien, Sade, Slash, Cameron Diaz, Geraldo Rivera, Elizabeth Vargas, Malcolm Gladwell, and Illinois senator and presidential hopeful Barack Obama. Forty-two percent of all persons choosing Hispanic as their national background in the 2000 Census chose no racial category at all, marking the box for "some other race" instead.[5] The traditional census categories no longer capture the diversity of racial identities by which many people are defining themselves.

Household diversity is exploding as well. In 2006, population surveys found that single households now outnumber married households.[6] By way of comparison, in 1950, married households accounted for 78 percent of all households.[7] That homogeneity of the past has been replaced by today's heterogeneous mix of household types.

Cultural styles are more diverse than ever, too. Hit TV shows are built around lifestyles and household settings that were virtually invisible or unheard of in the past. Multicultural fashions, music, symbols, and identities have wide-ranging appeal. In every high-school lunchroom or high-rise office building long-hairs, short-hairs, bald heads, skinheads, buzz cuts, braids, dreadlocks, mop-tops, ponytails, beehives, do-rags, hijabs, and more mingle and interact.

This diversity of life fosters self-invention. Increasingly, Boomers, like everyone else, encounter life as a blank canvas that rewards people for the flexibility and originality they bring to bear. Learning, openness, and un-relenting evolution are the cornerstones of success. The more that life de-mands the inventive participation of individuals, the greater the plasticity of self and the agility of mind that people must master. More and more, peo-ple must be creators and directors, not simply consumers and viewers.

Life is no longer so settled that people can stop learning or cease reinvent-ing themselves. Involvement and constant self-development are demanded. Youthful flexibility to explore and adapt is now required of adults, too. The world of self-invention is a constant unfolding of possibilities for which flexi-bility of response is essential.

The everyday experience of life is one of open-ended, self-determined invention. Even if one is not personally engaged in a particular form of self-invention, this is the broader context within which life unfolds and presents itself. It shapes expectations. It is a world in which things get done only through bottom-up, participatory involvement by individuals. Traditional authorities and institutions are ceding command and control to their cli-ents and constituencies.

Boomers bring with them a spirit of possibility, youthfulness, and en-gagement. This sort of middle age–less approach is exactly what it takes to handle the demands of contemporary life, so Boomers are well-equipped to occupy a central place of influence and impact in the years to come. Adults who think youthfully have the openness and flexibility it takes to cope suc-cessfully in the modern world. Boomers are sure they have the skills needed, as seen in Figure 4-1.

Boomers are confident that they have what it takes—the energy, the imagination, the technology skills, the ability to assess risks, the capacity to process information, and the savvy to know whom to trust. They think they know how to deal with whatever comes their way. Boomers are ready to take on the world of self-invention and master it.

In fact, Boomers are well-schooled in reinventing themselves. They

Using your imagination	80%
Handling whatever life throws your way	75%
Being able to process new information quickly	73%
Knowing how to get what you need when dealing with customer service	72%
Multitasking	72%
Being able to evaluate the trustworthiness of information	71%
Being able to work through negative emotions	71%
Making product and service selections that you don't later regret	70%
Recognizing what risks are worth taking	70%
Being able to say "no" when you need to	68%
Managing your time	68%
Finding enough time for friends and family	67%
Keeping your stress at a manageable level	67%
Maintaining a good energy level	66%
Being able to put your past problems behind you	65%
Handling forms and paperwork (e.g., health care, government)	64%
Knowing how to find a job	61%
Being able to handle whatever technology you encounter	59%
Knowing how to come out on top	58%
Sticking to a budget	57%

Top 3 box on 7-point scale
Source: Yankelovich MONITOR 2006

Figure 4-1: Boomers Rate Their Own Skills Highly

are the modern-day pioneers of identity shifting. Boomers have had multiples of everything—multiple jobs, multiple marriages, multiple families, multiple homes, multiple hometowns, multiple experiences, multiple brands, and more. Throughout their lives, they have had to be in command of keeping up with rapid change. Their experience and comfort with the accelerating pace of new things is longstanding and wide-ranging, covering new technologies, new media, new software, new jobs and job skills, new fashions, new friends, new relationships, and new brands of everything. Boomers have experienced far more mobility and variability than the generation before them.

Stability, fixed lives, and long-term commitments have never been part of the Boomer environment or mindset. For Boomers, life has been in continuous flux, both through their own initiative and because of external factors forcing them to change. As a result, youthful flexibility and contingency have long been central to their repertoire of life skills. Boomers are well-prepared for a future of self-invention that will put a premium on youthful dexterity and adaptability.

My Choice

Every aspect of life reflects the emergence of a culture of self-invention. Old limits now look laughable. The individual is in control, unconstrained by any need to find support or win approval from others.

The smart homes being built today enable people to live in interior environments that are actively responsive to their individual tastes and preferences. The tidal wave of renovation that swept through suburbia during the post-2001 mortgage refinancing boom turned home remodelers, in the words of science writer James Gleick, into home "systems integrators."[8]

Computer-enhanced fashions, or so-called wearable computers, are going to make it possible for people to completely determine the environments within which they spend their days. MP3 players already wrap people in self-customized soundscapes of personal playlists. Modern medical procedures give them affordable control over their physical appearances.

Surgical self-invention is now so commonplace that people no longer expect to see the same person the next time they get together. In response to a question from host Terry Gross during an interview on her public radio show *Fresh Air*, Clint Eastwood agreed that "cosmetic surgery is a problem if you're casting a person in a film." In the past, he said, you knew what someone looked like. Not so any longer. You now have to bring people in to see "how they are today." With cosmetic surgery they may have a whole new look that, as Eastwood said, "is not the look I was expecting . . . not what was in my imagination when I thought of casting that person."[9]

Even religion is being self-invented. People feel free to pick whatever religion best fits their personal tastes. Dean Hoge, professor of sociology at Catholic University of America, has noted that so-called religion switching is "more common now" than at any point in American history.[10] Martin Marty, the former dean of the University of Chicago Divinity School, has written that the choice of a church and even a denomination is no longer based solely on religious beliefs. Instead, it has come down to "a choice [about] a way of life."[11]

Gender, too, is becoming a matter of self-inventive choice. On Election Day 2006, a front-page headline in the *New York Times* declared, "New York [City] Plans to Make Gender Personal Choice."[12] As long as people have lived as their "adopted gender" for two years, New York City now allows them to change the sex on their birth certificates "even if they have *not* had sex-change surgery [emphasis added]." Although this policy was reversed just a few weeks later because of unanticipated complications related to segregating people by gender in jails, schools and hospitals, once these problems are resolved this policy is likely to be reinstated.[13] What's most important is the fact that this change was even contemplated in the first place because it betrays the underlying presumption that self-invention, even for something like gender, is now the norm.

Self-invention gets the most attention in the realm of media, something affecting the context of life for everyone, young and old alike. Broadly speaking, the new media are inherently participatory.

With the old media, the one-way framework of delivery encouraged the perception that effective communication, advertising included, was like a lecture to an audience taking notes. The new media have swept away this framework of delivery by giving individual audience members control over content, exposure, and response, thus putting an end to the fiction of a lecture. The new media are better thought of as a conversation in which all participants can invent for themselves the ways in which they want to participate.

Marketing Thought-Starter:
Zero Time or Slow Time

Advertising in the new media is about getting into the conversation, not just about delivering a message. This means rewarding time and attention. People will show up to participate in the conversation only if the experience is worth it.

Time is the new currency of the marketplace, trumping money and things as the epitome of success. The Yankelovich MONITOR finds that people feel increasingly pressed for time, a source of stress that is the single biggest detriment to the quality of their otherwise comfortable and productive lives. John Robinson, a professor of sociology and the past director of the Americans' Use of Time Project at the University of Maryland, has been studying how people use time since 1965. Robinson reports that in his 1998 survey, for the first time ever, more people said they were pressed for time than for money.[14]

People will be even more pressed for time in a world of self-invention. The downside of control is the time it takes. Boomers are particularly sensitive to this, because they place a disproportionate value on their time. The 2006 Yankelovich MONITOR Perspective study "Finding Time" asked people to place a value on one minute of their time. Boomers valued their time the most at $2.00 per minute, double every other generational cohort and much more than the $1.25 per minute average.

As the demands of self-invention grow, so, too, will the need for time solutions. These solutions will fall into one of two buckets, with nothing in between: zero time solutions or slow time experiences. In a time-starved world, if something is not worth the time it takes, people don't want to spend any time on it at all. These activities should take zero time. This is the best use of technology. If something is worth the time, then even in a time-starved world people are willing to slow down to savor it and enjoy it. These interactions should deliver high-quality experiences.

For Boomers in particular, companies must identify which of their touch points need zero time solutions and which provide the opportunity for value-added, premium-priced slow time experiences.

When hyperbolic Internet boosters wax poetic about the digital revival of oral culture, what they mean is the simple yet profound notion that the new media are more interactive and less mediated.

Information Control

Self-invention is here to stay. It is rooted in a fundamental, lasting change in marketplace roles and resources. It is more than mere access to technology and tools. This is necessary, but inventing one's self takes more than that—it takes access to information.

The crucial shift in the marketplace is that access and control over information have passed from institutions to ordinary people, from the elected to the electorate, from marketers to consumers. Individuals are now able to see and utilize data previously inaccessible to them. This is a profound change.

Mohanbir Sawhney, the McCormick Tribune Professor of Management at Northwestern's Kellogg School of Management, refers to this as a shift from "information asymmetry" to "information democracy."[15] With more information in hand, consumers are able to do things they have never been able to do before. Sawhney lists them: get product information from sources other than manufacturers and retailers; initiate requests for information; design customized offerings; use buying agents; unbundle offerings; pay by usage; and communicate directly with peers and experts.

These kinds of information opportunities create wholly new relationships between marketers and consumers; specifically, consumers are no

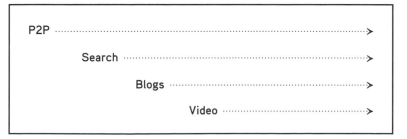

Figure 4-2: Growth of Consumer Information Access

longer dependent upon marketers for feedback, knowledge, and decisions about products. Marketers are now taking direction from consumers because consumers have the information it takes to assert control. Information in the hands of consumers has put an end to their dependency on marketers.

The end of dependency makes way for the rise of self-invention. No longer at the mercy of marketers or other institutions, people are inventing for themselves what they want. These days, savvy shopping takes ingenuity and imagination—not only about where to go and what to do, but what to invent and how to create. This is more than the trend of the day; self-invention is the future.

Aging Happens

The personal qualities associated with achieving success in an age of self-invention are not those traditionally associated with old age. When asked outright, Boomers often describe themselves in ways that, taken at face value, might suggest they will not be prepared for a future of self-invention.

In the Yankelovich Boomer Dreams study, respondents rated the extent to which certain words and phrases applied to their generation in the past and then again as they are likely to apply in the future. As shown in Figure 4-3, for many "young-at-heart" characteristics, fewer Boomers think these will be true in the future compared to the past. Several differences between future and past are sizeable.

Boomers see themselves becoming something different in the future than they were in the past, particularly when it comes to rock'n'roll, sexual freedom, experimentation, risk-taking, protesting, fashion and style, and drugs. If, indeed, these kinds of things are the exclusive purview of youth, then Boomers don't see themselves as being youthful in the future.

Other generational descriptors parallel these, as shown in Figure 4-4.

Most striking is the dramatic shift from liberal to conservative. Boomers are much more likely to characterize their past selves as liberal and their future selves as conservative. These were not mutually exclusive

Describes Boomers...	In the past	In the future
Rock'n'roll	92.8%	59.4%
Sexual freedom	88.4%	50.4%
Experimentation	87.9%	48.5%
Challenging the status quo	87.7%	57.4%
Youthfulness	87.6%	73.3%
Risk-taking	85.7%	54.1%
Playing hard	84.7%	61.6%
Making a difference	84.5%	70.6%
Taking on new challenges	84.1%	66.3%
Equality	83.3%	72.4%
Social causes	82.7%	74.3%
Protesting	80.6%	45.2%
Fashion and style	79.7%	59.7%
Drugs	77.0%	44.3%
Being self-absorbed	70.3%	54.7%
Radicalism	70.3%	42.9%
Celebrity	68.3%	48.6%
The underdog	68.6%	54.8%

Top 3 box on 7-point scale
Source: Yankelovich Boomer Dreams Study, 2006

Figure 4-3: Boomer Self-Perceptions

choices in the survey, so it is possible to rate Boomers as high or low on both. The key factor is that, on balance, Boomers see the general idea of being liberal much less applicable in the future and that of being conservative much more applicable.

These self-assessments of past and future are consistent with changes in attitudes over time. In 1973, Yankelovich surveyed Boomers ages sixteen to twenty-five. Those who would have been sixteen to twenty-five in 1973 can be looked at separately in the Boomer Dreams study to assess how a few key attitudes have evolved over time. Figure 4-5 shows these results, which are broken out by education in the way that they were reported in 1973.

Boomers report a stronger grounding in traditional American values

Describes Boomers . . .	In the past	In the future
Liberalism	78.6%	56.3%
Conservatism	45.6%	60.8%
Home and family	65.5%	80.1%
A quiet lifestyle	38.8%	67.0%
Luxury	74.2%	75.8%
Spending	76.0%	77.2%
Debt	48.2%	74.3%

Top 3 box on 7-point scale
Source: Yankelovich Boomer Dreams Study, 2006

Figure 4-4: Boomer Self-Perceptions

today than they did in the early 1970s—more respect for private property, more commitment to duty first, more belief in hard work, more disdain for casual sex, and less focus on oneself. They are more likely to agree today that they have a sense of purpose in life.

Concerns about privacy are somewhat lower today, though still high. Attitudes about patriotism and law and order are pretty much unchanged from the early 1970s, and, frankly, were a lot stronger then than the stereotype of young Boomers would lead one to believe.

As Boomers assess their opportunities for the future, more of them voice self-doubt today than in the past about their potential for making money or being successful.

Add these research results together and it looks like a cohort getting old. Other organizations have reported similar research results, on the basis of which most conclude that Boomers are getting old just like every generation before them. The best way to plan for Boomers, these studies recommend, is to think of them in this way—as old people.

But this is a mistake. This interpretation confuses the manifestations of a youthful mindset with the mindset itself. Boomers are giving up certain things, but not their spirit of youthfulness. They are simply moving on to a

	1973		2006	
	Non-College	College	Non-College	College
People's privacy is being destroyed	84%	86%	71.7%	71.9%
Private property is sacred	74%	67%	93.7%	82.2%
Duty comes before pleasure	66%	54%	77.1%	68.3%
Hard work will always pay off	56%	44%	65.8%	61.7%
Casual premarital sexual relations are morally wrong	34%	22%	62.3%	49.1%
I am tired of hearing people attack patriotism, morality, and American values	78%	65%	80.5%	60.8%
There is too much concern with equality and not enough with law and order	71%	53%	72.2%	49.3%
Police should not hesitate to use force to maintain order	69%	55%	51.9%	42.1%
Have no doubts about being as successful as I want	72%	76%	56.9%	50.4%
I have a clear idea of what I want to do	63%	66%	79.6%	81.9%
Have no doubts about making as much money as I want	53%	57%	31.8%	36.7%

Top 2 box on 4-point scale
Sources: John D. Rockefeller III Fund Study, 1973, and Yankelovich Boomer Dreams Study, 2006

Figure 4-5: Social and Personal Values

fresh purpose. This is the plasticity of self and the embrace of continual reinvention necessary in a world of self-invention. Boomers are repurposing their youthfulness to new pursuits rooted in new hopes, dreams, and aspirations.

Boomers have a multidimensional view of themselves. They recognize that they are aging, so their attitudes about themselves reflect a sense of maturity. Still, Boomers also agree that youthfulness and making an impact are relevant to their future, maybe not as strongly as in the past, but quite strongly nevertheless. This dualistic view is evidence of the Boomer comfort with rule-breaking. Boomers see both self-descriptions as pertinent and in accord with who they think they are because they understand that they are free to invent themselves without being bound by convention or old-fashioned consistency.

Are Not

While it's important to understand what Boomers say they are, we mustn't overlook what they say they are *not*, because it is this that enables us to make sense of what Boomers mean when they say what they are. What we see from this is pretty clear. Boomers are not envisioning a future that entails a surrender to old age.

Figure 4-6 shows how Boomers answer when asked to choose between what they are and what they are not.

In every way, a preponderance of Boomers do not see themselves as out of the picture. They are not conformists. They are not overwhelmed by information. They are not dependent on experts. They are not resistant to

Identify most with:	
Individuality over conformity	88.7%
Hungry for information over overwhelmed by information	84.0%
Following your own instincts over listening to experts	80.4%
Comfortable with change over resistant to change	76.7%
Leader over follower	75.1%
Looking for answers over knowing the answers	70.4%
Challenge authority over accept authority	61.0%
Doing something completely new over settling into a routine	60.2%

Source: Yankelovich Boomer Dreams Study, 2006

Figure 4-6: Self-Identification

change. They are not followers. They are not sure of all the answers. They are not accepting of authority. They are not settling down into routines. In short, whatever Boomers say they are, what they are not is anything that might be thought of as getting old.

Boomers remain driven by a generational sensibility of youthfulness. It is demanded by the contingent, fast-changing, self-inventive nature of contemporary life. Boomers agree that certain youthful attributes no longer apply to them, but that does not mean they envision themselves as retiring or becoming old. Youthfulness is more than the whimsies of young people; it is a mindset about how to approach life's challenges and opportunities at every age.

The expressive self has lost its hold on the Boomer imagination. Boomers no longer seek to make personal statements through the expressive extremes of sex, drugs, and rock'n'roll. They have no more interest in rebellion for the sake of rebellion, difference for the sake of difference, or outrageousness just to provoke, goad, and incite. Their life still has a youthful character, but in entirely different ways. Boomers intend to stay on the journey of discovery, development, and reinvention. They are not settling down; they are simply redefining how they are involved.

Boomers may no longer think of themselves as experimental, risk-taking, or liberal, but they still see themselves as comfortable with change and willing to do something completely new. They may not want to rock'n'roll anymore, but they still see themselves as individuals following their own instincts. They may have more doubts about their future potential, but they remain in the hunt, hungry for information and looking for answers. Boomers may not describe themselves as protestors these days, but they still see themselves as challenging authority.

A less youthful point of view does not mean an old-age perspective in its place. A less fashion-forward outlook does not mean that an old-fashioned demeanor is the only alternative. A less challenging posture with respect to authority and convention does not mean allegiance to traditional doctrine. Boomers are aging; they are not aging out.

Boomers have grown into a more reflective midlife, but they have not given up their youthful spirit. They have rechanneled their sense of youthfulness, readying themselves for the prospects ahead.

Over the last several years, as self-invention has emerged full-blown, Boomers have thrived with flexible, creative, self-inventive ways of taking on the marketplace. Even as they get older, the trend is toward greater plasticity and youthfulness of style. Despite being more settled into a comfortable middle age, Boomers continue to live on life's frontier, self-inventing their way forward.

The Next New Adventure

The Boomer spirit of youthfulness is not being lost. A new purpose to which it can be dedicated is being found. A new adventure is in the offing.

For Boomers, life has always been about the next new adventure. No matter how old they get, they look at life with a youthful sense of exploration, discovery, and redefinition. This sense of adventure is seen in at least two ways. There is the physical adventure of participating in exciting activities, and there is the spiritual adventure of exploring new forms of well-being and fulfillment. For both, the underlying spur is one of living on the edge and pioneering new frontiers.

Aging Boomers are a large and often dominant part of the recent growth in demand for products across a wide variety of active leisure pursuits, including motorcycle riding, sky diving, scuba diving, snorkeling, windsurfing, sailing, bow hunting, boating, mountain biking, in-line skating, ballroom dancing, canoeing, and kayaking. SUVs have been an adventure surrogate for this generation.

The adventure travel industry owes its very existence to the jumpstart it got from the interests and demands of young Baby Boomers.[16] It is more popular than ever with aging Boomers, especially rugged, edgy adventure experiences that are exclusive and customized. The vice president for sales and marketing at adventure travel firm, Ocean Adventures, often travels with competitors to see what they're up to, and he reports that one Patagonia trip he took was a whitewater and fly-fishing expedition by day that morphed into "seven-course meals paired with vintage Chilean wines" by night.[17] The best adventures are demanding and indulgent.

Well-being comes not only from physical release but from spiritual enlightenment. In his study of religion and spirituality among Baby Boomers, Wade Clark Roof, the J. F. Rowny Professor of Religion and Society at the University of California at Santa Barbara, famously characterized them as a "generation of seekers."[18] Baby Boomers have never been content to accept their religious patrimony; instead, they have been on a continual adventure of spiritual exploration. The result has been the eclectic mix of spiritual fashions that Roof catalogs: Eastern religions, evangelicalism and fundamentalism, mysticism, New Age movements, Goddess worship, twelve-step recovery programs, environmentalism, holistic health and ancient religions, as well as mainline churches and synagogues. All of these Boomer interests continue, with no signs of slackening.

Boomers are now ready to invent their next big adventure. When appropriate and necessary, they are open to new options. As the Yankelovich MONITOR survey results in Figure 4-7 illustrate, more Boomers than ever are willing to chance it in the marketplace.

Consumers have more control over what they get from brands and more influence on the ways in which they can change (or self-reinvent) things they don't like. So why not be more open to novelty and experimentation?

Prefer or relate to more:	2002	2006
Something new and exciting over something familiar and comfortable	36%	52%

Important in personal life:	2004	2006
To follow your dreams	70%	79%
To stretch yourself to try new things	55%	70%

Top 3 box for agree/disagree questions on 7-point scale
Source: Yankelovich MONITOR

Figure 4-7: Openness to New Things

Marketing Thought-Starter:
Loyal to Experiences and Empowerment

Boomers will be no more and no less brand loyal in their old age than they have been before. Certainly they are increasingly interested in novelty and experimentation, but established brands can offer that just as well as new brands. Boomers are not thinking about brands; they are thinking about originality and freshness. They're not looking for brands so much as they are seeking imaginative solutions and experiences.

Boomers will make the same demands of brands as always: uniqueness, functionality, indulgence, service, and transparency. They know all the marketing tricks of the trade, so they know when to give in to impulse buying and when to hold back. They know when to let the right brain hold sway and when to rein it in with the left brain. Either way, Boomers like information with which to guide their decisions.

But the bottom line is that it's not about brands per se; it never has been. Boomers will be loyal, as they always have, to brands that deliver transformative experiences. One of the biggest opportunities to do this in an age of self-invention is for brands to deliver the tools and resources Boomers need to take control. Brands should look for opportunities to be tool-providers or facilitators of self-invented experiences.

This is a large part of the appeal of eBay. Customers control everything about their experiences in the context of shared, participatory interactions with like-minded others. What eBay does is make the tools available to do so. Not every business can be like eBay, but every business can look to deliver an empowering experience for demanding, self-inventive consumers like aging Boomers.

Belief in the opportunity to remake oneself, to become whatever one chooses, is an integral part of the American psyche. The self-made man is the acme of American success. The arc of American history has been a progressive, fiercely fought expansion of the opportunities for everyone to determine for themselves, free from impediments and intolerance, the character and purpose of their lives.

The new technologies, tools, and information resources of self-invention are carrying self-determination to unexplored heights. Expectations are being reshaped. Information access and technological developments are liberating people from dependence on others, particularly from long-standing ties to authorities and institutions.

Boomer expectations about all aspects of their lives, marketing included, now reflect a belief in the unbounded possibilities of self-invention. This has enormous implications for the ways in which middle age–less Baby Boomers will repurpose their lives in search of their next new adventures.

Psychological Neoteny

Traditionally, neither old, retired people nor young, developing people have enjoyed much of a say about things. Influence and impact belonged to those in the middle. That's where Baby Boomers want to stay—middle age–less.

There is another way to characterize middle age–less. It's a technical term and it applies only metaphorically, but it's a useful concept. The term is neoteny. The word comes from the Greek *neos*, which means "young," and *teinein*, which means "to extend." In short, neoteny is extended youth.

In biology, an organism is said to exhibit neoteny when it retains juvenile bodily characteristics after it has reached adulthood, meaning sexual maturity, or more generally, when sexual maturity is reached before physical maturity.[19] But what if neoteny were psychological instead of biological, i.e., the persistence into adulthood of a young way of thinking? This is the idea advanced recently by Dr. Bruce Charlton, editor-in-chief of *Medical Hypotheses* and a Reader in Evolutionary Psychiatry in the School of Biology and Psychology at the University of Newcastle upon Tyne.[20]

Psychologically, Charlton notes, children are learning, thus exhibiting maximum flexibility of attitudes and behaviors. Adults who display the same kind of mutability of mind and action are said to be immature. But these so-called immature adults, says Charlton, have now become both the norm and the most successful.

Charlton argues that contemporary society is so protean and is changing so rapidly that this "childlike flexibility" in adults is necessary and essential simply for survival, not to mention success. Today's most accomplished adults are those who retain these youthful cognitive skills. In a sense, says Charlton, many people never really become adults nowadays, at least not in the traditional sense of maturing into a fixed identity and approach to life. Increasingly, adults retain a youthful, constantly developing state of mind. This is the postponement of psychological maturation relative to physical maturation. Charlton calls this "psychological neoteny."

In Charlton's view, changing social and economic realities have made certain experiences much more commonplace than ever before: changing jobs, moving, making new friends, developing new skills, and prolonged education. These are pervasive elements of the modern world and they demand a greater plasticity of mind, reflexes, and disposition. Nowadays, success requires a commitment to possibility, not closure; to youthfulness, not maturity; to engagement, not detachment.

What Charlton hints at but never fully articulates is that this is a world of self-invention in which everything is contingent, variable, and transitory. Nothing is fixed in advance, awaiting consumption. Individuals give shape to things according to their own inventions, which are, in turn, subject to future revisions, modifications, adaptations, and reversals. For Boomers, psychological neoteny means being middle age–less.

This is more than theory; it is the way in which Boomers talk about themselves and their lives. *Wall Street Journal* career-advice columnist Ron Alsop responded to one reader's question about whether getting an MBA after fifty was worth it by quoting the words of a fifty-five-year-old Boomer who did so. The newly minted middle age–less MBA said that as a result of getting his degree, he now feels "a renewed sense of limitless capabilities."[21]

Endless possibility—read, psychological neoteny—is what Boomers want for their lives. It is what they look for in the things they buy and the activities they do.

While psychological neoteny, or being middle age–less, is an advantage these days, it also carries with it all of the associated baggage. Charlton lists these as shortened attention spans, novelty-seeking, fad mania, and "cultural shallowness." The "profundity of character," wisdom, and maturity characteristic of prior generations is rarer these days, too.

Both the good and the bad seem to exactly describe middle age–less Baby Boomers—driven by possibility, committed to a youthful spirit, focused on being engaged and influential, interested in experimentation and originality, seeking guidance and wisdom from prior generations, continually searching for spiritual and personal fulfillment, and determined to not get old. Boomers have lived their lives in a constant state of change, adaptation, and transition, and they will continue to do so in the face of a self-inventive marketplace.

In a biting yet sympathetic profile of upper-class Baby Boomers, writer and social critic David Brooks called them Bobos, short for bourgeois bohemians (*Bobos in Paradise: The New Upper Class and How They Got There*, New York: Simon & Schuster, 2000). These Baby Boomer Bobos, writes Brooks, represent a historically unique mixture of styles: the youthful bohemian spirit of the 1960s along with the midlife bourgeois ambitions of the 1980s. The result is a paradox of conflicting sensibilities that are combined in the same subculture, the same neighborhoods, the same workplaces, the same shopping venues, the same people: Luxury consumption is now practiced by those who were once its fiercest critics. Counterculture stances are being adopted by its most unlikely followers, business leaders. Moneyed environs have been redecorated with the symbols and icons of protest and rebellion. Left and right politics are reconciled by a Third Way. In the process, all the old rules of privilege, inclusiveness, and etiquette are found wanting, replaced by new rules with new combinations of elements that come across as unintentionally ironic and easy to mock in their clash of ideas and attributes traditionally antithetical to one another.

Charlton cites the Bobo sensibility as an example of psychological neoteny.[22] The fading of bourgeois wisdom and maturity paralleled by the rise of bohemian flexibility and vitality means that today's adults root themselves in a psychology of youthfulness, exactly what middle age–less Boomers want to carry forward into their older years. Charlton sees these kinds of incongruities as the very essence of cogency in contemporary society.

Baby Boomers get singled out for criticism, even scorn, because of their incongruous attitudes and behaviors. But these critiques presume a world of pressures, choices, and demands that no longer exists. In today's world, plasticity is a virtue, not a vice. Flexibility is smart, not cynical. Adaptability, even to the point of inconsistency and paradox, is superior to ardent rigidity.

Boomers bear the brunt of these harsh evaluations because they are the first to be fully immersed in the demands of a protean world in which endless possibility is the fundamental requirement for success. But Boomers are just the vanguard. They will be the first to live middle age–less, but they won't be the last.

Boomers embody many inconsistencies that are explicable, even laudatory, when it is recognized that their mindset is not fixed, closed, or finished. What was true at one time in their lives need not be true or practiced today. Boomers are not being hypocritical when they take up the very things they put down decades ago. They live with a sense of self that is still developing. They remain open to new possibilities dictated by swiftly evolving circumstances and pressures. Things they once rejected may now be those that are most fulfilling, meaningful, and valuable.

This plasticity of self is oftentimes seen as the root of the moral and cultural relativism for which Boomers get the most criticism. Even Charlton worries about the absence of any "fortitude of conviction." Brooks describes Bobos as "spiritual reactionaries" who long for traditional comforts while rejecting the norms and commandments that are the underpinnings of traditional solace and certainty. What's important is to understand that this is not a moral failing. As the Yankelovich Boomer Dreams research shows, Boomers have a strong moral core. They want to do the right things and live morally virtuous lives. But they make judgments contingently and flexibly because they bring a wholly new mindset to these decisions. Plasticity is a psychology and lifestyle appropriate to modern life. Boomers have taken it up out of necessity. It is not degeneracy; it is an openness that is imperative to success.

Life no longer affords Boomers the luxury of being settled. The only mindset that works is one of possibility. Boomers live in a constant state of "becoming." The style best suited for success is one of plasticity. Youthfulness is the spirit of possibility and plasticity, and so that's what all middle age–less Boomers will use to transform old age.

The neotenic mindset or plasticity of self that Charlton ascribes to to-day's adults is also the quality Brooks admires most about Bobos. In closing his book, Brooks notes that "potential" is their definitive characteristic, "more striking" than anything else about them or what they have achieved. It is this potential, this commitment to endless possibility, that he concludes will enable them to master the challenges of the modern world, and per-haps, thereby, even lead America into its next "golden age."

five

Marketing Immortality

*T*he fitness industry has a new rallying cry these days: age management, which is to say, helping Baby Boomers not get old. Why? Because that's where demand is going to come from in the future. Just as Boomers fueled the aerobics boom of the 1980s (think back to Boomers John Travolta, born 1954, and Jamie Lee Curtis, born 1958, in the 1985 movie *Perfect*), so too will they drive a wellness and fitness boom in the future.

According to American Sports Data, a sports research firm, from 1998 to 2004 the fastest-growing group exercising at least one hundred days per year was people fifty-five years of age and older. The 33 percent growth in this age group was far greater than the zero growth over the same period among people eighteen to thirty-four years of age and the mere 13 percent growth among people thirty-five to fifty-four years of age. People fifty-five and older also account for roughly one-quarter of all health club memberships sold each year.[1]

This is where many of tomorrow's jobs will be found. The Bureau of Labor Statistics estimates that fitness and health club jobs will increase 27 percent over the next decade, and health-care and social assistance jobs 30 percent.[2]

But there's a lot more to the business of age management than selling health club memberships. The broader opportunity is found in the area of wellness, and that includes many business sectors such as nutritional supplements, nutraceuticals, personal trainers, nutrition specialists, dieticians, home exercise equipment, plastic surgery, hip and knee replacements, yoga, strength training, Pilates, boxing, elliptical trainers, recumbent cycles, indoor cycling, gene repair, stress management, and more. Everything associated with age management is headed upward because middle age–less Baby Boomers are determined not to get old.

A whole category of so-called "anti-aging medicine" has sprung up to enable middle ageless Boomers to not get old. Controversy surrounds whether or not this kind of medicine really works, but with $50 billion in sales per year, it's got a lot of people convinced. Predictions are that annual revenues will top $71 billion by 2009.[3]

Perhaps the best measure of this enduring Boomer interest to stay in the game is the new malady known as Boomeritis, a term coined by orthopedic surgeon Dr. Nicholas DiNubile to describe the sports-related injuries that are now the second-most-frequent reason, behind the common cold, that Baby Boomers visit a doctor. Boomeritis accounted for 488 million lost work days in 2002.[4] Baby Boomer sports injuries were up 33 percent from the beginning to the end of the 1990s. This is only going to become more common.[5]

What's worse than a fitness injury, though, is being unfit, something many Boomers know and fear all too well. The MacArthur Foundation study cited in chapter 2 found that, to greater or lesser degrees, being fit can offset other health risk factors, even smoking. Dr. Michael Roizen, professor and chairman of anesthesiology and critical care at the University of Chicago, has developed a diagnostic test to calculate a person's so-called real age by looking at various health behaviors, fitness included, that affect known health factors. (Get your own calculation at RealAge.com.) It's a tool for Boomers to determine and track whether their "real age" is above or below their chronological age. More help for their ambitions to stay youthful, birth years be damned.

Boomers don't think in terms of age; they think in terms of age nullification, not only for fitness but for everything. They don't think that anything they do should be dictated by their chronological age. To Boomers, age is merely descriptive, not proscriptive or prescriptive. Age should not limit possibilities or restrict opportunities. Age should not stipulate roles or reduce potential or curb enthusiasm . . . or rein in anything. Boomers want to do away with age as a factor germane to the possibilities available to them.

Age nullification means a felt sense of permission to do anything in which one is interested, whether or not it's age-appropriate. This rebellious sensibility is seen in many ways, even in something like the use of illegal drugs. It might be thought that Boomers have finally aged out of recreational drug use. Yet in the 2005 survey conducted by the Substance Abuse and Mental Health Services Administration, the use of illicit drugs since 2002 had gone up among Baby Boomers while going down overall. The percentage of twelve- to seventeen-year-olds using drugs dropped from 8.2 percent in 2002 to 6.8 percent in 2005, while the percentage of fifty- to fifty-nine-year-olds doing so increased from 2.7 percent to 4.4 percent.[6]

No matter what it is, Boomers refuse to let age get in their way. Age is simply not relevant, so nullifying age is not a major act of rebellion for them or some defiant fist in the face of the existential void. Boomers take it for granted that age doesn't apply. They do whatever they want without any regard to traditional expectations about age.

Certainly, the physical incapacities of age matter, but when faced with them, Boomers look for ways to compensate for their limitations or for techniques to augment their capabilities, and fully expect that medical advances, improved information technologies, innovative product designs, and other types of support and personal enhancements will enable them to do so.

Talking Middle Age–less

The marketing of immortality to Baby Boomers is a pretty straightforward proposition: Give them what they need to continue to matter forever. Be a facilitator of being middle age–less. Most obviously, this means helping them push back or overcome biology. But there's more to it. Middle age–less is a state of mind, too. For both physical and psychological reasons, Boomers are looking for solutions that enable them to live younger longer.

There is a burgeoning market for tools to facilitate an active, energetic maturity. As more Boomers cross the unavoidable biological thresholds of their fifties and early sixties, this market will get even bigger.

Boomers are also wondering about where they will find the resources they are going to need in their middle age–less years. Where to live that has the right resources? Where to shop? Where to work and play? Where to travel for what they're looking for? Where to go online? Certain places will offer more than others of what middle age–less Boomers need and want. These places will be better able to support the youthful inclinations of this generation.

Many things can be done to make the situations in which aging Boomers live, work, play, and consume more attractive and compelling—less noise, fewer crowds, wider passageways, less glare, larger signage, better lighting, places to sit, and talking kiosks and signs. Whatever the context, though, Boomers won't respond unless the marketing language resonates with their sense of self. They need more than functional benefits; they need a psychological boost of reassurance and confidence. There are well-worn pieces of advice for talking to Boomers—"Portray Boomers as active" and "Don't say 'senior' "—but a few other guidelines are relevant, too:

- *Emphasize personal relevance.* This is a general marketing principle, but it's especially important for Boomers. One of the two strongest predictors of a new product's potential is whether people rate it highly as being "for people like me." (The other is being "unique.") For Boomers, though, everything has always been about "me," so personal relevance is an even more important thing to demonstrate to them.
- *Use aspirational language.* Boomers are not finished. They have done many things, but they have not done it all. They are looking forward to many more years of engagement and influence as they press their agenda for the future. Inspire them with what's yet to be accomplished.
- *Reference life stage, not age.* Boomers accept age, but they don't allow themselves to be defined by it. Life stage touches them more directly. The situations in which they find themselves, not age, shape their orientations to the possibilities awaiting them.
- *Make marketing itself an experience worth the time.* Boomers grew up with modern marketing. They have seen all the tricks of the trade and are very marketing savvy. Results from the 2004 Yankelovich study on consumer marketing resistance[7] first

presented at the Management Conference of the American Association of Advertising Agencies found that only 40.9 percent of Boomers agreed they "enjoy advertising," while 60.7 percent agreed it was accurate to describe them as "a person who tries to resist being exposed to" marketing. Just over half (52.2 percent) wished for less marketing than there is today. Two-thirds professed a desire for more "limits and regulations" on advertising. GenXers are much more comfortable than Boomers with the marketing saturation characteristic of the contemporary marketplace. But Boomers are not closed to marketing. After all, they have always loved shopping. Boomers are so marketing-savvy, though, that it takes something extra to truly engage them and hold their attention. As we wrote in our last book, *Coming to Concurrence: Addressable Attitudes and the New Model for Marketing Productivity* (Chicago: Racom Communications, 2005), superior marketing nowadays takes better precision and relevance as well as more control and greater value for their time and attention. Not marketing that promises future value after the sale, but marketing that is worth the time it takes. Advertising itself must be an experience worth having.

- *Make it age-appropriate.* Older people process information differently than younger people. While aging Boomers want to stay youthful, information should be presented to them in a manner that is best suited for their age. University of Massachusetts at Amherst marketing professor Charles Schewe has made a specialty of studying marketing to elderly consumers. From his review of research into the cognitive processes of older consumers, he has developed a number of practical guidelines.[8] Three are particularly important: One, allow self-pacing. When older people process information at their own pace, their learning ability is significantly enhanced. Two, use visual cues. Visual memory declines more slowly than verbal memory, so visual aids are preferred. Three, avoid sensory overload. The capacity for coordinating information from multiple senses is lower for older people, so keep the message and the medium focused and uncomplicated.

Getting a Boost

Energy and vitality are hallmarks of youthfulness and reassuring markers to Boomers that they are not getting old. Boomers recognize that they will lose a step or two as they get older, but they don't expect to become less vigorous or less animated as a result. They want to maintain the spirited look, feel, and performance of being middle age–less.

Boomers take comfort in their Viagra-fueled rescue fantasies of pharmaceutical breakthroughs. These are not idle daydreams. Besides Viagra, Boomers have witnessed the introduction of a plethora of so-called lifestyle drugs that promise to cure their ills as well as sooth their vanity. The roll call of recent new drugs runs the gamut of ailments and alphabet: Cialis, Levitra, Caverject, Rogaine, Propecia, Xenical, Meredia, Seroxat, Prozac, Zoloft, Paxil, Lexapro, Zyban, Lipitor, Vytorin, Crestor, Zocor, Aricept, Botox, and Renova. Whether it's erectile dysfunction, hair loss, obesity, depression, anxiety disorders, high cholesterol, Alzheimer's, or skin aging, all are now addressed by one or more of the latest advances in pharmaceutical research and development. Other mood, energy, and physical enhancements aren't far behind.

New York Times writer James Gorman has observed that pharmaceuticals are now being used to treat physical and psychological conditions once thought to be outside the purview of medicine. The use of such lifestyle drugs has grown to the point that Dr. Christian Daughton, chief of environmental chemistry for the Environmental Protection Agency's National Exposure Research Laboratory, worries that water supplies are becoming polluted with dangerously high levels of still-potent medications being introduced through careless disposal and normal human waste.[9]

Miracle drugs are just one part of the medical advances driving Boomer expectations. Improved surgical procedures have made new knees and new hips easier and less risky to get, just in time for the creaky joints of aging Baby Boomers. The demand is expected to be so great that the American Academy of Orthopaedic Surgeons worries that there won't be enough qualified doctors to perform the operations. Based on the demographics of an older yet active population, the scientific consulting firm Exponent projects a 673 percent increase in knee replacements by 2030, as well as a 174 percent increase in hip replacements and a 54 percent increase in partial joint replacements. This is in addition to a doubling or more of revision surgeries to fix or replace the artificial joints people already have.[10]

Cosmetic plastic surgery has become so commonplace and affordable that several popular TV shows have been built around it, including *Nip/Tuck*, *The Swan*, *Extreme Makeover*, and *I Want a Famous Face*. The American Society for Aesthetic Plastic Surgery reported 11.5 million cosmetic surgical and nonsurgical procedures in 2005, compared to only a little more than 2 million in 1997. Boomers account for the bulk of these procedures, with nearly half (47 percent) performed on people between the ages of thirty-five and fifty and almost another one-quarter (23 percent) for fifty-one-to sixty-four-year olds.[11]

If Boomers harbor any doubts about the power of modern medicine to keep them active and vigorous as they age, headlines in the popular media put these doubts to rest. Like the feature stories in the May 1999 issue of *Esquire* about immortality and what life will be like living forever, including tips on how to outsmart aging and provocative opinions from experts to the effect that Boomers might be the last generation to die or the first to live forever. Or like the surprise announcement that Janise Wulf, a sixty-two-year-old great-grandmother, gave birth in 2006 to her twelfth child through in vitro fertilization.[12] Or like the front-page news that recent declines in cancer deaths are real and continuing, not a statistical anomaly.[13] Or like the widely reported research of Jim Oeppen of Cambridge University and James Vaupel of Duke University published in a 2002 journal article in *Science*, in which they concluded that in sixty years, average life expectancy in some developed nations will exceed age one hundred, and that even though eternal life may be beyond our reach, there is no natural upper limit capping our life spans.[14] All the water-cooler talk and forwarded e-mails are about beating the odds and pushing past limits—exactly what Boomers have always sought.

The decoding of the human genome has raised expectations even higher. Baby Boomers look forward to the coming explosion of genomic advances that will give them the ability to reprogram or override their inherited make-ups, at which point we will all be able to ask ourselves questions about our health that we've never been able to ask before. For example, how healthy do we want to be, and what is that worth? Is a 5 percent improvement in one's health a good investment? Ten percent? Fifty percent? We will be able to ask even more unusual questions, too, like what kind of stamina we should give ourselves—the Winston Churchill kind of stamina (the constitution to eat too much, drink too much, smoke too much, lead his country through two World Wars and still live to ninety) or the Michael Jordan kind of stamina (the fitness to play all-out for the entire game while still having enough left at the end to clinch a sixth title with a clutch shot at the buzzer).

Medical advances are making it possible for people to be in greater control of their physical bodies, thus empowering them to make conscious, deliberate decisions about the kinds of bodies they would like to inhabit,[15] which opens up new personal possibilities and invites new lifestyle expectations. Boomers figure that even if they don't live forever, they will at least be able to augment their store of energy and stamina enough to outrun the Grim Reaper for a lot longer than generations before them . . . and look good while they're doing it!

Gene therapies are on the horizon. This is projected to be a $6.5 billion business by 2011. Research breakthroughs are pushing the envelope. A scientist at the University of Pennsylvania has reversed muscle decline in rats by injecting them with extra copies of the gene that develops muscle mass. A researcher at Southern Illinois University has genetically engineered mice that live to an age equivalent to 180 human years. Stanford researchers have genetically engineered vaginal bacteria to protect against HIV. A Princeton researcher has developed a breed of mice that learns at twice the normal rate.[16] To Boomers, nothing seems impossible anymore.

When time does run out for Baby Boomers, it is likely to catch up with many of them at work. Whether work is for enjoyment or for money, vigor is needed and will become a greater need as Boomers stay at work longer. To stay at the top of their game, Boomers will need to sustain their energy and vitality, which will send more and more of them in search of lifestyle drugs and medical procedures to keep them animated, vigorous, and looking good.

A hearty, attractive appearance is not unimportant. Economic researchers have found that people who get above-average ratings for their looks earn more than average. University of Texas economist David Hamermesh has studied the impact of appearance on earnings in the United States, Canada, and China. By his calculations, better-looking people earn an average of 12 percent more over the course of their lifetimes.[17] This good-looks bias is true of height as well. The Social Issues Research Center in Oxford, England, estimates that in the United States, each inch of height is worth an additional $600 of salary per year.[18]

Boomers know that as they age, a youthful appearance will be more important than ever to sustain a competitive edge at work. Already, the American Academy of Facial Plastic and Reconstructive Surgery reports that in 2004, work was the reason for plastic surgery among 22 percent of men and 15 percent of women.[19]

The American Society for Aesthetic Plastic Surgery reports that cosmetic surgeries totaled 11.5 million in 2005, an increase of 119 percent from 1997. All procedures, surgical and nonsurgical, are up 444 percent over this period. The top three surgical procedures in 2005 were liposuction, breast augmentation, and eyelid surgery. Over 3 million Botox injections were performed in 2005, making it the top nonsurgical procedure. Baby Boomers accounted for the largest proportion of these surgeries—fifty-one- to sixty-four-year-olds had 24 percent of these procedures in 2005; thirty-five- to fifty-year-olds had 47 percent.[20]

Stomach stapling grew ninefold from 1998 to 2004, with twenty-fold growth among fifty-five- to sixty-four-year-olds and a tenfold increase among forty-five- to fifty-four-year-olds.[21] Boomers have been a big reason behind the popularity of Lasik eye surgery and as they get older, interest is expected to grow stronger.

Aging Boomers will keep demand high for all of these procedures and more, and in the process make it unwise to write them off because they are aging.

Youthful Shopping

Aging Boomers do not act their age today, so why would we expect them to do so tomorrow? Their youthful mindset is most evident in the ways in which they have defied all expectations with their shopping. Boomers have refused to be typecast in their shopping preferences based on their chronological ages.

As shoppers, Boomers look like youthaholics. They can't seem to stop themselves from shopping and buying in ways that satisfy a generational craving to project and embrace a youthful spirit. Boomers buy products designed for younger consumers that they then accommodate to their own midlife needs and interests. They also buy products designed for older people that they then adapt to reflect their more youthful sensibility. In their shopping choices, there is almost no end to the manifold ways in which Boomers display their resolve to stay young at heart.

For example, the new cars introduced in recent years for younger drivers have been "hijacked" by Baby Boomers, says Art Spinella, president of CNW Marketing Research, a consulting firm that tracks trends in the automobile industry.[22] The targeted median age for the Toyota Matrix driver (not purchaser) was 28.8, but it has actually turned out to be 42.7. The target for the Honda Element was 28.6; it is actually 44.7. The target for the Pontiac Vibe was 30.2; it is actually 48.2. The target for the Dodge Neon was 22.7; it is actually 39.2.[23]

Even when Boomers shop their age, they reinvent the category in more youthful ways. Boomers are largely responsible for the 58 percent increase since 1980 in the number of households owning at least one recreational vehicle.[24] But the contemporary RV lifestyle is no longer a minimalist retirement escape. Now, it is reflective of the luxury tastes and preferences of Boomers who want an experience that has the youthful feel of adventure and novelty without having to sacrifice any adult comforts or conveniences. High-end RVs are the fastest-growing segment of the RV market, and many RV campgrounds now sell high-priced camping spots for hundreds of thousands of dollars that come complete with amenities like tennis courts, health spas, yoga classes, coffee shops, and golf courses, all behind gates manned by security guards that enclose a complex of manicured lawns.[25]

As Boomers look for new things to do, they are rediscovering many of the old things they used to do in their youth. Seattle-based Underdog Sports organizes adult leagues for the old schoolyard sports of kickball and dodgeball. There are 150 participating teams in the kickball league with adults of all ages, including people in their sixties.[26] Half the visitors to Disney World are adults who come for their own enjoyment with no children in tow.[27] According to the 2006 report of the Entertainment Software Association, 25 percent of video game players are over fifty,[28] up from only 9 percent in 1999.[29]

Mattel is now targeting Boomers with a sexier line of dolls called Barbie® Pin-Up Girls™ meant to be adult collectibles, not play toys. First on the market were Way Out West™ Barbie®, a cowgirl decked out in red boots, denim shorts, and a fringed leather vest, and Hula Honey™ Barbie®, a tropical girl with a wraparound skirt and an optional second ensemble of a grass skirt and a coconut-shell bra.[30] Mattel has also forged alliances with cutting-edge fashion designers to offer an adult line of Barbie apparel called Barbie™ Luxe. This clothing line is "designed for women who grew up with Barbie," meaning Baby Boomers.[31]

AFOL is an acronym for the Adult Fan of Lego, a major consumer group of Lego hobbyists who can be more passionate about Legos as adults than they were as children. The Lego company specifically recognizes the AFOL as distinct from the KABOB, or the Kid with A Bunch Of Bricks, and treats the two groups quite differently in its marketing, product design, and customer service. For example, AFOLs prefer smaller bricks while KABOBs want larger ones. There is an international community of AFOLs who stay in touch online through Lego Web sites, magazines, marketplaces, and photo galleries. Additionally there are regular exhibitions where AFOLs come to meet in person and display their elaborate Lego models.[32] As a spokesperson for Lego has noted, for Boomer enthusiasts, Legos are a "link to their past," a youthful connection that has helped make them just as popular today as ever.[33]

Boomers are making a difference for types of entertainment traditionally dominated by young consumers. For example, music buyers forty-five years of age and older comprise the biggest part of the market for CDs, double that of older teens. Music buyers over fifty account for nearly 24 percent of online music sales.[34] Boomers are a growing audience for movies, too. Moviegoers fifty years of age and older were 23.9 percent of the total audience in

2005, compared with 21.3 percent in 2001.[35] This is in contrast to flat or declining attendance among younger moviegoers over that same period.

Viacom's TV Land cable network targets Boomers with classic TV programs and related online tie-ins. The attraction is exclusively nostalgia appeal, but it taps into the continuing interest of Baby Boomers to be engaged with any medium carrying programming that caters to their tastes.[36]

These youthaholic buying patterns are particularly evident when it comes to housing. Shuffleboard and bingo retirement lifestyles no longer resonate with older homebuyers, so the homebuilding industry has updated its approach to this market, even its lingo. No more retirement communities; now the term is "active adult communities." This better describes members of a generation ages fifty and up who eschew any ambitions of retiring in the manner of their parents in favor of lifestyles that continue to be active, engaged, and youthful.

Today's new developments for older homebuyers are focused on active recreation. The old warehouse-style rec centers and clubhouses are passé, replaced by fitness centers, health spas, running paths, biking trails, and technology centers located alongside more upscale versions of the traditional amenities of golf courses, swimming pools, and tennis complexes. Social engagement is a key element in these communities as well. Book clubs, motorcycle clubs, RV clubs, musical clubs, political clubs, and more are typical parts of these communities, as are volunteer organizations of all sorts. Mixed-use communities with restaurants, retail shops, and office space as well as a diversity of housing types ranging from single-family homes to condominiums to town homes to multifamily apartments offer the feel of close-knit lifestyle villages, especially when they can be easily negotiated on foot or by bike. The mega–retirement development is giving way to more intimate communities with a neighborhood feel and high-end homes.

To accommodate a greater diversity of tastes among older homebuyers, the one-size-fits-all retirement ranch house has given way to highly tailored homes, a trend that homebuilders expect to be significantly accelerated by aging Boomers. More space, more bedrooms, and more high-tech hook-ups have become essential. Patios, courtyards, and porches have been turned into rooms. Home exteriors are being customized with special trim, details, color, and materials. Landscaping has become as important as interior decorating; streetscapes as important as elevations.

The experience of the home must mirror that of a life in progress, not a life on the decline, with gourmet kitchens, spas connected to the master bedroom, big rooms, media rooms, fine craftsmanship, and designs with artisan appeal and character. Boomers are not downsizing their lives as they get older, so they do not want to downsize their homes, either. Aging Boomers are looking for more space in which to indulge themselves, not less. And they want something that shows off an individual sense of style.[37]

While some older Boomers prefer age-qualified communities, this is not true of most. Boomers want to live in areas that are vital and active, so in addition to active adult communities, urban areas and micropolitan resort and college towns are seeing spikes of interest by aging Boomers.

Small towns like Oxford, Mississippi, and Thomasville, Georgia, have launched aggressive recruiting campaigns to attract aging Boomers.[38] In addition to raising their visibility with Boomers, towns like these are remaking what they have to offer in order to satisfy the urbane tastes that Boomer newcomers will bring with them. College towns like Conway, Arkansas, home to Hendrix College, are updating their "bucolic" appeal with a new "urban buzz," not only to attract students but to be more appealing to "retiring" Boomers as well. Similar efforts are in the works in Storrs, Connecticut, home to the University of Connecticut, and South Bend, Indiana, home to the University of Notre Dame. Furman University in Greenville, South Carolina, is building a retirement center on campus. Hampshire College in Amherst, Massachusetts, is building condominiums on campus for working people and retirees. The University of Pennsylvania in Philadelphia is building apartment complexes on university property that will be open to the public.[39]

This recitation of youthaholic shopping and buying by Baby Boomers could go on and on. Boomers have long been consumed by a need to bring a youthful orientation to their marketplace choices and personal lifestyles. Youthfulness has been lauded, valued, and rewarded for so long that it is now second nature to Boomers. It is not going to vanish just because they are aging.

The Tools It Takes

Boomers are looking for the tools it takes to stay younger longer. These cover a wide range of things to facilitate an enduring youthfulness. The market is growing for new and better tools. The overarching marketing principle is simple: Be a provider of tools to enable Baby Boomers to be middle age–less.

Make things easier to handle. Oxo is the best known, most frequently mentioned example of a company committed to making things that are easier for older people to use. The Oxo Good Grips line of kitchenware was developed for people with arthritis who have greater difficulty handling utensils, cutlery, and other kitchen tools. However, they have a wider appeal. In addition to ease of use, they have a sleek, contemporary look that is aesthetically appealing. Oxo's kitchenware does not look like cheap, serviceable stuff for old people. This combination of practical usability and artful polish is ideal for Boomers, who see no reason why functionality and youthfulness shouldn't go together.

After observing people with rheumatoid arthritis using its products, Whirlpool developed the Duet front-loading washer and dryer, which is mounted on a raised pedestal and has angled baskets and enlarged doors.[40] It is well-suited for all consumers, but especially aging Boomers who are looking for its combination of usability and artfulness.

Automobile manufacturers have already incorporated many features into their cars to make them better designed for older consumers: ignition switches on the dashboard instead of the steering column, extended door openings, higher seats, larger trunks, thicker door handles with contoured grooves, and dashboards with bigger knobs and larger displays. Swiveling seats and back doors hinged at the rear, among other ideas, are being considered as well.[41]

Sunbeam's new electric blanket controller has a distinctive figure-eight shape that makes it easier to find in a room, a white color scheme that is easier to see, and oversized buttons that are easier to use. Snapware containers have grips and lids that are easier to open and close.

Marketing Thought-Starter: Designs for Life

Age-appropriate designs provide remedies for the deficiencies and infirmities of old age. But Boomers are skittish about anything associated with old age, even if it is a useful fix. They want solutions that facilitate active lifestyles. When incorporating or promoting age-appropriate designs, it is best to represent these designs as facilitators, not fixes.

Boomers have always looked for things that boost their capacities to get the most out of life. These are things that enhance and optimize youthfulness. Remedies for the ailments of old age are enhancements, too, but they tend to be seen as things to keep the aged hobbling around rather than things to energize middle age–less Boomers off to the next new adventure.

The best approach to designing for Boomers is to follow a "universal design" strategy of simplicity, flexibility, and ease of use.[42] Universal designs are intentionally inclusive of all age groups and thus are age-appropriate for older people while having a streamlined, cutting-edge look and feel that appeals to younger people. This is the way to finesse the paradox of appealing to Boomers—designing something with a youthful vibe that better fits the abilities of people the age of Boomers.

Fiskars makes pruning shears with a gear system that increases cutting power with little or no extra effort by the user. The Folgers AromaSeal coffee cannister has an easy-grip handle that is endorsed by the American Arthritis Foundation.

One of the fastest-growing fashion retailers in recent years is Chico's, a chain that offers stylish clothing for Boomer women who want a looser fit without a frumpy look. Women's clothing retailer Eileen Fisher built its recent success in much the same way. Others are following suit. Liz Claiborne and J.C. Penney have introduced lines to better fit the contours of aging Boomer women. Success in attracting Boomer women will be well rewarded. They outspend younger women each year, having spent a total of $27 billion on clothing in 2004.[43]

Keep Boomers from showing their age. Boomers want a youthful appearance. They understand its value in the workplace, but more than that they don't want anything to do with old age, wrinkles in particular. Products that maintain or restore a youthful appearance like cosmeceuticals—skin-care products with medicinal, not merely cosmetic, benefits—offer this to Boomers.

Cosmeceuticals are projected to grow 11 percent per year through 2008, to reach $7 billion in annual sales. Skin-care products, including anti-aging and sun-care products, are the biggest part of this market, accounting for over 60 percent of sales.[44] By 2010, this market could reach $16 billion.[45] Boomers are driving this demand.

Revlon introduced Vital Radiance in 2006, a line of cosmetics for older women. This new product is targeted at the biggest segment of the cosmetics market. Women over forty-five account for 69.3 percent of cosmetic sales at mass retailers.[46] Early sales were beating expectations, causing other cosmetic marketers to take a second look at this market.[47] Other products to mask aging, such as color cosmetics or products with natural or organic ingredients, will be helped by Boomer demand, too.

There is no reason for this to be limited to skin-care products. Any sign of old age—gait, gray hair, balding, fashion sense, pop culture savvy, vocabulary—provides opportunities to offer Boomers tools to keep them from showing their age.

Keep Boomers mentally sharp. Little could be more important to Boomers than tools to keep their minds sound and clear. Mental acuity is fundamental to any hope they have of continuing their interests and passions. More generally, though, Boomers worry about suffering mental declines as they age. A research team of senior scientists from several leading institutions that study the health of older people estimated in 2003 that the number of people sixty-five and older afflicted with Alzheimer's disease would grow from 4.5 million in 2000 to 5.5 million in 2020, and then to 7.2 million in 2030.[48]

Certain leisure activities can help prevent dementia, though. A twenty-one-year study of people seventy-five and older led by researchers at the Albert Einstein College of Medicine in New York City and funded by the National Institute on Aging found that playing board games, reading, playing a musical instrument, and dancing significantly reduced the risk of various types of dementia, including Alzheimer's, especially among people who frequently engaged in these leisure activities.[49]

There is a natural fit between the Boomer interest in active lifestyles and the need for keeping their minds active to ward off mental decline. Product offerings that facilitate dynamic thinking and lively mental engagement will be well-suited to Boomers in their middle age–less years.

Supplement what Boomers don't have but need in order to remain active. There is strong demand across all generations for dietary supplements and functional foods, which are foods, fortified and nonfortified, with health benefits beyond basic nutrition. The term "nutraceuticals" is often used to broadly refer to all foods that promise a medical benefit, including supplements, functional foods, and other medical foods.

In 2004, the Institute of Medicine estimated that the market for dietary supplements was nearly $16 billion, with over one thousand new products introduced each year.[50] *Nutrition Business Journal* estimates that by 2010, the U.S. market for functional foods will equal $34 billion, or 5.5 percent of total food sales.[51]

The future of supplements and functional foods will be largely determined by the preferences of an aging population of Boomers. Typically, an aging population leads to a drop in food sales. But this is likely to be offset by demand from aging Boomers for supplements to replace or boost the nutrition and medicines they need.

The principle at work is that Boomers want things to supplement what they are losing to aging and what they will need to counter the declines of aging. Just look at dark chocolate, long a poor relation to milk chocolate until research found that it improved cardiovascular health. From 2003 to 2005, dark chocolate sales jumped 29 percent, reaching $1.62 billion. One-quarter of U.S. households have dark chocolate in the pantry, up from only 8 percent in 2003.[52]

This principle goes beyond food. Anything that supplements something essential for staying active, energetic, and engaged will be keenly sought.

Take the risk out. The corollary to supplements is permissible indulgence. While not replacing something that's missing or being lost, permissible

Marketing Thought-Starter:
Focus on Customer Value, Not Shelf Price

The logical question about adding product features or additional services is whether consumers will pay more for these sorts of value-added extras. The answer is no, they won't, because extras are now expected. Today's basic product looks a lot like yesterday's deluxe offering. Consumers demand more even as they shop around for the lowest price. But this doesn't mean that extras are loss-leaders. In fact, consumers will pay more if the value added is compelling. Discount retailer Target provides the best example.

Target is able to command slightly higher prices than industry leader Wal-Mart because the design intangible it delivers is worth it. It's not worth a substantial premium, but it is worth somewhat more to many consumers.

But shelf price is not the only, or even the most important, measure of value. Lifetime value is a better gauge of productivity and profitability. The ultimate aim is to have loyal customers who buy again and again with little prompting. When customers seek out brands, margins are much bigger than when brands must constantly inveigle people to buy. What brings people back with less coaxing is continuously enhanced value-added. It may not command a premium price but it can significantly reduce the costs of marketing, sales, and service, thus contributing as much as, if not more than, a higher price to the bottom line.

Boomers are particularly experienced consumers who know how to shop around on price. Notwithstanding that, value-added products and services are essential even if they won't pay a higher price. Giving Boomers a reason to keep coming back on their own initiative will pay off on the bottom line.

indulgence is a way for Boomers to treat themselves guilt-free. Instead of putting something good in, this requires taking all the bad things out.

Healthier doughnuts (no trans-fats), healthier chocolates (sugar-free), and even "reduced-risk" cigarettes are attempts to tap into this interest. Of course, there is nothing new about this sort of thing. But the opportunity created by aging Boomers gives renewed potential to this strategy.

In particular, Boomers want risk-free indulgence, not just risk-free commodities. "Safe adventure" is the Boomer watchword—something special to reward themselves without exposure to risk.

Portion-controlled packaged foods are a good illustration of this principle. Kraft ignited this trend with its 2004 introduction of 100-calorie snack packs of products like Oreos and Chips Ahoy! First-year sales exceeded $100 million, a feat accomplished by less than 1 percent of new packaged-goods products.[53] Kraft now offers 100-calorie packs of Wheat Thins, Cheese Nips, Honey Maid Cinnamon Grahams, and Ritz crackers as well. Procter & Gamble, the Coca-Cola company, Frito-Lay, and Hershey, among dozens of other food and beverage companies, have followed with their own 100-calorie or reduced-size packages. This is an offering well suited to Boomers looking for indulgence without risks. Boomers are particularly interested in portion control, a preference that carries over to all settings, including restaurants, where they are "the most frequent diners to order small plates and multiple appetizers."[54]

Reduced-size, low-calorie packs are tools of convenience for Boomers because they enable them to use to their advantage a psychological dynamic that social psychologists refer to as "the unit bias." The unit bias is the tendency of people to presume that an appropriate serving is whatever unit size they are presented with, no matter how large. People don't eat a certain amount; rather, they consume the "unit" with which they are presented.

In one widely reported set of experiments led by researchers from the University of Pennsylvania, people were offered smaller and larger sizes of various food products (Tootsie Rolls, soft pretzels, and M&Ms).[55] In every instance, they consumed the "unit" or size with which they were presented, whether it was the size of the food itself or the size of the utensil provided to scoop the food. People did not leave some of the larger sizes uneaten, nor did they eat multiple units of the smaller sizes. The observed pattern was one of consumption by unit, not by weight, which is a pattern consistent with a unit bias.

By swimming against the tide of recent decades and reducing rather than increasing the size of the package, marketers of 100-calorie packs have put a tool in the hands of Boomers that is more than a gimmick. It is a true tool for satisfying the craving for indulgence while minimizing the risks of overindulgence.

Give Boomers the ability to keep track of themselves. Aging brings with it the need to be more vigilant about monitoring and managing one's health. Boomers will be eager users of the tools and systems available to them. With information and feedback systems, they will be better able to negotiate the demands of being active, vital, and middle age–less.

The market for in vitro diagnostics is growing rapidly. Tests for detecting and managing diabetes, cancer, cardiovascular health, infectious diseases, and other medical conditions represent a $13.2 billion category that is projected to grow 6.1 percent per year over the near-term.[56] Similarly strong growth is projected for home health monitoring. Home-based digital systems to monitor and report the health of remote patients will grow from $461 million in 2005 to $2.11 billion in 2010.[57] In both cases, the aging population of Boomers is the primary driver of demand.

More generally, Boomers find value in all systems that enable them to process information more efficiently and govern the flow of sensory inputs more intelligently. An increasingly data-rich world puts a premium on managing, organizing, and filtering information and experiences. Wearable computers and advanced artificial intelligence systems to do this are being developed by many academic and corporate researchers. The Institute for the Future, a Palo Alto, California–based think tank and consulting firm, calls this "personal sensory management."[58] In its 2006 review of trends to watch, IFTF identified this as one of the primary societal dynamics unfolding over the next ten years.

As Boomers age, they will need smarter systems to help them keep up with the mounting and constantly changing abundance of data and sensory inputs. As information becomes richer and more multisensory, aging Boomers will increasingly turn to technology systems for help. They don't want to retreat from this data-rich environment; they just need better ways to cope and thrive in order to be self-inventive and in command.

"Do it for me." Motivated by an interest in individuality and a desire to experience things firsthand, Boomers have been the driving force behind the success of the do-it-yourself market over the past three decades. But now

they have new priorities on which they want to spend their time, and in many cases Boomers can no longer do much of what they once did themselves, either because of physical limitations or because the sophistication of technology has outrun their abilities to keep up. The emerging opportunity is one of "do-it-for-me," or DIFM.

The DIFM market is being actively pursued by the leaders of the do-it-yourself, or DIY, market. Both Home Depot and Lowe's have put greater emphasis on installation services. Neither is abandoning DIY, but both see DIFM as a stronger growth engine for the future given the aging of Boomers. Already this is paying off, as both chains have seen stronger growth in recent years from DIFM services than from their old-line DIY offerings.[59]

Best Buy's purchase and expansion of the Geek Squad is another example of a leading retailer pursuing the growing DIFM opportunity. Technical support delivered in-home is exactly what Boomers, and others, need in order to stay abreast of rapidly changing technologies for which frequent security enhancements are of critical importance. Like Home Depot and Lowe's, Best Buy is placing big bets on the potential of DIFM to drive its future growth.[60]

Boomers are looking for solutions and experiences facilitated by others that empower them by putting them in control of support resources rather than putting them in charge of doing it for themselves.

Make Boomers smarter. As middle age–less Boomers look ahead, they want to feel prepared for taking on the challenges of a self-inventive world. Consequently, they recognize the necessity to immerse themselves in a lifelong process of learning and self-development.

In the Yankelovich Boomer Dreams study, 71 percent expected to devote more time and energy over the next five to ten years to "learning a new skill or hobby." Similarly, 64.8 percent anticipated "developing new skills and expertise" and 62.8 percent "taking courses to learn something new." This is reflective of the underlying desire expressed by 63.1 percent for "unleashing your personal potential."

Aging Boomers will be lifelong and voracious consumers of educational offerings and developmental seminars. The online distance learning industry for students of all ages is booming already. It was a $5 billion busi-

Marketing Thought-Starter:
Empowerment Does Not Mean Going It Alone

Boomers want to be in charge but not to do everything themselves. Taking on too much is the surest way to get nothing done. Even in a marketplace of extreme self-reliance, there is a key place for advice, guidance, and solutions.

While a pop culture icon like the Lone Ranger might seem to be an apt expression of the American ideal of self-reliance, the reality has always been more along the lines of a football quarterback. People are able to determine their own affairs and accomplish things for themselves as part of a bigger team effort, not as isolated free agents. The successful quarterback wins not by doing everything himself but by organizing and directing a team of skilled players. Each team member plays a key role in supporting the success that the quarterback leads. Thus, the American strain of self-reliance has always been a matter of getting the best help and of having the best resources, not of being independent of all ties and connections.

Boomers want to call the plays, not run the ball on every down. They are looking for brands that can provide needed skills and services to make them into better managers of their own affairs. More self-reliance does not mean an end to outside resources or external authorities; it merely means that Boomers want help that doesn't require relinquishing control. DIFM must be about implementation, not takeover.

ness in 2004, up 38 percent that year. Traditional distance-learning powerhouses like DeVry and the University of Phoenix—which has nearly 300,000 students, making it the largest institution of higher leaning in the United States[61]—now face competition from major universities of all types, including leading institutions like Harvard, MIT, and Stanford. Nearly all public universities offer courses online. In 2004, three million students took at least one course online; 600,000 completed all of their coursework online.[62] Boomers will keep demand high for these sorts of offerings.

Corporate education and training programs are other avenues by which Boomers can pursue continuous learning. The benefits of corporate education are reciprocal: Employees learn new skills while company performance is improved. An Accenture Survey of Corporate Learning Executives found that well-executed training programs could boost revenue growth by as much as 40 percent and net income growth by 50 percent or more.[63] Corporations are placing more emphasis on this as Boomers near retirement. The dual need to retrain Boomers and to transfer knowledge to younger workers will help fuel future growth in this $16 billion-per-year industry.[64]

Boomers want to stay current, be smarter, and maintain their competitive edge. They are keen for anything that offers them greater knowledge, whether it's training for a job or exploring new interests and leisure-time activities.

The Resources Required

In addition to tools they can use, Boomers are interested in resources to transform the experience of aging into one of being middle age–less. Aging Boomers will look to many places to find resources like time, money, community, and health care. The overarching marketing principle is straightforward: Connect Boomers with the resources needed to be middle age–less.

Pooling resources in a cooperative or communal setting is one approach being taken by many middle age–less Boomers. A growing number of elder housing cooperatives are in place or in the planning.[65] Glacier Circle in Davis, California, was begun by a group of twelve friends who worked together to build a housing development for themselves in which they could share the costs and duties of caring for one another in their old age. Each person or couple lives in a separate house in a development bound together by a "common house" where residents share meals and spend time together. The properties are designed to accommodate the special needs of older people, and the development is located near a greenbelt area with a walking path and a pond, a major hospital, access to mass transit, and shops.

In a similar vein, the Silver Sage elder housing development in Boulder, Colorado, promotes an active lifestyle for older people in a communal setting. The ElderSpirit Community in Abingdon, Virginia, offers the same kind of communal approach to elder housing. Other ElderSpirit Communities are in development in places including St. Petersburg, Florida, and Wichita, Kansas.

The Elder Cohousing Network provides information about and links to environmentally sensitive and sustainable communities designed to enable active older adults to "live independently and 'age in community' within a close-knit group of neighbors."[66] While intergenerational cohousing communities have been around since the late 1980s—they even have their own industry organization called The Cohousing Association of the United States—elder cohousing is more recent and will be driven in the years to come by aging Baby Boomers concerned about resources.[67]

The Burbank Senior Artists Colony offers another model for elderly communal living.[68] It is a residence-based community for older artists located in a 141-unit apartment building in Burbank, California. The artists living there support a theater group, an independent film company, a fine-arts collective, and an arts mentoring program for local schools. Not only does this colony help these older artists pursue their art; it is a resource for them to live longer lives as well. Studies have shown that older people who regularly participate in arts programs make fewer visits to the doctor, have less need for medication, and are less likely to suffer from depression.

While these communal cohousing developments are an important trend, most Boomers, like generations before them, will age in place. In the Yankelovich Boomer Dreams study, 51.2 percent indicated that they plan to stay in their current residences upon retirement, so resources will need to come to them.

Boomer numbers will create an increasing number of geographic pockets in which large percentages of older people are clustered. These are known as NORCs, or naturally occurring retirement communities.[69] The challenge within a NORC is getting needed services to the older people living there. To meet this need, Supportive Service Programs (SSPs) of various sorts have been created to organize and coordinate relevant social service organizations, public and private. However, there is a lot of variability in the breadth and stability of SSP offerings around the country. As Boomers age in place, their numbers will create a much more critical need, and thus a big market, for reliable, high-quality SSPs.

Boomers are looking online for resources as well. TeeBeeDee.com and Eons.com are Web sites with resources customized for people fifty and older. Hundreds of communities connect older people with similar interests on every topic imaginable. Advice is available on interests ranging from money to wellness to relationships to travel. At Eons.com, Boomers can learn how to live longer with the Longevity Calculator, exercise their minds with BrainBuilders, tell their life stories through LifeMap, or use the cRANKy™ search engine that ranks results by relevancy to those fifty and older. C-Boom.com is a shopping site for Boomers with a tagline that brags it's where "the cool boomers surf!" Boomers International maintains the Web site BoomersInt.org as a clearinghouse for hundreds of other sites that track or market to Boomers.

Boomers are willing to travel to find the resources they need. For example, spiritual tourism is a burgeoning travel niche.[70] A 2006 survey by the Travel Industry Association found that 25 percent of adults were interested in spiritual travel. While this is not an interest exclusive to Boomers, Boomers in search of spiritual fulfillment are a significant part of the interest in travel for spas, yoga, meditation, wellness centers, astrology, mythology, and pilgrimages to holy sites. National and regional travel associations are now emphasizing spiritual attractions in their marketing.

Spiritual tourists want more from travel than a place to visit; they want to "get" something out of it. Travel is their means of accessing the resource they need, and they want to make the journey without sacrificing comforts and luxury touches.

This combination of high luxury and high adventure (of both the spiritual and corporeal varieties) has been described as "wanderluxe"—thrills plus luxury; "wanderlust as well as . . . pampering"; and adventure without "grim accommodations."[71] Boomers will go to whatever extreme it takes to get the resources they need as long as they can indulge themselves in doing so. Indeed, this is a consistent pattern with Boomers—doing the right thing by doing right for themselves. It is a pattern rooted in their focus on self and will shape the ways in which they meet the future, no less in their agenda of interests and priorities than in their quest for continued impact and relevance.

Morality

six

Having a Purpose

*B*aby Boomers get a lot of credit, good and bad, for things they didn't invent. That's because when they put their numbers and enthusiasm behind something, they make it important. So even if it wasn't their idea, they get the credit or blame.

Much of what shaped Boomers as they grew up became important and influential not because they created it, but because they adopted what others had conceived. Maybe these things would have emerged anyway without the commitment of millions of Boomers, but there's no way of knowing since they signed on in droves.

It's not as if Boomers haven't had their own ideas; it's just that by and large they have been most captivated by the ideas of others. It's no surprise, then, that when the *New York Times* in 2006 got 124 leading critics and literary authorities to name the best American fiction of the last twenty-five years, only two of twenty-two novels that received more than two votes were authored by a Baby Boomer. The top five novels were all by authors born in the 1930s. By way of contrast, the *Times* noted that a 1965 list compiled through a similar exercise conducted by the *New York Herald Tribune* included mostly novels by authors who were then under fifty years of age. The *Times* called it "startling" that Baby Boomers have not produced a single great novel.[1]

Every generation takes guidance from prior generations, but Baby Boomers have done this to a fault. Just look at three of their biggest passions: sex, drugs, and rock'n'roll.

The sexual revolution and free love were well under way by the time teenage hormones started raging in Baby Boomers. Hugh Hefner (b. 1926) launched *Playboy* magazine in 1953. Helen Gurley Brown (b. 1922) published *Sex and the Single Girl* in 1962 and took over as editor-in-chief of staid *Cosmopolitan* in 1965, transforming it from a literary and advice magazine for family women into a provocative glamour magazine for young single women. Burt Reynolds (b. 1936) posed in it for a nearly nude centerfold in 1972.

Boomers honed their lovemaking techniques from how-to guides penned by their elders. Dr. David Reuben (b. 1933) published *Everything You Always Wanted to Know About Sex (But Were Afraid to Ask)* in 1969. Under the enigmatic pseudonym J., Jean Garrity (b. 1940) published the classic woman's how-to *The Sensuous Woman* in 1971. And Alex Comfort (b. 1920) published the bestselling *The Joy of Sex* in 1972.

The women's movement of the 1960s and 1970s was inspired by Betty Friedan's (b. 1921) classic, *The Feminine Mystique*, first published in 1963, when the oldest Boomers were seventeen and Friedan was forty-two. Friedan was one of twenty-eight women and men who founded the National Organization for Women in 1966. She and Episcopal priest Reverend Pauli Murray (b. 1910) wrote NOW's first Statement of Purpose. Gloria Steinem (b. 1934) was founder of *Ms.* magazine. Jane Fonda (b. 1937) gave a celebrity face to the cause of feminism.

Many of the notable critics of the sexual revolution and feminism are of the generation before Baby Boomers, including political activist Phyllis Schafly (b. 1924) and marriage therapist Marabel Morgan (b. 1937), whose 1974 book *The Total Woman* advocated that women "surrender" themselves to their husbands.

Similarly, Baby Boomers were followers, not leaders, of the 1960s and 1970s psychedelic culture of hippies, LSD, be-ins, and mysticism. Timothy Leary (b. 1920) was the former Harvard professor who famously told Boomers to "turn on, tune in, drop out" at the January 14, 1967 Human Be-In at San Francisco's Golden Gate Park.

Ken Kesey's (b. 1935) band of northern California Merry Pranksters invented the psychedelic look of vibrant, swirling Day-Glo designs—painted first on Kesey's 1939 International Harvester school bus Furthur in preparation for a cross-country trip to the 1964 World's Fair—and conducted legendary "acid tests" throughout the Bay Area in the mid-1960s. Fellow Prankster Vic Lovell (b. 1935), who told Kesey about the Stanford research program where Kesey first took LSD, credits their circle with pioneering all the "hallmarks" of the hippie lifestyle, including LSD, body painting, light shows, strobe lights, mixed-media shows, exotic-looking clothes, "freakouts," and "the rebirth of hair."[2]

Psychedelia and politics came together in the Yippies, the Youth International Party, co-founded by, among others, Jerry Rubin (b. 1938), Abbie Hoffman (b. 1936), and Paul Krassner (b. 1932). Rubin and Hoffman were among the defendants in the Chicago Seven trial accused of conspiracy, inciting to riot, and other crimes during the 1968 Democratic National Convention. Other defendants included Dave Dellinger (b. 1915), Rennie Davis (b. 1941), and Tom Hayden (b. 1939). Hayden, later a California state legislator and ex-husband of Jane Fonda, is the author of the 1962 Port Huron Statement, the political manifesto of the Students for a Democratic Society, a liberal student organization started in 1960 that that led many student protests in the 1960s and was the precursor to the more extreme Weather Underground group.

The counterculture has had many intersections and left many legacies, not the least of which, according to ex–Merry Prankster, business consultant, and global futurist Stewart Brand (b. 1938), is the modern cyber-revolution of PCs and the Internet. Boomers Bill Gates (b. 1955) and Steve Jobs (b. 1955) were computing trendsetters, earning billions and their places in history along the way. But as Brand notes, Boomers, inspired by cultural observers like Marshall McLuhan (b. 1911), Buckminster Fuller (b. 1895), and sci-fi author Robert Heinlein (b. 1907), found in PCs and later the Internet a haven for personal expression and freedom from central authority.

Says Brand, the hippie mantra to do your own thing turned into the entrepreneurial one of start your own business, a creative imperative that inspired even such nonhippies as Gates. (Although it is worth noting that in the late 1970s Microsoft co-founder Paul Allen, born 1953, sported a hippie look with long hair and a full beard,[3] and he has used his fortune to amass a large collection of Jimi Hendrix memorabilia.) In short, while the PC revolution is Boomer-led, it is nevertheless, argues Brand, "a flowering remnant" of the open-minded values and politics of the hippies,[4] a cultural phenomenon begun by leaders from the prior generation.

Rock'n'roll has roots in blues, R&B, folk, bluegrass, and rockabilly that date back decades before Baby Boomers. But the incarnations that enthralled Boomers during the 1960s and 1970s—and that still command their ears—emanated as much from the trailing edge of the prior generation as from Boomers themselves. A short, illustrative list of these musicians (including some non-American artists) would include Sonny Bono (b. 1935), Glen Campbell (b. 1936), Grace Slick (b. 1939), John Lennon (b. 1940), Ringo Starr (b. 1940), Bob Dylan (b. 1941), Harry Nilsson (b. 1941), David Crosby (b. 1941), Joan Baez (b. 1941), Jimi Hendrix (b. 1942), Paul McCartney (b. 1942), Leon Russell (b. 1942), Carole King (b. 1942), Roger McGuinn (b. 1942), Jerry Garcia (b. 1942), Lou Reed (b. 1942), Graham Nash (b. 1942), Janis Joplin (b. 1943), Keith Richards (b. 1943), Jim Morrison (b. 1943), Joni Mitchell (b. 1943), John Denver (b. 1943), Mick Jagger (b. 1943), George Harrison (b. 1943), Jimmy Page (b. 1944), Ray Davies (b. 1944), Stephen Stills (b. 1945), Neil Young (b. 1945), and Bob Seger (b. 1945).

Promoter Bill Graham (b. 1931) built his empire staging rock concerts for Baby Boomers, introducing them to the music that is now the soundtrack for their generation, first at the Fillmore on the edge of the Pacific Heights neighborhood in San Francisco and later at Fillmore West across town and at Fillmore East in New York City's East Village.

Atlantic Records co-founder Ahmet Ertegun (b. 1923) shaped the music of this generation by recording or otherwise working with many of the classic rock bands of the 1960s and 1970s, including Led Zeppelin; the Rolling Stones; Crosby, Stills, Nash & Young; Cream; King Crimson; Yes; Emerson, Lake & Palmer; and the MC5, along with many celebrated R&B and soul music acts of the 1950s, 1960s, and 1970s such as Ray Charles, Aretha Franklin, Wilson Pickett, Otis Redding, Solomon Burke, Clyde McPhatter, the Drifters, the Clovers, Archie Bell & the Drells, and the Coasters. Ertegun's influence included helping other leading producers and agents, including billionaire mogul David Geffen (b. 1943), start their own labels. Ertegun was a key figure behind the founding of the Rock and Roll Hall of Fame, into which he was inducted in 1997.

Many of the other notable passions of Boomer youth were also led by members of the prior generation.

The bloody struggles of the civil rights movement during the 1960s and 1970s, to which many Boomers committed themselves, were organized and directed by leaders from the prior generation, including leading lights such as Rosa Parks (b. 1913), Reverend Martin Luther King (b. 1929), James Meredith (b. 1933), Reverend Fred Shuttlesworth (b. 1922), Reverend Ralph Abernathy (b. 1926), Medgar Evers (b. 1925), Bob Moses (b. 1935), John Lewis (b. 1940), Reverend Hosea Williams (b. 1926), and Stokely Carmichael (a.k.a. Kwame Ture, b. 1941). Bobby Seale (b. 1936) and Dr. Huey Newton (b. 1942) were co-founders of the Black Panther Party, of which Eldridge Cleaver (b. 1935), author of the 1968 racially galvanizing memoir *Soul on Ice*, was also a member.

The contemporary environmental movement found its first voice in Rachel Carson's (b. 1907) 1962 classic *Silent Spring*, the book that started the global environmental movement of the late twentieth century. Former Vice President Al Gore recounts in his bestselling book *An Inconvenient Truth: The Planetary Emergency of Global Warming and What We Can Do About It* (New York: Melcher Media, 2006) his childhood awakening to environmental threats as his mother read passages from Carson's book to him and his sister at their dinner table.

David Brower (b. 1912) was executive director of the Sierra Club during its fight to save the Colorado River through the Grand Canyon from plans to build two dams and a diversion tunnel. In 1969, he founded Friends of the Earth. Senator Gaylord Nelson (b. 1916) came up with the idea for Earth Day after seeing the effects of the 1969 oil spill off the California coast near Santa Barbara. Ed Abbey's (b. 1927) 1975 book *The Monkey Wrench Gang* was the intellectual inspiration behind the 1980 founding of the radical environmental group Earth First!

Boomers followed the lead of the older generation not only when it came to the well-being of society, but when it came to their personal well-being as well. Jane Fonda moved beyond politics to spark a Boomer aerobics craze with her 1982 workout video. Jim Fixx (b. 1932) fueled the running vogue with his 1977 bestseller *The Complete Book of Running*. Phil Knight (b. 1938) capitalized on the burgeoning Boomer interest in running, fitness, and sports when he started Nike in 1972 with University of Oregon track coach Bill Bowerman (b. 1911) by selling shoes out of the trunk of his car.

The tax revolt of the last quarter of the twentieth century was ignited by Proposition 13, a California ballot initiative approved by voters in 1978 to reduce and cap property taxes. Proposition 13 was the brainchild of Howard Jarvis (b. 1903). It fomented a nationwide tax revolt that found resonance with Baby Boomers and helped build support for Ronald Reagan's (b. 1911) bid for the presidency. This taxpayer revolt has had the continuing support of many Boomers, affecting the policies of both Boomer Presidents Clinton and Bush.

Obviously, Baby Boomers have been caught up in a lot more than just these few things, and not all were caught up in these particular movements. But these are some of the central passions that have consumed Boomers throughout their lives. What gave these movements power was not the vision of Boomers but their numbers and enthusiasm. Boomers found their agenda of interests in the ideas of the prior generation, which they then made into dominant social and marketplace forces through the overwhelming force of their cohort. Boomers manned the barricades erected by Matures.

After being derivative for so long, Boomers are finally ready to reinvent the world according to their own ideas. They are in command and can no longer look to the prior generation for guidance. Their numbers will still matter, but these numbers will drive what Boomers bring to the table, not what they borrow from the prior generation. Through the weight of Boomer numbers and the energy of Boomer commitment, these ideas will be the dominant priorities for everyone in the decades ahead.

Comfortably Righteous

As Boomers migrated from Beetles to Beemers to Hummers, many observers began to wonder what had become of the generation on the other side of the generation gap. The generation that thrived on breaking rules and defying convention looked as if it had sold out. There seemed to be no fight left in

Boomers, no ambition left to make things right, only a rapacious appetite for over-the-top accumulation and consumption.

What's never changed about Boomers is their youthful focus on self. At every stage of their lives, they have flourished through a spirited focus on self-discovery. They have done so in different ways as times have changed and as they themselves have matured. As Boomers faced up to a world of limits, the expressive self took a backseat to the indulgent self. The righteous self with its willingness to make a stand on principle remained, especially for certain smaller groups of Boomers, but it was overshadowed by the allure of self-indulgence.

Nowadays, the expressive self is fading as Boomers come to terms with physical age, and the indulgent self has been sated, or at least satisfied to the extent that it no longer dominates the Boomer agenda. On the other hand, the righteous self is making a comeback.

Boomers never renounced their moral concerns and interests; they simply found themselves balancing other obligations and priorities. What they seemed to have lost was actually just below the surface. Now that their life situations are changing, this moral sensibility is reemerging along with a renewed interest in fighting the good fight.

A few exceptions notwithstanding, Boomer protests in the past were dissents about the ways in which they believed the "system" was betraying basic American values (such as disallowing free speech, conducting a war of uncertain legitimacy, failing to treat all people equally). Boomers believed in these core values, just not in the way the system was operating. The self-indulgence that has been criticized as inconsistent with these protests was nothing but Boomers enjoying the fruits and rewards of a social order in which they have always believed. Their protests were as much a demonstration of allegiance as their shopping.

Boomers now want to go back to making the system better rather than just taking advantage of what it has to offer. A commitment to moral values is something that all Boomers share, as shown in Figure 2-5, and it is a commitment that has grown over the past thirty years, as shown in Figure 4-5.

The righteous self of the past was combined with an expressive self more focused on lifestyle experimentation and inner frontiers. Rule-breaking

Marketing Thought-Starter: Naughty Boomers

Boomers may be older, but they are no less interested in being disobedient. Conformity has never been attractive to them. Boomers like shortcuts, angles, and mischief, particularly when they believe in the righteousness of the cause or the personal benefits. Yankelovich MONITOR data finds Boomers no less interested than younger generations in decadent, sinful treats. Nor are they any less attracted to every sort of personal indulgence. Boomers seek out opportunities to be disobedient and naughty.

As Boomers have matured, business managers have struggled to abide by the mantra that the customer is king. Finding themselves in this spotlight has reinforced to Boomers that they are entitled to treat themselves. Age is no barrier to a little playful, willful disobedience. Permission to break the rules continues to resonate with Boomers, particularly if it involves naughtiness behind closed doors.

Popular TV shows like *Desperate Housewives* have implicitly legitimized the idea that it's okay for women over forty to act coquettish and to think of themselves as comely and thrilling. These are not idle fantasies. One of the fastest-growing genres of video pornography is the so-called mature woman category, a phenomenon that is said to be rooted in the interests of younger, not older, men.[5] Boomers still seem to have that youthful appeal.

Ben and Jerry's, a Boomer icon of safe, fun insubordination, continues to connect with their spirit of disobedience. It now offers for sale on its Web site the Ben and Jerry's Euphori-Lock, a combination lock for a pint of ice cream designed to keep naughty roomies from pilfering the Cherry Garcia. Boomers know naughtiness firsthand, so presumably they know it's a good idea to be vigilant about one's favorite treats. The Euphori-Lock idea is a lighthearted poke at the sensibility of nonconformity and disobedience that has long been pivotal for naughty-minded Baby Boomers.

was the vogue. Social causes were another area in which tradition, authority, and established rules needed to be challenged, if not abolished. Righteousness was another form of self-expression.

The righteous self of tomorrow will be combined with an indulgent self more focused on personal pleasures and pampered well-being. Doing good for others that is also good for oneself will be preferred. Righteousness will provide another sort of self-indulgence.

For Boomers, the expressive self has been seen in lifestyles, the indulgent self in shopping, and the righteous self in causes. When righteousness was another form of self-expression, lifestyles were as much a form of protest as marches and sit-ins. Long hair made a statement, too. As another sort of self-indulgence, though, righteousness will be channeled through shopping. Brand choices will signal sympathies.

Increasingly, Boomers are going to protest and dissent, even vote their conscience, through the ways in which they participate in the consumer marketplace. Consuming will come to be more than a source of indulgence; it will emerge as the chief means by which middle age–less Boomers voice their protests, register their dissent, and act to make the system better . . . while making themselves better at the same time.

Many companies are trying to win the loyalty of aging Boomers through corporate social responsibility initiatives. However, Boomers aren't likely to choose one brand over another solely for the cause it supports. As an increasing number of companies commit to various causes, supporting a cause will not be distinctive. At best, it will be the cost of entry.

Boomers are willing to support causes to the extent that it is good for

Once Was	Now Is
Mini-skirts	Minivans
The pill	The little blue pill
Anti-establishment	Anti-aging
Hippies	Hip replacement
Changing the world	Changing the will
Radical	Radicchio
LSD	Lipitor
Easy Rider	Easy does it
Getting high	Low Impact

Figure 6-1: Boomer Culture

them, too. Good causes are of interest to Boomers, but sacrifice is of no interest whatsoever. The righteous self is in ascendance, but the indulgent self remains strong.

Taking up the Gauntlet

Aging Boomers have a lot of fight left in them. In the 2006 Yankelovich MONITOR survey, respondents were shown a list of various activities and asked which one or more they had done in the past year as a form of activism. As Figure 6-2 shows, Baby Boomers were more likely than the younger Generation X cohort to have participated in nearly every activity in the list.

Over the last five to ten years, a steadily growing number of Boomers have expressed an unwillingness to be taken in by compromise, hype, and convention, as shown in Figure 6-3. With the time and resources these days to do so much more, they want to make sure they don't wind up doing far less than they could or should.

In years past, Boomers have been partisan to a fault. Their approach to

Done in past year as a form of activism (Partial list)	Boomers	Xers
Voted	64%	50%
Refused to buy a product or service	49%	47%
Had phone number added to Do Not Call list	49%	37%
Contacted a business to complain	45%	41%
Signed a petition	41%	33%
Told friend/co-worker not to buy from a company	36%	40%
Refused to shop at a particular store	35%	38%
Contacted a business to give a compliment	34%	27%

Source: Yankelovich MONITOR, 2006

Figure 6-2: Activism

	1994	2005
In this world, you sometimes have to compromise your principles	65%	47%
Important to be seen as someone who...	**2001**	**2005**
Can always see through exaggeration and hype	37%	56%
Is willing to defy convention	17%	35%

Top 2 box on 4-point scale
Source: Yankelovich MONITOR

Figure 6-3: Taking a Stand

addressing issues and solving problems has been highly polarized. This is seen most readily in their politics. The uncompromising political style of the past thirty years has arisen in parallel with the rise of Boomers in politics.

One measure of this has been reported by award-winning journalist Bill Bishop of the *Austin American-Statesman*. Bishop reports that politics have become bitterly polarized in recent years as communities themselves have become less politically diverse. In a study of county voting patterns in presidential elections since 1948, he found that in 1976, 26.8 percent of voters lived in a landslide county where one candidate received more than 60 percent of the vote. In 2000, the percentage had grown to 45.3 percent; in 2004, it was 48.3 percent.[6]

Boomers prefer communities that mirror their way of thinking. The result is de facto segregation by politics and ideology. When asked in the Yankelovich Boomer Dreams study whether they preferred friends with different values or friends who shared their values, 80.3 percent preferred friends with shared values. As Bishop notes, insulation from competing ideas breeds more extreme opinions and less willingness to compromise. Since the mid-1970s, according to the data cited by Bishop, voters have become more partisan, less independent, and more likely to vote along straight party lines.

This partisan edge may or may not soften as Boomers proffer their agenda for the future, but it will not disappear. It is going to endure. Boomers will tackle every issue as a moral issue, and will do so with a moralistic edge. They will invest this partisan passion in shopping as consuming becomes their outlet for making a stand.

Notwithstanding the stated desire of many to move beyond partisan politics, no firm resolve to compromise is yet in evidence. The Pew Research Center for People and the Press released a report in early 2007 with the headline that survey results showed that people were ready for compromise.[7] Yet while this hopeful news describes the general wish that people have for the transformation of politics, the survey results show that on "contentious" issues they continue to be unwilling to yield any ground. The so-called political wedge issues continue to polarize them. No one, Boomers included, is ready yet to give ground.

Perhaps the most revealing results of this Pew Research Center study, though, were those showing that Republicans thought Democrats should compromise with them just as Democrats thought Republicans should compromise with them.[8] One-sided sacrifices do not constitute a meeting of the minds, nor do they encourage less partisanship. People want to get beyond political polarization, but they are unwilling to facilitate this by being less polarized themselves.

Boomers are not the only generational cohort involved in these highly polarized ideological struggles. After all, it was conservative Pat Buchanan (b. 1938) of the Mature generation who famously proclaimed from the podium at the 1992 Republican National Convention that Americans were fighting a "cultural war" for the "soul" of America.[9] But Boomers didn't need coaxing; they understood this perspective already. This is the Boomer style. While they have not been the only generation caught up in the politics of partisanship, Boomers have been the generation most deeply involved in it.

Boomers of all stripes have subscribed to the view that "the personal is political," a battle cry made famous by feminist activist Carol Hanisch in a 1969 essay bearing that title.[10] The original idea was that personal problems are actually rooted in political arrangements, so problems are not personal but political. Over time, this idea carried over into the broader culture as

Marketing Thought-Starter: Niche News

When the Fox News Channel was launched in 1996 by media tycoon Rupert Murdoch and TV producer and political consultant Roger Ailes, it introduced a new sensibility to late twentieth-century news broadcasting, that of "corrective news." Concerned that a liberal bias pervaded other broadcast news reporting, Fox News promised to present both sides of an issue or story so that viewers could decide for themselves. In this way, it hoped to counterbalance or correct for the purported liberal bias. In practice, though, this has meant a conservative tilt to its reporting. Even so, Fox News found a niche, quickly becoming the most-watched cable news channel.

This bias is not exclusive to conservative politics. Air America offers liberal-minded syndicated radio programming. Niche media and information promoting a particular political ideology have become more popular.

More than ever before, people have the tools and resources it takes to wrap themselves in a cocoon of news and information that reflects their existing beliefs and preconceptions. People have always done this, but nowadays there is much less content that they share and much more self-sorting into enclosed niches.

As a generation steeped in both political polarization and self-indulgent lifestyles, Boomers will provide a huge market for ever more narrowly bounded news and information niches. The marketing imperative will be one of finding cost-effective ways of aggregating a highly disaggregated audience.

What consumers are likely to share in the future will be physical needs more than psychological benefits and values. The only way to manage marketing messages productively in a marketplace demanding extreme customization is to facilitate the ability of consumers to customize for themselves. The future is not one of customization; it is one of self-customization. In this future, business models change, not simply consumer needs. The old model of studying consumers and predicting demand will have to be replaced by a new model of facilitating their ability to voice their preferences and then responding by producing one highly customized item at a time. Niches are the new norms, the new mass market, the new context for understanding how to connect with Baby Boomers.

the notion that all personal choices, even those about lifestyles and consuming, have political consequences. Political correctness comes directly
from this.

With the indulgent self in ascendance, the connection between consumption and creed was less patent, but it was still there. Political strate-
gists have rediscovered it. In *Applebee's America* (New York: Simon &
Schuster, 2006), journalist Ron Fournier, Clinton strategist Douglas Sos-
nick, and Bush strategist Matthew Dowd outline the ways in which commercial third-party databases are transforming election campaigns.
Voters are no longer targeted solely on traditional criteria like geography,
income, race, union membership, gun ownership, anti-abortion group
membership, and the like. Instead, brand choices are used.

At the Web site www.applebeesamerica.com, visitors are invited to answer twelve profiling questions. For example, do you prefer Dr. Pepper or
Pepsi? Audi or Saab? Wal-Mart or Whole Foods? Bourbon or gin? Each answer has a certain probability of predicting party preference. Someone who
drinks bourbon, for example, is more likely to be a Republican voter; a gin
drinker, Democratic. Altogether, these twelve questions generate a good
prediction of political party. In other words, our brand choices reflect
lifestyle preferences that are rooted in our underlying ideological leanings. The personal is political even when we are doing nothing more than
choosing things we like to buy and do. Much of the success enjoyed by
Republicans in the elections of 2002 and 2004 has been attributed to the
deployment and use of these kinds of lifestyle models.

A flurry of news stories during the midterm elections of 2006 reported
on the advanced modeling systems being used by both parties to predict voting preferences from lifestyle and consumption data. The GOP's Voter Vault
provides local organizers with detailed information about the hobbies, interests, brand choices, and club memberships of individual voters.[11] Former Clinton Administration deputy chief of staff Harold Ickes has launched
a for-profit company called Catalist to do the same for Democratic candidates.[12] Other for-profit companies like Spotlight Analysis are developing
lifestyle- and values-based models for Democratic candidates.[13]

Baby Boomers are poised to lead the marketplace in the direction of shopping for causes. It has always been implicit in their lifestyle choices. They are now ready to make it a more explicit part of how they consume.

Corporate Purpose

More and more, the marketplace presents itself to Baby Boomers as a set of ethical choices masquerading as brand choices. In an effort to cash in on this, many companies are aligning themselves with certain social values and causes. Of course, there is nothing new about corporate social responsibility. But many companies are now going beyond merely supporting worthwhile causes to centering the very purpose of their businesses on a certain set of social values and causes.

Rarely is social responsibility a product attribute that motivates consumers to buy. Consumers make product choices on the basis of performance and price. A good cause won't make up for a bad product. Social responsibility matters when it is the broader purpose of a company. Businesses with good products that are aligned with good causes are what Boomers want. They enable consumers to get the best products to meet their needs while also declaring their allegiance to certain values and causes.

The best-known example of such a company is Whole Foods. Co-founded in 1980 by Boomer CEO John Mackey (b. 1954), Whole Foods is a $5.6 billion high-end grocery retailer specializing in a wide array of organic and natural food products. Mackey is outspoken that business should have a purpose beyond maximizing profits. In the November 2005 issue of *Reason* magazine, he engaged in a debate about this issue with Milton Friedman, the late Nobel prize–winning economist who once famously denounced the concept of corporate social responsibility as "pure and unadulterated socialism."[14]

Mackey believes that a business is responsible to all of its stakeholders, which is to say everyone who adds to the infrastructure of operation and exchange that makes a business possible—investors, customers, employees, suppliers, and community. Only investors, argues Mackey, have maximum profits as their top priority. Other constituencies seek other things, all of which are important, too. The job of management is to balance the interests

of all constituencies such that everyone wins. Not that profits are unimportant; Mackey is adamant that a business must be profitable. But, he asks,
profits to what end?

The mission statement of Whole Foods states that the company will do-
nate 5 percent of net profits to philanthropy. Thus, shopping at Whole Foods
shows an affiliation with that policy and with the causes the company
supports.

Other companies have similar programs. Salesforce.com, founded in
1999 by trailing Boomer Marc Benioff (b. 1964), pursues a so-called one
percent solution in which one percent of profits, equity, and employees'
time are given back to local communities. Patagonia pledges one percent
of its sales revenues to environmental causes through a self-imposed
Earth Tax.

In 2001, Yvon Chouinard, the sixty-eight-year-old founder of Patagonia,
and Boomer Craig Mathews (b. 1951), a world-famous angler and owner of
Blue Ribbon Flies, started 1% For The Planet®, an alliance of businesses contributing one percent of sales revenues to one or more of the affiliated environmental organizations. It includes more than four hundred member
companies in forty-three states and twenty other countries. The World
Business Council for Sustainable Development brings together over 180
companies from more than thirty countries and twenty industrial sectors to
work toward sustainable development that balances economic growth,
ecological balance, and social progress.

The chairman of the textile manufacturer Interface, Ray Anderson, was
profiled in *Inc. Magazine* for his corporate and personal commitment to the
environment.[15] Spurred by customer inquiries about the environmental
impact of his company's products and inspired by Paul Hawken, the environmentally committed founder of the garden supply company Smith and
Hawken, who wrote *The Ecology of Commerce: A Declaration of Sustainability* (New York: Collins, 1994), Anderson became a passionate advocate of
sustainability, even penning a book of his own about the topic (*Mid-Course
Correction: The Sustainable Enterprise: The Interface Model*, Atlanta: Pere-
grinzilla Press, 1999). Interface is now a leader in environmentalism, but not
to the detriment of its bottom line. As Anderson emphasizes in his speeches

to other business leaders, he is just as "competitive and profit-minded" as anyone. He simply believes in the necessity and duty of running a profitable, growing business within the context of broader responsibilities and purpose.

Marketing professors Rajendra Sisodia of Bentley College and Jagdish Sheth of Emory University, along with business consultant David Wolfe, undertook an assessment of companies on a variety of "soft" criteria such as the ways in which they treated employees, suppliers, environmentalists, communities, and the government and whether the CEO led by inspiration or by fear. They then looked at the market performance of the thirty companies scoring highest on their criteria. The detailed results were published in their book *Firms of Endearment: How World-Class Companies Profit from Passion and Purpose* (Upper Saddle River, N.J.: Wharton School Publishing, 2007). The bottom line is compelling: the ten-year market return for the thirty "firms of endearment" was 758 percent, compared to 128 percent for the S&P 500.[16]

Many companies are looking to do more than maximize profits; they make money for the purpose of something bigger. While these companies are strong competitors with good products and services, they are good for society at large, too, because they are committed to a mission that transcends the category in which they compete.

Whole Foods is not just about grocery shopping. It is a connection to design, community, diversity, exclusivity, luxury, and philanthropy. Shopping at Whole Foods is more than a grocery-shopping errand. The company sells intangibles like purpose and experience. Indeed, the experience of Whole Foods means that there is no sacrifice in shopping there. Boomers can contribute to others while getting an experience for themselves. The indulgent self is sated as much as the righteous self.

Milton Friedman objected to any distraction that would keep a business from a single-minded focus on satisfying its customers. But customers are different nowadays. They want to buy into a good purpose as much as buy a good product. So social responsibility is not a distraction; it's a central concern. Boomers are leading the marketplace through this fundamental shift in priorities. Intangibles now top the agenda.

The Claustrophobia of Abundance[17]

Superabundance defines our times. Not that we have all that we might want, but in general our lives are crowded with stuff. Store shelves are overflowing. Retailers are everywhere. Pop culture venerates stuff in word, deed, and setting. The media pour out a nonstop stream of glittering images, tempting us to buy.

But superabundance has bred a longing for something more than just more stuff. We are looking harder than ever for meaning and purpose in the material glut. The result is burgeoning interest in nonmaterial values, an interest intensified by the dawning realization that money and material things do not bring happiness or fulfillment.

Boomers are the vanguard of this shift in priorities. The Psychology of Affluence that characterized their formative years gave them an early focus on intangible satisfactions. Decades of immersion in material abundance have left Boomers yearning for something more. The intangibles in life are now their primary interest.

The paradox of superabundance is that it does not ensure happiness. This puzzle was examined in detail by emeritus Yale University political scientist Robert Lane in his turn-of-the-millennium synthesis, *The Loss of Happiness in Market Democracies* (New Haven, Conn.: Yale University Press, 2000). Notwithstanding rising indicators of social and material well-being like gross domestic product, equality for women, old-age pensions, a free press, democratic institutions, greater education, and more access to media and information, survey measures of self-reported happiness have been declining for decades. Additionally, depression and teen suicide rates are up. The old saw turns out to be true: Money can't buy happiness.

This is not to say that people in abject poverty are happy. More money does bring more happiness, but only up to a point, a threshold calculated from the World Values Survey of 1990–91 by University of Michigan political scientist Ronald Inglehart to be roughly equal to the per capita GNP of Ireland in 1990.[18] Above that, there is no correlation between the average wealth of a country and its average level of happiness.

Has Been	Has Come to Be
Mad Magazine	*Modern Maturity*
Pink Floyd	Pink ribbon
Poli Sci	Polident
Senior prom	Senior moment
GI Joe	GI series
Orthodontist	Orthopedist
Oil crisis	Oil of Olay
Jonathan Livingston Seagull	Crow's feet
Nanu nanu	iPod Nano

Figure 6-4: Boomer Culture

There are many reasons why money and happiness are unrelated. Lane concludes that the primary reason is that the pursuit of prosperity takes time away from personal relationships, yet it's relationships with others that make people happy.

Other characteristics of the consumer economy play a part as well. Various researchers have cited things like too many choices, an overemphasis on instant gratification and selfish interests, the overarousal of appetites, spiraling levels of expectations, more stress, less free time, too much focus on the future and too little on the here and now, worries about debt, and the unrelenting pressure to buy. Indeed, it is difficult to envision a market-driven society in which people are perfectly content. A certain amount of dissatisfaction is essential to demand.

No one wants to give up material things; rather, people want plenty of nonmaterial things to go along with stuff. Boomers in particular no longer believe that nonmaterial values require material sacrifices. The quest is for both at once. Boomers will connect with intangibles through their choices in the consumer marketplace.

As a result, first priorities have shifted from quantity, tangibles, and money to quality, intangibles, and time.[19] Not that people are walking away from more tangibles and money, only that things per se have been eclipsed in importance. Of course, it's not as if quality, intangibles, and time have ever been unimportant. The difference now is that intangibles are the emerging opportunities in the marketplace and thus the best vehicle for growth and expansion. In today's marketplace, material characteristics like reliability, comfort, convenience, performance, and functionality are taken for granted. Only intangibles make the difference that matters.

Boomers are demanding something more from the marketplace than stuff per se. Their agenda of priorities focuses on purpose and meaning—a way to do good for others while doing good for themselves.

The element that Boomers have brought to their agenda is the convergence of causes and consuming. While their priorities continue to reflect many of their old interests, they are now looking to marry the shopping savvy of their indulgent selves with the moralism of their righteous selves. These are the two things Boomers do best: shop and protest. These are the two things they will forge into one as they face the future.

seven

A Healthy Attitude

Since 1959, U.S. commercial airline pilots have been required to quit flying at age sixty. That suited Baby Boomers just fine. There were lots of them, and they needed turnover at the top of the seniority ladder to make room for their own advancement. But now that Boomers themselves are topping out, the mandatory retirement age has been rethought. After all, Baby Boomers don't see themselves as getting too old to fly just because they are aging.

In late 2006, the International Civil Aviation Organization changed its rules, allowing pilots to fly until age sixty-five as long as their co-pilot is under sixty. This forced the U.S. Federal Aviation Administration to reconsider its policy, and on January 30, 2007, the FAA announced that it would initiate the process for changing its rule to conform with the ICAO rule.

The wisdom of this proposed change was hotly debated. It was even opposed by the Air Line Pilots Association, the pilots' union. But grassroots pressure had been building for years, led by Airline Pilots Against Age Discrimination (APAAD), an organization of pilots from all major domestic airlines that cast its position in terms of age discrimination. Those resisting the change argued in terms of diminished safety due to poorer pilot health and lessened physical capacities. Ultimately, an FAA study group concluded that there was no evidence of any health-related safety risks, hence the start of the process to raise the retirement age for pilots from sixty to sixty-five.

There is much to learn from this about the impact that middle age–less Boomers will have on the ways in which the future unfolds. As discussed already, Boomers are going to reignite the fight against age discrimination once it starts to impinge on their own plans and opportunities. Boomers want to remain active, engaged, and influential, and if denied the ability to do so, they will change the system. Not to overthrow the system but, as always, to make it better for everyone by making it better for themselves.

The battle over the retirement age of airline pilots is a just one front in the bigger battle that will be fought by aging Boomers. In every case, these battles will entail the same dynamics: resisting age discrimination, doing for others in order to do for themselves, challenging tradition, breaking rules, reinventing old age, staying involved in work and life, and defying expectations about health and physical capacities.

Health was at the center of the debate about the retirement age of commercial pilots. The FAA concluded that "experienced pilots in good health can fly beyond age 60 without compromising safety."[1] It's an interesting conclusion, because all airline pilots, whatever their age, have to be in good health. So what the FAA is saying is not that pilots over sixty have to be in good health, but that it is now abandoning its presumption that people over sixty have health issues that could compromise airline safety. In other words, Boomers have forced the rethinking of the old-age stereotype guiding previous policy and have shifted the burden of proof from people over sixty having to prove their good health to oversight agencies having to prove their poor health.

For Boomers, health is more than a need to be addressed. It is a moral issue connected to the rights of older people and the fairness of policies and regulations that affect their opportunities to control their own destinies and to self-invent their futures.

Frailty

The youthfulness, impact, and possibility that constitute the shared beliefs of Baby Boomers depend upon continued good health. Concern about health defines another area of shared Boomer values and attitudes.

In the Yankelovich Boomer Dreams study, respondents were asked to rate the extent to which they were worried about twenty-one different things that might affect retirement. On a seven-point scale of concern, eight of these were given the highest ratings—5, 6, or 7—by half or more. These are shown in Figure 7-1.

The top five are particularly significant because they are important both in general and to at least half of every subgroup of Boomers. But all eight concerns are of a piece. The overarching concern of Boomers as they look to the future is *self-sufficiency*. While certainly a concern of older people of every generation, it is particularly worrisome for Boomers, who are the first generation of older people to face a future of self-invention in which self-sufficiency and self-determination will be essential.

Topping this list of eight is concern about being able to afford the health care that Boomers know will be critical for sustaining their energy, acuity, and capacity. Above all else, Boomers want assurances about access to health care, for it is health care that holds out the promise of making their old age middle age–less. Health care in their older years, not income security, is the biggest concern for aging Boomers.

Parallel results were found by the 2006 Yankelovich MONITOR survey. In

Having sufficient health care insurance coverage	70.4%
Getting sick and frail	66.5%
Having enough money to get by	63.9%
Being able to live independently	62.8%
Not being mentally sharp	62.8%
Being short of energy and vitality	59.4%
No longer being able to live life to the fullest	51.8%
Being in charge of your affairs	50.1%

Top 3 box on 7-point scale
Source: Yankelovich Boomer Dreams Study, 2006

Figure 7-1: Worried About in Retirement

that research, health-care costs topped the list of things Boomers said were causing stress in their lives. It was the only area mentioned by a majority of Boomers. By contrast, only 37 percent of Boomers said they were stressed about the actual state of their health, far fewer than the 60 percent stressed about health-care costs. The percentage of Boomers mentioning health-care costs was the highest of any generation, even Matures, among whom only 49 percent mentioned it.

As Figure 7-1 shows, frailty is another key concern. Boomers worry about mental sharpness, energy, vitality, and independence—concerns that are all tied to health.

In fact, health is tied to every priority or ambition that Boomers have for the future. Whatever Boomers pursue, support, or advocate, good health is a necessary requirement; absent that, nothing else matters. While always true of older people, it is more vital for Baby Boomers because they face a world of self-invention that demands they take charge and stay in control. Their health as older people is not about coping with their decline but maintaining their engagement. Their generational character demands nothing less and abides no other expectation. Health takes on a special urgency with Boomers. It becomes moral issue number one.

Fighting Frailty

The importance of health is underlined when the top eight concerns shown in Figure 7-1 are contrasted with the ratings given to the other thirteen concerns included in the Yankelovich Boomer Dreams study. These are shown in Figure 7-2.

The first thing to note is the gap between the eighth-highest concern and the ninth—just over 10 percentage points. Other than the gap between the bottom two items, this is the largest gap between any two items, signifying a definitive break in attitudes. Health concerns stand far above anything else. Boomers want to be taken seriously, stay off the sidelines, keep busy, do new and different things, lead a vibrant, exciting life, be in charge,

Not being able to live in your current home	39.6%
Being treated as an old person	37.9%
Not being taken seriously	37.7%
Being bored with your life	35.4%
Being relegated to the sidelines	33.9%
Having enough to do and keep busy	33.8%
Being stuck doing the same old things every day	33.7%
Living somewhere that is not vibrant and exciting	29.4%
Being taken advantage of in some scam	28.5%
Not having the opportunity to be in charge of something	26.3%
Finding a community of other people to be with	26.2%
Not being involved in social causes	25.4%
Not being current on what's in style	8.7%

Top 3 box on 7-point scale
Source: Yankelovich Boomer Dreams Study, 2006

Figure 7-2: Worried About in Retirement

be involved in social causes, and more. And they do not want to be treated as old people or taken advantage of in scams. But few Boomers are "worried" about these things. They know that they can get what they want and live however they choose . . . health permitting, that is.

Boomers are worried about health. If their health is assured, then there is nothing else to worry about. They will see to it that they get what they want. They will get the rules about retirement age changed. They will stamp out other limitations or restrictions. They will defy stereotypes. They will stay engaged and take up causes. They will do all of these things and more as long as they can be assured of their health.

The central worry of Boomers as they look toward the future is becoming too frail to live out their self-inventive hopes, dreams, and aspirations. Because everything depends on it, health tops their list. And not merely staying healthy, but staying healthy enough to be youthful even as they age. Boomers don't want the good health of old people; they want the kind of good health that will enable them to live as middle age–less people. Boomers will fight for this, and when Boomers fight for something, it becomes a moral issue.

Taking Charge

The singular importance of health to Boomers is readily apparent in the "Generation V" study that The Segmentation Company, a division of Yankelovich, completed for Bayer Consumer Care. Bayer sponsored this research to dig into the health-care perceptions and priorities of Baby Boomers. The results were first released in January 2007 and revealed a generational focus on "vitality," especially among a highly involved segment of Boomers. In short, it's Generation V for vitality along with the corollary dimensions of vigor, verve, vivacity, and joie de vivre.

Boomers don't think about good health merely as not being sick; they think about it as being "vital." Good health care is not simply restorative; it is an enhancement. Good health care doesn't just cure, fix, and repair; it invigorates, energizes, and enlivens. Living well is not just being free of disease or disability; it is being free to keep going or even start fresh.

Vitality is the way in which Boomers think about their health. They want the vitality it takes to stay engaged and pursue their agenda of interests and causes.

Nothing is more important to Boomers than good health. In the Generation V research sponsored by Bayer, good health was the overwhelming choice among other priorities, as seen in Figure 7-3.

Not only do Boomers want good health; they take pride in it, as seen in Figure 7-4.

The majority of Boomers believe their personal vitality exceeds that of their parents and peers. In the Generation V study, 91 percent agreed that they would like to stay active and vital. Absent vitality, Boomers lose their middle age–less lives. Sustained engagement takes vitality.

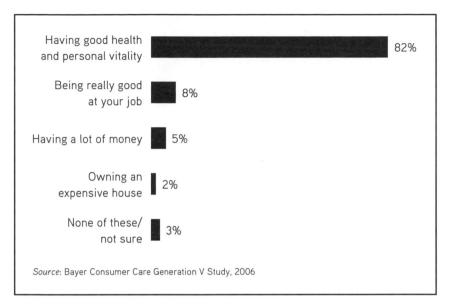

Figure 7-3: Most Important in Life

I take pride in what I do to maintain my health and vitality	84%
I define myself by my ability to remain active and do the things I enjoy	84%
I have so much going on in my life that I have to stay healthy to keep doing the things that I enjoy doing	81%
I am more healthy and full of vitality than my parents were at my age	65%
I have more energy and vitality than most other people my age	65%

Top 2 box on 4-point scale
Source: Bayer Consumer Care Generation V Study, 2006

Figure 7-4: Vitality and Health

Health My Way

To maintain their vitality, and thus their health, Boomers want to take charge themselves. This is a consistent theme in all Yankelovich research. For example, in the 2005 Yankelovich Preventive Health Care study, 85.2 percent of Boomers agreed that they are personally responsible for their own health, higher than the 78.4 percent of Generation Xers who agreed.

The Generation V research sponsored by Bayer echoed this theme of personal responsibility. Almost every Boomer—98 percent—agreed with the statement that "my future health depends on how well I take care of myself." As far as Boomers are concerned, it is all up to them, which is why 81 percent say they will spend whatever time is needed on maintaining good health and 74 percent say they will spend whatever money it takes.

Boomers try to keep up with the information it takes to maintain their vitality. Nearly all, 92 percent, feel they are informed about the amount of physical exercise they should be getting. Nearly as many, 89 percent, feel they are knowledgeable about the amount of sleep they should be getting. And 84 percent feel they are informed about government dietary guidelines and the benefits of vitamins and supplements.

The Boomer style of managing their health is characterized by the very result Boomers are seeking. Every aspect of health, from what it is to how it's managed, is about vitality.

Vitality Is the Best Medicine

When asked what they do regularly to stay healthy, Boomers were most likely to mention things that are active and vital. Figure 7-5 shows the percentage of Boomers mentioning each of the choices included in the research.

Topping the list is having fun. Seeing a doctor once a year is fourth on the list, behind hobbies and stress management. Diet is next. Exercise is second to last, although cited by a majority.

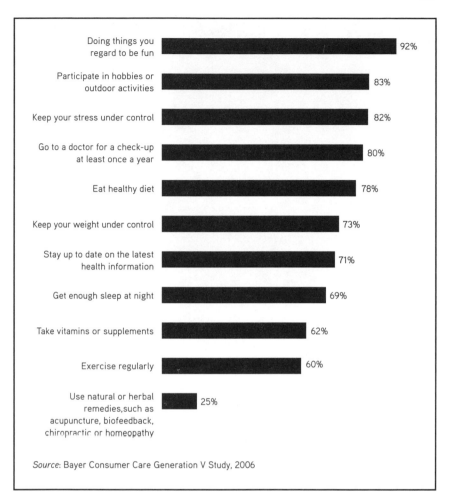

Figure 7-5: Regularly Engage In to Stay Healthy

Boomers do not see good health in the same way as medical professionals. For Boomers, it's less about the things you do and more about how you do things. Doctors, diet, and exercise play a part, but they believe the main thing is to have fun and be engaged in one's life. Get outside, relax with hobbies, and have fun. Do these things and you'll be healthy, because good health is about being vital in these ways. Restrictions, limits, and guidelines aren't unimportant, but first and foremost is to live life with vitality.

Marketing Thought-Starter: Put Them to Sleep

Sleep is a health issue for Boomers. In the 2006 Yankelovich MONITOR survey, 74 percent of Boomers reported that getting eight hours of sleep is a health-related behavior they care about, yet only 52 percent reported doing so. This is the same percentage reporting they feel well-rested when they wake up in the morning, down from 64 percent in 2004.

The swiftly rising demands of a 24/7 world are keeping more and more Boomers awake at night. Unfortunately, sleep deprivation compromises health. A growing body of research shows a connection between too little sleep and diseases such as colon cancer, breast cancer, heart disease, and diabetes, as well as health risk factors like obesity, high blood pressure, bodily inflammation, reduced melatonin, and stress.[2]

This is not to mention the thousands of automobile accidents caused each year by sleep deprivation. The National Highway Traffic Safety Administration estimates that these accidents result in an average of fifteen hundred fatalities each year.[3] Fortunately for Boomers, older people are at lower risk for sleep-related traffic accidents.[4]

Boomer vitality will depend upon getting enough sleep. In the near future, it is likely that Boomers will rebel against activities or demands that cause them to lose sleep and thus put them at risk of losing the vigorous edge they are determined to carry into their older years. At the same time, they will look for more products and services to ensure that they are well-rested and thus able to sustain the vitality that is the epitome of good health to them. Already, this is a huge market.

Sales of prescription sleep aids were $3.6 billion in 2006, up 29 percent from the year before and expected to reach $4.3 billion by 2010.[5] The wholesale market for mattresses grew almost 40 percent from 2000 to 2005, reaching $6.4 billion in sales, driven largely by the high-end mattresses favored by many Boomers. Luxury mattresses were 21 percent of total sales in 2005. Fifty-six percent of bedding sales were for the premium products made for luxury mattresses, up from 37 percent in 2000.[6] Aging middle age–less Boomers will push sales of these and related products and services like over-the-counter sleep aids, sleep centers, and stays at hotels offering superior sleep experiences even higher.

Just Okay

Just because Boomers are in charge of their health doesn't mean they are doing a top-notch job. In the Generation V study, only 12 percent graded their efforts an "A." Fifty-four percent gave themselves a "B." Not too bad, but that leaves 34 percent doing a "C" job or worse. Most Boomers would probably prefer that their doctors, nutritionists, and trainers do an "A" job—as the old adage goes, nobody wants a "C" student for a doctor—so 88 percent of Boomers giving themselves anything less suggests that they are doing little better than an okay job.

In the 2006 Yankelovich Food For Life research, ony 47.4 percent of Boomers rated their diets at home higher than 70 on a 0-to-100 scale. A mere 17.4 percent rated their diets away from home higher than 70.

Contrast these ratings of how well Boomers say they care for themselves with their ratings of their overall health in the Preventive Health Care study. Boomers have yet to reach the older ages at which disease, illness, and disability become more prevalent and debilitating, so it's not too surprising that 69.6 percent rated their health higher than 70 on a 0-to-100 scale. Even so, in response to what they do to maintain good health, only 43.3 percent reported getting regular health screenings to test for high cholesterol, high blood pressure, or cancer and only 44.9 percent reported getting regular medical check-ups. Nearly as many, 41.4 percent, said they practice prayer and meditation to maintain good health.

Topping the list of ways to maintain good health was personal hygiene, mentioned by 69.3 percent of Boomers. Next was positive attitude, at 63.8 percent; good family relationships, at 57.4 percent; managing stress, at 52.4 percent; and staying active, at 50.2 percent. Nothing else was mentioned by a majority of Boomers.

Only a minority of Boomers worry that they are not doing enough. In the Yankelovich Boomer Dreams study, only 40.8 percent agreed that their "health over the next ten years will restrict [their] abilities and capabilities." Leading-edge Boomers born in the 1940s worry more—52 percent agreed—but this is far from universal. By and large, Boomers feel pretty good about the sort of approach they're taking to maintaining good health.

Good health is a matter of feeling vital. Visits to the doctor, sweating at the gym, or pushing back from the table don't provide that feeling to the majority of Boomers. They turn elsewhere to get the vitality boost that they associate with good health, and in doing so don't follow the preventive measures urged by health professionals.

Even in the little things, Boomers can't bring themselves to make sacrifices that would detract from vital, youthful experiences. When asked in the 2006 Yankelovich MONITOR survey about things they do when they want to treat themselves, 32 percent of Boomers said they "eat something decadent or sinful." The nature of the permission these Boomers are giving themselves is easy to decipher—enjoy life now; fix any complications later.

Fix-It Mentality

Obesity is a problem for many Boomers. A 2005 study conducted by researchers at Beth Israel Deaconess Medical Center and Harvard Medical School found that Boomers are living large in midlife. Compared to the prior generation, more Boomers at thirty-five to forty-four years of age were overweight. Among Boomers, 28 to 32 percent were obese at those ages, compared to only 14 to 18 percent among the generation before them.[7]

In the Generation V study sponsored by Bayer, 62 percent of Boomers said they were at least ten pounds overweight. In the Yankelovich Preventive Health Care study, 36.4 percent of Boomers reported that they had been diagnosed as being obese or overweight. As noted in chapter 2, self-reported height and weight collected in the Preventive Health Care study were used to calculate BMI for each respondent. Based on these calculations, 34.4 percent of Boomers would be considered overweight and 31.3 percent obese. A BMI calculation in the Yankelovich Food For Life study yielded similar results. In both studies, the percentage of Boomers classified as obese on the basis of BMI was the highest across all generations.

Obesity is a serious risk factor for many things. In fact, it is the biggest wild card for Boomer life spans. Higher obesity rates could slow or cap the increases in average life spans to which Boomers are looking forward.[8] The question is whether they will be able to fix whatever problems arise, because too few Boomers are doing enough to prevent them. Fix-it, not prevention, is the Boomer mentality.

Quick fixes have long been an integral part of the Boomer scene. Throughout their lives, Boomers have presumed good health, courtesy of medical breakthroughs in vaccines and antibiotics. Their experience of health has been one of "fixing" oneself when the need arises, whether through diet, exercise, or mental discipline. From brown rice to biking, from tofu to Tarot, Boomers have thought of health and wellness as a combination of physical, spiritual, and emotional fixes.

The expectation that remedies will be available whenever the need arises continues to shape how Boomers plan for the future. Prevention, while important, helpful, and maybe even fun, is not considered absolutely essential. Whatever it takes—drugs, surgery, therapy, whatever—the generational experience of Boomers has been that cures will make things as good as new. Nothing bad or unpleasant is inevitable or irremediable.

This fix-it mindset is a holdover from their formative years, when the future seemed assured. No need to worry about the future today; it will take care of itself when it arrives. The ensuing onset of limits made Boomers more competitive and selfish about ensuring a secure future for themselves, but it did not cause them to rethink how they approached the future. Enjoyment of the moment has always been most important. After all, Boomers have reasoned that problems can be fixed when necessary but lost time and opportunities can never be recovered.

A fix-it approach is embedded in the health-care system itself. Doctors are rewarded more for fix-it tests and procedures than for preventive therapies and counseling. And in some cases, the economic trade-off between the costs and benefits of preventive care are insufficient to prompt greater emphasis on prevention (occasionally due to morally questionable calculations such as people without preventive care dying before they reach an age when it costs more to care for them).[9] The fix-it focus of Boomers is thus reinforced by the nature of the system they face.

The world of self-invention further reinforces this fix-it mentality. What one can become is not a function of what one is or is not, nor how well or how poorly one has lived before; it is only a matter of what someone is willing to do right now with tools and information that are readily accessible. Self-invention is a world of continuously unfolding possibilities in which one's future self can be reinvented as necessary at any point in time. One's present self need focus only on what's relevant and required today, not on what the future may or may not hold.

Medically speaking, a fix-it mentality is probably not the best approach, but for Boomers is feels entirely appropriate. It fits the world of self-invention they face and it resonates with their deeply felt generational experiences.

Using medicine to reinvent themselves as technologically enhanced creatures makes perfect sense to Boomers. They cut their pop-culture teeth on movies, comic books, and TV shows in which ordinary people were transformed by medicine or misbegotten laboratory experiments into superhumans with supernatural powers, sometimes for the better, sometimes for the worse. Boomers followed their stories and saw that deep down, even mutants, androids, cyborgs, and genetically enhanced humans are just like ordinary people. Nowadays, the creatures with artificial limbs and organs who are fortified by pills and supplements and in command of special equipment and machinery are not superheroes like the X-Men or Captain America or the Six Million Dollar Man but themselves! Those whom Boomers used to think of as alien super-beings are now their friends and neighbors.

Prevention to Fix-It

Boomers think of everything as a fix-it, even things that might be more precisely defined as preventive. For them, preventive activities are fixes, too. It's not so much the distant risk that motivates many Boomers to practice preventive measures; it's a mental calculus that translates risk in the future into something wrong today that also happens to create that future risk. So, whatever that is, it needs a fix. This shift in terms is not a bad thing; indeed, it is probably the best way in which to make an abstract, future risk real enough for people of every age to take action today. But for Boomers, this is the only translation sure to work, because it recasts prevention in a way that resonates with the Boomer fix-it mentality.

For people to help themselves, they must believe in the efficacy of their own actions. If people don't think that anything they do can make a difference, then no matter how much they agree that something needs to be done—for example, save for retirement, quit smoking, lose weight—they won't do anything. They see it as beyond their control. Preventive actions for the future often seem this way because feedback can be hard to get or highly ambiguous. By tying future prevention to fix-it today, people—Boomers especially—are better able to see some impact from their own efforts. They may not see the effects on their future selves, but they see the effects on their current selves and thus get reinforcement that their actions can make a difference.

Prevention makes sense to Boomers when it is part of creating something vital and smart for today. For example, running, in addition to being preventive, has its own chic. Yoga, Pilates, aerobics, and other types of exercise have enticed Boomers through panache as much as prevention. When prevention is part of defining one's contemporary self, not just one's future self, it becomes, in effect, something to do as a fix-it for today.

This paradox of reconceptualizing the future as the present applies in many domains. For years, Yankelovich has recommended that when it comes to Boomers, the future should be reimagined in terms of the present: How to age without getting old? How to retire without quitting? How to save while spending? This is not terribly difficult to envision or implement. A couple of nonhealth examples illustrate the power of connecting with Boomers in this way.

In 2005, American Express launched One from American Express℠, a card that offers the unique benefit of contributing one percent of a cardholder's purchases to a high-yield savings account. It is a card for saving while spending.

Bank of America did something similar with a debit card program called Keep The Change™. For every purchase made with the Bank of America Visa® Check Card, the difference to the next dollar up is charged and deposited in the customer's savings account. Bank of America matches this amount penny for penny for the first three months. It's another card for saving while spending.

While these are not health-related examples, they illustrate the mastery of paradox needed to motivate Boomers to engage in preventive behaviors of any sort, particularly when it comes to health. The primary focus of Boomers is on what they can make of themselves today, not on what they are making of themselves for the future. A focus on the future must be connected with enhancing oneself today.

For prevention to take hold with Boomers, it must be offered and perceived as another fix-it. Fix-it is how Boomers think, so that is the context within which to motivate and appeal to them.

The fix-it mindset of Boomers is another reminder that they are passionate about things that deliver instant gratification. Boomers want to engage with things that immediately reward their commitment, and not with things that require a long-term sacrifice. Prevention means sacrifice and postponement of rewards. It suits them just fine to deal with their health by waiting until it's time for a cure or a remedy.

By contrast, staying vital pays off right away. It is an animated style of life, not a constraint on life that pays off in the ways in which life can be enjoyed and the ways in which one is regarded by others. Vitality means setting your own discipline, not having it set by someone or something else. It means having fun.

Fun

Above all else, the spirit of Baby Boomers is about having fun. Fun is central to Boomer lifestyles. It's even what Boomers say about work: If it's not fun, it's not worth doing.

This is not to say that Boomers want to be lackadaisical; it is only that they want some carefree time that just feels good. As *U.S. News & World Report* noted at the turn of the millennium, many Boomers have watched their parents "retreat into retirement cocoons" where the "fun has drained

Past	Present
Going to hear the Rolling Stones	Going to hear the Rolling Stones
Listening to Bob Dylan	Listening to Bob Dylan
Watching James Bond Movies	Watching James Bond Movies
Reading Danielle Steel	Reading Danielle Steel
Playing along with *Jeopardy!*	Playing along with *Jeopardy!*
Driving a Beetle	Driving a Beetle

Figure 7-6: Boomer Fun

out of their lives." Not so for Boomers, this article reported. Boomers are "determined" to have fun as they get older.[10]

Adult summer camps have long waiting lists for the Boomers who want to relive as adults the summer fun they had as kids. Fantasy camps for hockey and baseball are thriving. The Disney Institute offers adult programs in TV production, gardening, cooking, design, and storytelling, among many others. Boomers flock to the reunion tours of old rock'n'roll bands to such an extent that these shows are consistently the highest-grossing live acts in the music business. They are paying a premium for the thrills of sleek, fun cars like the Chrysler PT Cruiser or the new Volkswagen Beetle or the Jaguar S-Type or the Honda S2000 roadster. The way to have this kind of fun is to remain vital, which in turn means staying healthy.

While countless books, life coaches, and pop psychologists counsel Boomers to stop and smell the roses, the fact of the matter is that they are a leisure generation, not a laboring generation. Sure, Boomers work hard, but they play hard, too.

For Boomers, there has always been more to work than clocking the hours to put something aside for the future. Work has been about affording fun today. Boomers have worked hard but never to the exclusion of fun, particularly in comparison to other generations. In the late 1990s, 62 percent of young GenX workers clocked more than forty hours per week on the job. Among young Boomers in 1977, the figure was only 37 percent.[11] Most Boomers were out having fun.

Marketing Thought-Starter: Send Them Abroad

Boomers' demand for health care is likely to outstrip both the capacity of the medical system to care for them and the ability of Boomers themselves to pay for the care they want and need. But this doesn't mean that they will go without care. As they have always done, Boomers will break the rules to invent something new. In this case, many of them will become medical tourists.

Medical tourism is a booming business already. People going abroad for medical procedures unaffordable at home is a $40 billion-a-year global industry. In 2006, a half million U.S. citizens went to India, Costa Rica, the Philippines, China, the Dominican Republic, and Thailand for a variety of surgeries and medical procedures that cost 30 to 80 percent less than at home.[12] Medical tourism is an important sector of India's economy, second only to technology in driving growth, with medical tourists growing 15 percent annually and 2012 revenue projected at $2.3 billion.[13]

Middle age–less Boomers will add to the flood of medical tourists. The Gordian knot of the aging Boomer cohort is health care. The problems of Social Security are child's play compared to those of Medicare. Figuring out how to marshal the resources, financial and otherwise, needed to support the health-care needs of the largest and soon-to-be longest-living generation in American history is a confounding policy enigma. As Boomers find themselves priced out of the market for many procedures, especially elective procedures that are a matter of vitality rather than life or death, they will look for other options, and in doing so will find medical tourism beckoning.

A confluence of forces is going to make medical tourism easier, safer, and more attractive to Boomers. Destination countries are investing in infrastructure, training, and oversight. Travel agencies are moving aggressively into this niche because it is one of the few full-service travel areas left with growth potential. Companies facing higher insurance costs, especially medium-size and small businesses, are looking into this as an option for their employees. For similar reasons, state governments are considering it as well.

Medical tourism is not appropriate for all surgeries and procedures. An analysis published in the *New England Journal of Medicine* suggests the cost savings net out to be worth it for less than 2 percent of all spending in the U.S. on noncosmetic medical procedures. Mostly, these are major cardiac and orthopedic procedures.[14] Even so, this is a lot of people and a lot of spending, and when elective and cosmetic procedures are included, the potential is much greater.

Boomer interest in elective procedures will add fuel to the fire of medical tourism. Boomers like to travel and want to stay vital. Medical tourism harnesses these two interests together, along with the Boomer interest in continuing to make a difference.

Eventually, medical tourism will put pressure on the U.S. health-care system, making the practice of medical tourism a way in which Boomers can contribute to policy and social reform. Many Boomers will think of it as another form of ethical consuming. With fewer profits from uninsured elective surgeries and medical procedures, hospitals and physicians will be forced to make the care they provide more efficient and more affordable, thus improving the health-care system for everyone.[15] Yet again, Boomers will lead the way for all by focusing first and foremost on themselves.

This is not to suggest that work hasn't been important to Boomers or that they haven't worked equally long hours in recent years. As discussed in chapter 3, work was regarded as a major source of meaning for young Boomers. But work itself was never the point. Meaning and fulfillment were the point, which everything in life, work included, was supposed to provide. Work has been important to Boomers, but so has time off. Boomers have made sure to get plenty of both.

The centrality of fun puts an edge on how Boomers think about basic health care. Good health care must do more than keep them alive and free of disease; it must enable them to remain vital in order to have fun.

The broader social environment of self-invention hones this edge even sharper. Vitality is the whole point of health care for Boomers swimming in a sea of possibility that requires active engagement and attention. Vitality is not a side benefit of basic health care or something extra provided by elective lifestyle procedures. Electives become necessities when vitality is necessary to cope in a world of self-invention.

With vitality a matter of survival, Boomers will insist on more than basic care from the health-care system. They will demand fixes to revitalize themselves and to rev up their ability to keep going. Increasingly, Boomers will view this kind of health care as a right.

A Right to Health Care

There is no explicit guarantee of health care in America. Yet if health care is thought by Boomers to be indispensable to their very ability to exercise initiative and hard work, it's no surprise that in practical terms they feel it is a right. From there, it is only a small conceptual leap to conclude that there are no other rights absent health care, particularly in a self-inventive world where success takes a special kind of individual initiative. Boomers believe in health-care access as the only way to fortify themselves to earn their own way.

In the Yankelovich Boomer Dreams study, 69.3 percent agreed that "the best medical care" is something that people should be "entitled to as a social right." Not simply medical care, but the "best" medical care. Just like everything else that arouses their attention and involvement, Boomers see health care as a right. It is a moral issue, not just a policy debate.

Boomers are demanding both the opportunity to be self-inventive and the opportunity to continue to work (just as they have with the retirement age of pilots). These opportunities depend upon good health care, so in demanding them, Boomers are demanding the right to good health care as well. They aren't making these demands to seek handouts or impose obligations on others, but they are coming to see that their ability to earn their own way requires the more basic guarantee of access to health care. As they always have, Boomers will be passionate about the issues directly affecting them, turning these issues into moral struggles about fundamental principles and rights. As Boomers get older and have more need of revitalization, the health-care debate will be more than a legislative policy dispute.

The numbers and determination of aging Boomers will bring a lot of pressure to bear on health-care access and affordability. As their involvement in the health-care system picks up, so, too, will the attention they devote to it. Aging Boomers are on the offensive across many fronts. The same moral imperative characteristic of every issue on their agenda will shape their demands on the health-care system. Not having undertaken preventive measures will not, in the eyes of Boomers, disqualify them from the care they feel they deserve. After all, there is a fix-it bias in the modern, self-inventive world, not to mention the current method of insurance compensation.

It is not clear, however, that the increasing draw of Boomers on resources like health care will precipitate the intergenerational struggle for control anticipated by so many. In the 2006 Yankelovich MONITOR survey, respondents were asked to rate the extent to which they thought certain things were likely to be true in ten years. Roughly half believed that there would be "greater resentment of Baby Boomers using more than their share of government resources"—51 percent of Baby Boomers, 54 percent of GenXers, and 52 percent of Echo Boomers (generally speaking, the generation born 1979 to 1990). While this is a big percentage, there is no universal concern about looming intergenerational antipathy, in all likelihood because other generations see that Boomers will do as they have done before and fight for changes that help everyone as much as themselves.

The greater share of health-care resources that Boomers need will enmesh them and their moral outrage in issues of concern to all. This reflects how Boomers see themselves—68.2 percent agreed in the 2006 Yankelovich Boomer Dreams study that "many of the best things about life today were pioneered and made possible" by Boomers.

If necessary, Boomers are willing to break the rules and find good health care outside traditional institutions. As churches, employers, and retailers begin to offer health care, both in-house and for sale, through medical professionals directly contracted by or working for them, Boomers will be first in line. They will have powerful negotiating leverage in a world frantic for their labor, their patronage, and—especially—their votes.

An Emerging Divide

The Boomer focus on vitality means increasing demand for lifestyle medicine. Beyond addressing hair loss, impotency, and obesity, this is medicine to keep Boomers vibrant, energetic, youthful, and perhaps even living so long that it seems like forever. Already, Boomers are flocking to this kind of care. As they age, demand will grow, and this pressure on the health-care system has the potential to bring on an unanticipated crisis.

With only a few exceptions, insurance does not foot the bill for lifestyle medicine. As Boomers look for care to keep them vital in addition to disease-free, the ability to pay will become a much bigger issue for them than it is today. Unless insurance policies change radically, insurance simply won't cover most of what Boomers are going to feel they need to stay middle age–less. Those able to afford it will be the small percentage at the top of the wealth distribution—more than just the super-rich, but still far short of everyone.

When more vitality, better looks, and greater energy are accessible only to the wealthy few, a new health-care divide will arise. This gap, like compound interest, will grow with accelerating speed. Social psychology has shown time and again that looks matter. Hale, hearty, ruddy people earn more and have better prospects. So those who can afford lifestyle medicine will accumulate ever more of the wealth it takes to pay for still more lifestyle medicine.

Lifestyle medicine is not just about feeling good and looking good; it's about life itself. Breakthroughs in the biochemistry and genomics of aging may not bring eternal life, but they will certainly bring much longer lives, and much more active longer lives. Value-based pricing for medicine that extends our life spans to 120 or beyond will put the age of Methuselah beyond the means of all but the richest Boomers.

If nothing changes, during this generation of aging Baby Boomers we could easily wind up with a society in which most pay dearly to live well into their seventies while those who control most of the wealth spend freely to live actively and energetically well into their early hundreds or beyond. This may sound fantastic, but it is not fantasy. As this gap begins to materialize, a broader social crisis could ensue.

These kinds of gaps threaten not only social cohesion but physical health and well-being. In a telling study conducted in the 1950s, medical research-ers examined a small Pennsylvania town that had a significantly lower rate of heart attacks than surrounding towns despite no differences in diet, smoking, or exercise.[16] The only noticeable difference was a higher level of social cohesion enforced by local norms that discouraged and downplayed public displays of differences in wealth and income. Over time, though, the social taboos against conspicuous consumption weakened and even though every other factor stayed the same, the rate of heart attacks in this town eventually rose to the same levels as those in nearby towns.

British economic historian Richard Wilkinson has conducted a compre-hensive study of the correlates of life expectancy in developed countries.[17] One of the most important is income inequality—more so than absolute wealth—which is why, Wilkinson argues, life spans in the United States are shorter than those in developed countries with less wealth but also less inequality, such as the Netherlands, Israel, Spain, Sweden, Canada, and Japan.

Whenever social cohesion is undermined by large public gaps in income and lifestyles, the engagement people feel with the wider community suf-fers. The resulting sense of disconnection has an impact on people's health and well-being.

Lifestyle medicine is not an extravagance to Boomers. In more ways than one, it is exactly the kind of medicine that delivers what is essential to their health and well-being. Above all else, though, vitality is what they want. Find-ing themselves unable to afford access to this care will make health-care re-form a top priority for Boomers. The passion and sense of righteousness they are sure to bring will make this more than a policy issue to them.

The gap in health-care coverage today is not insignificant. Tens of millions are either uninsured or underinsured. Studies show that most personal bankruptcies are brought on by unaffordable medical bills, and the bulk of these involve people who had insurance at the time they became ill.[18] Rising costs are likely to push more people over the brink, including many aging Boomers.

Yet as serious as today's gap is for so many people, when aging Baby Boomers finally come face to face with the financial realities of the health care they believe they need and deserve, a far-reaching reassessment of our system will follow. It is likely that policies will move closer to a redistributive model in which each pays to ensure coverage for all and away from the current actuarial model in which each pays according to individual risk.[19] Boomers will use their numbers and indignation to force change for all, although not because they want to carry the flag on behalf of others but because they want to keep themselves vital and in command.

eight
Reconnecting

Young Boomers are always remembered in crowds—overcrowded classrooms, anti-war demonstrations, en masse streaks, Woodstock and Altamont, communes, cults, lined up around the block for the premieres of *Jaws* and *Star Wars*. But they are not remembered for community. Boomers venerated self. They were surrounded by others but joined the crowd in order to pursue their own individual bliss. In the midst of others, Boomers were utterly unto themselves.

The primacy of the indulgent self at the beginning of the 1980s intensified this thoroughgoing self-absorption. As part of the New Realism, the focus on self became more aggressively competitive and selfish. Today, the imperative of self-invention ratchets up this insular focus yet another several notches.

Boomers put self above everything else. For their generation, it has always been self over sacrifice. Any other concern must benefit self as well. Every other allegiance must first pass muster with the authority of self. Unsurprisingly, then, community has suffered under the ascendancy of Boomers.

The decline of community did not go unnoticed as Boomers were coming into prominence. Parker Palmer of the American Association of Higher Education, honored in 1998 as one of the decade's ten key agenda-setters in education, witnessed this at the time and spoke out about it critically in his 1981 classic *The Company of Strangers: Christians and the Renewal of Public Life* (New York: Crossroad Publishing Company). In the late 1970s and early 1980s, Palmer saw an urgent need to reassert the value of public life as a rebuttal to the prevailing feeling at the time that only the private life had value. The Me Generation was in full flower, a bloom that has never quite faded but one that was particularly heady during those times. Palmer extolled the virtues of a life spent in the "company of strangers" as opposed to one spent in the company of self.

Around the same time, historian and social critic Christopher Lasch warned of the growing "culture of narcissism" sweeping through American life (*The Culture of Narcissism: American Life in An Age of Diminishing Expectations*, New York: W.W. Norton & Company, 1978). Lasch lamented the degeneration of the American ideal of "competitive individualism" into one of a "narcissistic preoccupation with self" in which both community and self suffer. As noted earlier, Dan Yankelovich chronicled this same development when he wrote in the early 1980s about the ways in which self-fulfillment had gained the upper hand in American life.

It is important to differentiate, as Lasch did, between selfishness and a focus on self. Selfishness is an age-old human weakness. Self-sacrifice can be and often is undertaken for selfish reasons. The Boomer focus on self is the exaltation of self as the principal spirit of life. Others are not disregarded or dishonored; rather, they are simply not that relevant to defining the purpose and focus of life. Others may well be aided, but less for their own sake and more because doing so is in harmony with the nature of self. Others provide an admiring mirror to reflect the self. Personal preoccupations are all that matter. Personal reasons—not political reasons, not religious reasons, not civic reasons—become the only motive force for action. The vocabulary of self is the lingo of life.

Lost Community

Boomers have committed themselves to self without reservation, no matter the cost, one of the biggest of which has been the diminishment of community. Robert Putnam, a professor of public policy and former dean of the Kennedy School of Government at Harvard, has documented the decline of community or social capital in his aptly titled bestseller, *Bowling Alone: The Collapse and Revival of American Community* (New York: Simon & Schuster, 2000). Using longitudinal attitudinal data from many sources—especially the Roper Social and Political Trends Archive, the DDB Needham Life Style survey archive, and the Yankelovich MONITOR—Putnam lays out in detail the ways in which people have been spending less time with community over the last century, particularly since the end of World War II.

In dissecting what's behind this decline, Putnam considers a number of explanations before narrowing the list to four factors: the greater time demands of work, extra time spent commuting and running errands due to sprawl, more time spent watching TV, and the ascendance of a new generation. Of these four, Putnam estimates that over half of the decline in community is a result of the generational factor, which is to say that the replacement of a "civic generation" with a "private generation" has undermined the resilience and appeal of community organizations.

The generational shift about which Putnam writes is largely the rise of Baby Boomers (although Putnam finds it to be somewhat characteristic of those born in the 1930s, too). Boomers have always wanted to do things on their own individual initiative apart from others. The self-made man, a central idea in the American national character, has been more like the self-centered man for Boomers. The prior generation was characterized by a stronger commitment to teamwork, community engagement, and individual contributions to the collective success. The members of this generation joined together and made sacrifices to battle fascism and communism and to erect the physical infrastructure of contemporary American life. The massive engineering triumphs of dams, interstates, rural electrification, suburban housing, the space program, the A-bomb, and even the Internet were the result of that generation's collective muscle and sweat. It was a generation willing to be the cogs turning the wheels that advanced the greater good.

Not so for Boomers. Boomers were heir to the fruits of this labor, inheriting a world in which rationing and self-sacrifice were stories in history books. The collective effort had been made. Boomers were free to enjoy it, as, indeed, their parents so encouraged them to do. They grew up feeling individually special and privileged, and during those times, in fact, they were. Boomers started out on that path and have never left it.

This self-focus of Boomers contributed the most to the deterioration of community. Even family has suffered. Divorce rates, latchkey kids, and

blended families ballooned as Boomers moved into their thirties and forties, in keeping with the pop culture legitimizing new lifestyle choices like
the extended stepfamily on *The Brady Bunch* or the divorced single moms
on *One Day at a Time* and *The Partridge Family.*

Boomers have a long history of disengagement with others. Yet notwithstanding their history, they are now yearning for reconnection and a renewal of engagement with others.

Reconnection

There is a growing, strengthening revival of interest in connection, engagement, and interaction in American society, particularly among Baby Boomers. Over the past decade or so (*not* only since 9/11) Yankelovich data show
a greater interest in connections, especially connections with friends and
family.[1]

Just to cite a few illustrative numbers, the percentage of Boomers in the
Yankelovich MONITOR survey reporting that it is important to be seen as
a good neighbor has risen from 55 percent in 1999 to 83 percent in 2006;
the percentage mentioning being a loyal friend has grown from 78 percent
to 88 percent. When asked about home entertaining, as shown in Figure
8-1, the activities Boomers mention more frequently are not solo enter-
tainments but shared activities—cookouts, barbecues, games, cocktail
parties— things people do together in connection with others.

Of course, these trends are true of all generations, not just Baby Boomers.
What's noteworthy, though, is the fact that the most self-focused generation
is moving in concert with everyone else in the direction of more connection
and engagement. Attitudes about family are most illustrative of this shift.

In 1979, only 45 percent of Baby Boomer women agreed that "having
a child is an experience every woman should have." When asked the same
question in 2002, 59 percent of women the same age as the Boomer women
in 1979 agreed. In 1981, 50 percent of women ages twenty-five to thirty-four
agreed that people should live for themselves rather than their children;
in 2001, only 33 percent agreed. Young women feel differently today than

Shared -generational marketplace (handwritten, right margin)

(Partial list)	1999	2005
Watch movies or videos	51%	42%
Watch sporting event on TV	36%	32%
Cookouts/barbecues	56%	61%
Family get-togethers	55%	61%
Holiday parties	33%	43%
Potluck dinners	18%	24%
Cocktail parties	14%	18%

Source: Yankelovich MONITOR

Figure 8-1: Home Entertaining Done Regularly

Boomer women felt when they were a comparable age, reflecting a different starting point. Today, however, Boomer and GenX women feel the same way. Like everyone else, Boomers want more connection, a significant reversal from their previous opinions.

This shared generational interest in connection has had a big impact on the marketplace. The most consistent pockets of strength in the consumer economy of late have been things that facilitate connections with others, especially home-centered connections: DVD players. Decorating and home cable TV shows. Home renovations. Cell-phone family plans. Barbecue grills. Microwavable pot roasts. Crafts like knitting and hobbies like scrapbooking. Lifestyle villages. Driving family vacations. Even Ping-Pong tables and board games.

At the same time, people are reinventing the ways in which they connect. More and more, new social ties are being formed in various venues: Coffee bars. Book clubs. Talk radio. Chat rooms. Blogs. Social-networking Web sites. Wiki Web sites. Auction Web sites. Virtual reality Web sites. Micropolitans and downtown revivals. Home concerts. Poetry slams. Volunteering. Adult education. Support groups. Yoga. Pilates. Dog runs. Penguin brigades. Bible study groups.

The emotional comforts of connection are more important than ever, particularly in a world of global terrorism, shrinking safety nets, and economic uncertainties. People are turning to one another for the guidance they no longer trust government or business to provide. More than ever, they are searching for fulfillment and happiness, something that comes mostly from personal relationships. Boomers want more connection, a desire that has been growing during recent years as *über*-Boomer then–first lady Hillary Clinton clearly demonstrated when she penned her 1996 bestseller, *It Takes a Village: And Other Lessons Children Teach Us* (New York: Simon & Schuster).

This is a trend with legs. Aging Baby Boomers are now in the life stage in which people always think more about nonmaterial priorities. Add to that the mainstreaming of affluence, which has created a glut of inexpensive, high-quality goods and is now taking people well beyond the post–World War II scarcity marketplace of materialism. And underlying it all, global geopolitical uncertainty is fueling a pervasive, low-grade fever of anxiety for which the comforts of connections are the best cure.

The bottom line is that Boomers no longer want self to smother connections. They want resources for connection, particularly more so-called third places where they can gather, both virtually and actually. Yet none of this presages a revival of community. Connections per se are not community, certainly not the kinds of connections being revived by Boomers.

Self Connected

Paradoxically, the ongoing revival of connections does not portend a renewal of community or a strengthening of social cohesion. Despite what some hopeful observers have read into these developments, the trend is a phenomenon of connections without community. The danger is that this revival of connections, led by Boomers and so coveted by them these days, will lead to a diminishment of community. The threat is that the coming together of Americans is splitting America apart.

Parker Palmer was careful to note in his analysis that community is more than connections with intimate associates. That's private life. Community must nurture private life, but community itself is about public life or, in Palmer's words, living in the company of strangers.

The turnaround of interest in connections has been about the character of private life and private interactions, not about civic or community engagement. Connections are being pursued nowadays in a way that is mostly about *living together in private* instead of living alone in private, not about a renewed interest in public spaces or in civic community. This is entirely in keeping with the longstanding Boomer interest in self. Boomers don't want connections to override self; they want connections that provide interaction without threatening the continued preeminence of self. The emerging dynamic is not the old one addressed by Parker Palmer, Christopher Lasch, and Dan Yankelovich of the private domain of self displacing the public domain of others but a new one in which people find the connections they want without any need of community. Boomers led the way during the first recession of community, and they are leading the way again.

Lifestyle interests, not community interests, are driving the connections people want nowadays. People are coming together around the lifestyle passions they share in common with certain others. In other words, they are eschewing even the least amount of the company of strangers in order to have ever more connection with like-minded others—people who share their interests, attitudes, values, and perspectives. These shared interests can run the gamut from entertainment to family to music to sports to politics to subdivisions to Web sites. As this kind of togetherness grows, the public space suffers. Lifestyle groups are insular, with exceedingly narrow interests that by and large can be satisfied without intersecting the interests of other groups in the public space.

Of course, in connecting with those who share their lifestyle interests, people are likely to interact with and get to know others with whom they would have had no contact in the past. Online lifestyle connections level traditional barriers of distance and demography. This is especially true to

Marketing Thought-Starter:
It's Not About the Product

The best way to market a product to Boomers is to *not* market the product. Not that Boomers don't care about products; it's just that they have always been most interested in the product experience. They want something beyond the product per se, so focusing only on the product misses the point with Boomers. Of course, it's basic marketing to focus on the benefits, not on the product, but for Boomers this is much truer, especially in regard to intangible benefits.

The greater opportunity provided by the Internet to indulge lifestyle interests makes the product even less central. Products will continue to be bought and sold, but the products commanding the greatest value will be those facilitating and delivering experiences.

Much has been written about this shift in the locus of value. The biggest shift, though, is in what should be branded. Traditionally, that's the product. But with products taken for granted and increasingly seen as commodities, they offer less attractive platforms for building a brand. Marketers must build brands where value is to be found. In the future, that will be experiences. They must brand experiences, not products.

Brands must look to product experiences, not product formulations, as the foundation on which to build and develop their brand identities. Experiences are what people care about, so they provide the basis on which people connect with brands. For aging Boomers who are looking to stay engaged with active, vigorous lifestyles, branded experiences offer the most compelling connection.

the extent that people forge connections across several of their lifestyle interests. Yet to the extent that these crossover connections stay confined to the lifestyle interests that forged them in the first place, there is no carryover to the broader community. Instead, they simply create a new form of insularity—one now based on lifestyles rather than race, class, or neighborhood. In fact, this is the general pattern seen with Internet communities. They create more intimacy among like-minded people, but they do not stimulate greater community engagement.

The many types of community engagement and social capital tracked by Putnam generally have a civic focus, not a lifestyle focus. They are outer-directed, focused on others. For Putnam it is the "wider" associations of civic engagement—residential, religious, organizational—that constitute community life. As Putnam puts it, these are the "weak ties" that enmesh us in a broader web of life. The "strong ties" of personal lifestyle interests do not engage us in real community. What's happening nowadays is that weak ties are being shed while strong ties are being strengthened. While people are more connected these days, the ties that are binding them more tightly together are not the weak ties that constitute community but the strong ties of direct interest to oneself.

Community is a life that includes others, not just self. It is the life that embraces the public good rather than only private interests. The connections being formed today do not measure up to community. In fact, by centering people ever more strongly on their own narrow interests, albeit connected with more like-minded people, lifestyle connections block out time and attention for any communal, or weak, interests. The strengthening focus on lifestyle connections will only further diminish community.

Recognizing that lifestyle connections are not authentic kinds of community helps account for certain findings that Putnam is able to describe only as anomalies. Putnam notes that associations in small groups, social movements, and the Internet are on the rise, thus seemingly contradicting his overarching hypothesis that social capital is on the decline. He calls them "exceptions to the trend toward civic disengagement" even as he notes in each case that there is little, or at best "tenuous," evidence that involvement in any of these types of associations actually contributes to public life or "offsets" the other declines he has documented. In assessing the Internet, Putnam laments the Internet "cyberbalkanization" whereby people "confine" their interaction to others with "precisely [their] interests"—in other words, connection without community.

What these "countercurrents" show is not an exception to the trends documented by Putnam but a foundation in personal lifestyle interests. All are forms of increasing balkanization. Thus, rather than being exceptions to the decline in social capital that Putnam laments, they are developments that will further erode social capital. There is no need for Putnam to accept them as exceptions; in fact, they are additional examples of his overall thesis.

The Internet Connection

Many researchers have studied the impact of the Internet on how people connect. Barry Wellman, the S. D. Clark Professor of Sociology and Director of Netlab at the University of Toronto, is perhaps the leading authority in this area, and he offers a counterpoint to Putnam's conclusions. In a detailed summary of the latest research on this topic, Wellman and co-author Anabel Quan-Hase distinguish three ways in which the Internet affects social capital: transforming it, diminishing it, or supplementing it. There are two senses in which Quan-Hase and Wellman define social capital. One is mere social contact; the other is civic engagement.[2] The consensus of existing research is clear.

The Internet has not diminished social contacts; in fact, it has transformed them by enabling people to transcend local geographies and establish far-flung networks of associations with others of like interests. Additionally, the Internet has strengthened existing networks of social contacts by providing another, even more expedient, way of keeping up with intimate associates.

But the data on civic engagement are different. While the Internet has enabled people to become more immersed in shared interests and closely knit groups, in the words of Quan-Hase and Wellman, "it does not appear to have radically transformed civic involvement in voluntary organizations and politics." This is not surprising. It is entirely consistent with the research cited by Quan-Hase and Wellman showing considerable growth in the breadth and depth of lifestyle-driven Internet associations. Connections centered on lifestyle interests do not boost engagement with the wider community; in fact, they orient people away from these kinds of "weak ties," exacerbating the present predicament of connections without community. Social capital is more than social contacts.

Marketing Thought-Starter:
Get Into the Conversation

The heart and soul of the Internet is peer-to-peer interaction. This has been true since its genesis. From the WELL, the first virtual community launched in 1985 by Stewart Brand and polymath philanthropist, doctor, and technologist Larry Brilliant, to MySpace.com, which Rupert Murdoch's News Corporation bought in 2005 for half a billion dollars, the Internet has put people in touch with others. The Internet gives people easy access to the sort of input and advice they crave most.

As social psychologists have shown repeatedly over decades of experiments and research, in situations of uncertainty, risk, and high cost, people look first to others like them for guidance about what to do and how to think.[3] The Internet has made this kind of peer-to-peer interaction easier and more accessible than ever before.

Prior to the Internet, cost, time, distance, and complexity made peer-to-peer interaction beyond one's immediate circle difficult, if not for all practical purposes impossible. With the advent of the Internet, these barriers have become moot. E-mail, file sharing, bulletin boards, blogs, user reviews and recommendations, chat rooms, instant messaging, social networking sites, Wiki sites, video sites, auction sites—all are merely different kinds of peer-to-peer interaction online.

Peer-to-peer interaction creates a new context for marketing communications. No longer is a message received by a single person. Now it is discussed, and thus in effect received by a group of people. The power of a marketing message lies not in how it affects a single person but in how it influences the conversation. A message is not processed by a single person but by a community of interacting people. To win customers, a marketer must target the conversation, not individuals, because it is the conversation that shapes individual decisions.

The key thing to understand about Boomers is that peer-to-peer interaction is not confined to young people. For everyone, the essence of the Internet experience is peer-to-peer. The Internet has opened up peer-to-peer information to all online users, young, old and middle age–less alike. Like every other user, when Boomers go online they are connecting with others. Mastery of peer-to-peer is what it takes for marketers to succeed on the Internet, with Boomers no less than with anyone else.

This fact is implicit within the term Wellman coined to describe how people interact online: "networked individualism." Individuals are connecting through broader, more extensive networks, but a network of connections alone does not make a community, particularly if the network primarily serves the private interests of individuals.

Boomers want connection, but they want it without losing sight of self and they want it only to the extent that it advances self. Self continues to dominate. Hence, when Boomers look to connect with others they are not looking for community; they are looking for connections that fit their private interests and enable them to maintain their insular focus on personal priorities and self-interests.

Marketing's Unintended Consequence

Many factors at work in the consumer marketplace are intensifying insularity and isolation even as connections are on the rise. Take, for example, the fast-growing marketing practice of CRM, or customer relationship management. One of the objectives of CRM is to give people more of what they already like. By tapping into detailed data about existing interests, CRM marketers are able to boost marketing precision and relevance. At the same time, though, this surrounds each person with an individual bubble of information and satisfactions that further entrenches him or her in an insular lifestyle niche.

The best part of CRM is that it better connects people to their own special interests and like-minded others. This is smart marketing and good for commerce. Its unintended consequence is that it further isolates people from broader exposure and contact. This is bad for civics, because it hastens the erosion of bonds to community—people feel less need to get caught up in what else is out there; CRM has got them covered. As CRM becomes more widespread and more sophisticated—as it will—people will have no problem finding what they want without having to endure the company of strangers.

While Yankelovich is one of the first observers of the contemporary consumer marketplace to recognize and critically assess these marketing developments,[4] others have begun to express concern about them as well. Teressa Iezzi, editor of *Creativity* magazine and AdCritic.com, wrote in a January 29, 2007 column in *AdAge* that the Web has created an "opinion cocoon" in which anybody can find some small group that will "justify" their beliefs, interests, and tastes. She describes it as a "contraction of worldview" and worries that the decline in serendipitous exposure to new perspectives or competing opinions will drag down creative excellence.

This sort of closure is reflected as well in the residential patterns paralleling the rise of Boomers that are mentioned in chapter 6. In his study of these migration trends, journalist Bill Bishop notes that people are more likely than ever to live in communities dominated by a single political party and philosophy. The result is a sharper edge that is less civil, less compromising, and less communal. This political segregation has increased even as racial segregation has decreased. Nowadays, we are sorting ourselves more by the color of our politics than by the color of our skin. As we share more in common by connecting with like-minded neighbors, we have less in common with the broader community of others.

Healthy Connections

While connections may not be community, that doesn't mean that there is no value in connections per se, with or without community. Personal connections are vital to one's health and well-being, something that has been documented time and again by medical researchers.

Dr. Lisa Berkman, the Norman Professor of Health, Social Behavior, and Epidemiology at the Harvard School of Public Health, led an intensive nine-year study of seven thousand adults in Alameda County, California. Her research found that people who were disconnected from others were roughly three times more likely to die during that period of time than people with strong social ties. The kinds of social ties didn't matter. What mattered was being nested in some network, whether family, friends, church, volunteer groups, or marriage, just to name a few. These findings held true irrespective of other risk factors such as smoking, drinking, obesity, or little exercise.[5] These results have been replicated several times in studies of other communities. Reaching out to others is the best way to do for oneself.

Researchers at the University of Michigan followed people over age sixty-five for five years and found that people who provided emotional support or actual help to others were half as likely to die during this period of time. In contrast, those receiving the support were no less likely to die than those receiving no support.[6] Simply put, the people who benefited from the support and help were those giving it, not those receiving it. People who did something for others got something back. Selflessness for others turns out to be a good way to maximize one's own selfish interests.

In seeking greater connections, Boomers are looking to get something back for themselves. They are looking for interactions that boost their sense of self and that directly benefit their own well-being. Connections that deliver this double dose of personal benefits are those that Boomers will value most. Boomers will help others because it helps them, psychologically and physically. Connections are all it takes; community is extra.

To get Boomers out of their connected isolation, there must be some attraction of community that benefits their self-absorbed interests. Clearly, there are health benefits, although connections alone can provide much of this without engaging the wider community. It is this paradox of doing the best for oneself by doing something for others that must be front and center.

Come Together

There is one connection that almost all Baby Boomers want to make as they move forward and that is family, grandchildren in particular. In the Yankelovich Boomer Dreams study, 80 percent of Boomers agree that they plan to focus more time and energy on their grandchildren over the next five to ten years. It is the number-one area for middle age–less Boomers. This is echoed by the number-two area of family, cited by 77.2 percent of all Boomers. As they look ahead, family looms large, something that was much less true for Boomers when they were younger.

While family was important to Boomers decades ago, they had other

[handwritten annotation: fams + grandchil / all interconnected / This __ PL __]

priorities that often took precedence—work, leisure, and self-improvement. Sometimes family had to take a backseat to these other interests. But no longer. As seen in Figure 8-2, everything else falls below family and grand- *X* children. Causes, creativity, adventures, friends, community, religion, politics, travel, charity, work, and more—all are important, but none measures up to family and grandchildren.

Boomers readily admit that they will be more focused on family as grandparents than they were as parents. When asked how well the notion of home and family describes Baby Boomers, 80.1 percent agreed it is applicable to Boomers in the future versus only 65.5 percent who thought it was applicable in the past.

Spending by today's grandparents on their grandchildren is substantial. The research firm NPD estimates that $26 billion was spent in 2004 on presents, toys, video games, books, and cash, 1.7 percent more than in 2001.[7] One-third of Boomers are grandparents today. As more Boomers have grandchildren to indulge, this spending is sure to grow. The demand for things Boomers can buy for their grandchildren is going to skyrocket. Certain categories of spending will become stronger, such as travel exclusively for grandparents and grandchildren, technologies that directly connect grandparents with their grandchildren, specialty restaurants that cater to "grand-parties," and financial-planning instruments that grandparents can manage for their grandchildren. Their numbers combined with their lifelong zeal for shopping and buying will make Boomers a potent generation of consuming grandparents.

Connecting for Me

This intense focus on family will further entrench Boomers in their cocoon of intimate connections. Family engagement is laudable and not to be disparaged, yet it is worth noting that family connections typify the broader pattern of connections that Boomers are pursuing. Boomers are focused primarily on the satisfactions and benefits that intimate connections can provide to them.

(Partial list – Items mentioned by fewer than 50% not shown)

Focusing more time and energy on your grandchildren	80.0%	Unleashing your personal potential	63.1%
Spending more time with family	77.2%	Taking courses to learn something new	62.8%
Reading more books	76.3%	Getting more involved in politics	62.6%
Getting more out of life	75.4%		
Taking more control over your future	73.6%	Exploring your potential in new and innovative ways	62.0%
Doing things I've always wanted to do	73.5%	Fulfilling your lifelong dreams and ambitions	61.1%
Having enough money to get by	72.6%	Traveling and seeing the world	60.3%
Learning a new skill or hobby	71.0%	Mentoring and helping young people	60.1%
Having new adventures that are exciting and fun	70.7%	Fighting against feeling old	57.8%
		Cutting back on spending, shopping and buying	57.5%
Planning your retirement	68.2%	Excelling in your job	55.0%
Making new friends	67.4%	Making more money	55.0%
Saving for/spending money on my grandchildren	67.4%	Contribute more time to charity	54.3%
Forgiving yourself more	66.7%	Testing yourself in new ways to prove yourself	54.0%
Getting more involved in social causes that matter to you	66.1%	Helping out my children financially	52.7%
Deepening and strengthening our relationship with God	65.3%	Finding something totally different to do in my life	52.4%
Developing new skills and expertise	64.8%	Working to help protect the environment	50.5%
Working to make your community a better place	64.3%		
Expressing yourself in more creative ways	63.6%		

Top 3 box on 7-point scale
Source: Yankelovich Boomer Dreams Study, 2006

Figure 8-2: Focus of Time and Energy Over Next 5 to 10 Years

When Boomers were younger, connections did not offer them the satisfactions they wanted for themselves. Now that they are older, they have come to value the benefits they can get from renewing and building connections. One key aspect of this is the change in the priority of family. Boomers will be more involved grandparents than they were parents.

As the focus of passion and energy for aging Boomers, grandparenthood will be pursued with the same righteous self that will be characteristic of everything they get involved with in the years ahead. Boomers will champion the rights of grandchildren, the accessibility of resources and venues, the prerogatives of grandparents, the inclusiveness and support of communities, and more.

In doing so, Boomers are likely to find themselves campaigning for initiatives that build and improve the broader community, but not because they are focused first and foremost on community. Rather, it will be because in their efforts to secure things for themselves, in particular to assemble the connections they are seeking, they will wind up doing something for others at the same time. When doing something for others delivers benefits to themselves, Boomers will pitch in.

The growing interest in corporate social responsibility and ethical consuming follows this formula, too. Boomers have a variety of social concerns, but not if these concerns require moderating their focus on self. Boomers will commit time, money, energy and attention to these priorities to the extent that there is a direct payoff to their own advantage.

The hopeful prospect is that in the course of renewing and strengthening connections, an unintended consequence will be the revival of community. This is not assured by any means. The contraction of outlook and associations being fueled by lifestyles, technology, marketing, and a broader polarization of ideological viewpoints is pushing Boomers into ever narrower spaces of engagement. Fortunately, though, many of these spaces have potential value for all and thus could affect the broader community. In this way, perhaps, Boomers can revive community for all by pursuing what they want most for themselves.

nine
Agendas for the Future

*B*aby Boomers agree universally on a number of things: self-perceptions about youthfulness, impact, possibility, and passion as well as zealous self-interests related to health, vitality, and social connections, especially with grandchildren. In other words, all middle age–less Boomers think in terms of things related to immortality and morality.

These shared attitudes constitute the major dynamics that will inspire Boomers as they set their courses for the next stages in their lives. However, in addition to this blend of core beliefs are a variety of areas in which Boomers are not in agreement, and these are important, too.

For the most part, assessments of Boomers treat the cohort as if it is an undifferentiated whole. This is not entirely inaccurate, but such treatments overlook numerous minority opinions that are no less important just because they are not shared by all. Few studies have probed the manifold character of the Baby Boom. One objective of the Yankelovich Boomer Dreams study was to look at Boomers in this way.

To examine the diversity of Boomer hopes, dreams, and aspirations, a segmentation analysis was conducted using the extensive attitudinal data collected in our study. Segmentation is a research procedure for clustering people into groups based upon the similarities and dissimilarities of their attitudes. Within any particular group or cluster attitudes will be similar, yet these shared attitudes will be different from those held by other groups. Segmentation is a widely employed statistical method that is used by marketers to identify pockets of consumers with specific, unique needs and preferences that can be targeted with customized products and advertising.

In our research we segmented Boomers into discrete attitudinal groups, each with a distinctive set of top or first priorities. Three broad dimensions of first priorities differentiate groups of Boomers: the spiritual, the personal, and the societal. All three have some degree of importance for every group, but what distinguishes one group from another is the greater or lesser importance of each.

These three priority areas identify six distinct groups of Boomers. Each group has its own way of thinking about what it wants from the future. These differences add up to a Boomer agenda for tomorrow that can be identified only by assessing Boomers as a diverse group.

Six Segments

The Yankelovich Boomer Dreams study included 174 items measuring attitudes across a comprehensive set of values and ambitions, including attitudes about new experiences, social activism, achievement, aging, spirituality, work, excitement, technology, personal appearance, social change, politics, comfort, duty, privacy, time, self, generations, limits, children and grandchildren, family, community, gender equality, stress, patriotism, legacy, openness to change, success, balance, meaning and fulfillment, the role of government, marketing, enrichment, tradition, home, the American Dream, style, morals, charity, spending, retirement, leadership, optimism, materialism, competition, marriage, aging, trust, authority, freedom, conformity, and many more topics. Segmenting Boomers on these dimensions yields six distinct groups. Thumbnail descriptions of these groups are provided in Figure 9-1.

These six groups differ in several key ways.

- *Straight Arrows.* This is the one group of Boomers for whom spiritual priorities are foremost. They make up one-third of Boomers. They are driven by traditional values and religion. They look forward to sharing their beliefs with others.

		Worldview	Thumbnail	Future Focus
Spiritual	**Straight Arrows** 33% ~25MM	Orthodoxy Balance	Traditional values define core beliefs as well as the focus on the future.	To find ways to enhance and share important personal beliefs and ethics.
		Big Idea		
		Morality		
Personal	**Due Diligents** 10% ~7MM	Worldview	Thumbnail	Future Focus
		Anticipation Prudence	Think things through and look out for pitfalls, then plunge into life.	To enjoy safe adventures that are protected and secure while radical and extreme.
		Big Idea		
		Safety Nets		
	Maxi-mizers 15% ~11MM	Worldview	Thumbnail	Future Focus
		More Meaning	Want to continue to achieve, accumulate, stay involved and hold center stage.	To push forward aggressively in order to stay active, engaged and in control.
		Big Idea		
		Relevance		
	Sideliners 20% ~15MM	Worldview	Thumbnail	Future Focus
		Detachment Presumptuousness	Aloof and separated, with less enthusiasm for anything except self-involvement.	To be as self-contained as possible for enjoyments that are moderate and undemanding.
		Big Idea		
		Self-Sufficiency		
Societal	**Diss/ Content-eds** 8% ~6MM	Worldview	Thumbnail	Future Focus
		Skepticism Comfort	Dissatisfied and challenging the status quo, but not to the point of spoiling comfort.	To connect with a broader vision or mission that restores and renews hope and trust.
		Big Idea		
		Purpose		
	Re-Acti-vists 15% ~15MM	Worldview	Thumbnail	Future Focus
		Social causes Self-discovery	Poised and ready to get heavily reinvolved in saving the world.	To re-engage with bigger ideals and movements before the chance is gone forever.
		Big Idea		
		Last Call		

PRIMARY DYNAMIC

Figure 9-1: Boomer Segments

- *Due Diligents.* This is one of three groups for which personal priorities are most important. They represent 10 percent of Boomers. They think ahead and plan for the worst. They are willing to take risks, though, as long as they feel protected.
- *Maximizers.* Personal priorities are at the top for this group. They account for 15 percent of Boomers. They want to do as much as possible and get the most from life. They seek fulfillment by immersing themselves in everything possible.

- *Sideliners.* Personal priorities matter most for this group, too. They make up 20 percent of Boomers. They are less involved in all activities and amusements. They are very private, self-contained, and undemanding.
- *Diss/Contenteds.* This is one of two groups for which societal priorities are highest. They account for only 8 percent of Boomers. They see social problems they would like to fix, and their sympathies are with protestors. However, they shy away from getting involved to the point of compromising their own comfort.
- *Re-Activists.* Societal priorities are highest for this group as well. They represent 15 percent of Boomers. They are ready to join campaigns in support of social causes. They want to get involved while they still can, before age makes it difficult for them to have an impact.

It's evident from these short summaries that these six groups have very different ambitions for the future.

The demographic characteristics of these groups are shown in the next series of figures, Figure 9-2 through Figure 9-6.

These charts contain a lot of data, so careful study is illuminating. But there are a few key points worth mentioning.

Figure 9-2 shows age differences across these six Boomer segments. The mean age for all groups is forty-nine, plus or minus one year. There are only modest differences when looking at the cohort partitioned by birth years. Middle Boomers make up the bulk of each segment.

These small differences by age and cohort subdivision directly rebut one criticism of looking at Baby Boomers as a unified cohort. The argument is that Boomers born in different decades are more different than alike and thus cannot be grouped together. Yet these results show that neither age nor birth year is a discriminating factor for attitudes. In other words, younger Boomers do not cluster by themselves in one segment with a particular set of attitudes while older Boomers cluster by themselves in another segment with a different set of attitudes. Younger and older Boomers are found in

	Straight Arrows	Due Diligents	Maximizers	Sideliners	Diss/ Contenteds	Re- Activists
Age (mean)	50.3	48.6	48.4	50.0	50.1	49.1
Leading Boomers (Born 1946-1949)	26.8%	21.3%	21.7%	25.9%	27.9%	20.2%
Middle Boomers (Born 1950-1959)	50.9%	50.0%	47.0%	51.2%	44.8%	46.7%
Trailing Boomers (Born 1960-1964)	22.3%	28.7%	31.3%	22.9%	27.3%	33.1%
Women	55.2%	57.5%	57.3%	42.5%	38.7%	56.0%
Men	44.8%	42.5%	42.7%	57.5%	61.3%	44.0%
White (non-Hispanic Caucasian)	83.9%	82.2%	51.7%	83.3%	84.5%	70.6%
African- American	9.3%	7.2%	27.6%	4.2%	4.4%	7.4%
Hispanic	2.8%	7.7%	17.2%	6.8%	2.5%	14.0%
Native American	0.7%	—	1.2%	0.4%	1.6%	3.2%

Source: Yankelovich Boomer Dreams Study, 2006

Figure 9-2: Age, Gender, Race/Ethnicity

roughly similar proportions across all attitudinal segments. Attitudes differ, but not as a function of age or birth year.

On the other hand, Sideliners and Diss/Contenteds are much more likely to be men, showing that Boomer men are a bit more likely than Boomer

	Straight Arrows	Due Diligents	Maximizers	Sideliners	Diss/ Contenteds	Re- Activists
Employed full-time	58.0%	55.1%	70.1%	69.9%	71.8%	63.4%
Employed part-time	8.6%	12.5%	4.8%	5.9%	5.2%	9.8%
Retired	7.9%	7.3%	3.7%	8.5%	6.9%	3.7%
Disabled	10.3%	13.2%	3.5%	3.9%	4.5%	5.2%
Temporarily unemployed	5.6%	2.2%	5.8%	6.5%	4.5%	9.1%
Housewife/ house- husband	9.5%	9.8%	12.1%	7.1%	8.8%	5.3%

Source: Yankelovich Boomer Dreams Study, 2006

Figure 9-3: Occupational Status

	Straight Arrows	Due Diligents	Maximizers	Sideliners	Diss/ Contenteds	Re- Activists
Some high school or less	5.7%	2.6%	3.8%	9.3%	2.4%	6.5%
High school Graduate	39.3%	32.3%	32.2%	43.0%	33.1%	22.8%
Some college/ graduate	40.6%	61.0%	52.0%	42.7%	46.1%	58.7%
Some gradu- ate school/ degree	14.4%	4.2%	11.9%	4.9%	11.6%	16.1%

Source: Yankelovich Boomer Dreams Study, 2006

Figure 9-4: Education

women to be found in groups that prefer a passive style of taking part in their interests.

Whites are the majority for each segment, but only by a small margin for Maximizers. African-Americans are concentrated in the segment consisting of people who want the most they can get from every aspect of life. Hispanics make up greater percentages of Maximizers and Re-Activists, both high-involvement, high-energy groups.

As seen in Figure 9-3, most Boomers in each segment are employed. Few are retired, especially among Maximizers and Re-Activists. The higher percentage of disabled Due Diligents may account for some of their caution and worry.

	Straight Arrows	Due Diligents	Maximizers	Sideliners	Diss/ Contenteds	Re- Activists
$49.9k/yr. or less	40.2%	34.2%	35.9%	36.3%	32.0%	26.5%
$50k to $99.9k/yr.	35.6%	47.5%	40.3%	34.6%	33.3%	37.9%
$100k to $149.9k/yr.	14.7%	13.8%	19.5%	19.5%	25.2%	21.7%
> $150.0k/yr.	9.5%	4.5%	4.3%	9.6%	9.5%	13.9%
Own home	84.6%	70.8%	69.8%	83.2%	86.8%	81.3%
Own second home	13.1%	9.8%	7.8%	9.4%	7.1%	15.7%

Source: Yankelovich Boomer Dreams Study, 2006

Figure 9-5: Income and Home Ownership

	Straight Arrows	Due Diligents	Maximizers	Sideliners	Diss/ Contenteds	Re-Activists
Married	67.1%	59.0%	57.2%	64.4%	61.8%	71.3%
Separated	1.2%	7.8%	2.5%	4.3%	1.8%	2.7%
Divorced	15.5%	14.8%	16.7%	15.3%	16.3%	12.8%
Widow(er)	4.3%	5.1%	2.8%	1.0%	1.4%	—
Unmarried couple	3.4%	5.8%	5.2%	2.1%	3.3%	4.6%
Single	8.4%	7.6%	15.7%	9.9%	16.7%	9.9%
Parent	85.5%	84.8%	89.2%	79.9%	76.6%	75.9%
Mean no. of children living at home	1.02	1.30	1.09	0.81	0.74	0.84
Grand-parent	38.0%	37.7%	36.0%	31.5%	26.1%	21.5%

Source: Yankelovich Boomer Dreams Study, 2006

Figure 9-6: Marital/Family Status

Figure 9-4 shows educational differences. Sideliners are less educated, perhaps accounting for their reluctance to be more actively engaged in a self-inventive world. Maximizers, Diss/Contenteds, and Re-Activists are the best educated, although the percentage of Straight Arrows with a graduate degree is high, too. The income differences shown in Figure 9-5 are consistent with these educational differences.

Most Boomers in each segment are married, as seen in Figure 9-6. Maximizers and Diss/Contenteds have higher proportions of singles.

These demographic characteristics do show some relationship to certain kinds of attitudes, particularly at the extremes. Figures 9-7 and 9-8 show political leanings and attendance at places of worship. Straight Arrows are a traditionally oriented group with a skew toward family households and greater attendance at places of worship. Unsurprisingly, they are also the most conservative.

Diss/Contenteds and Re-Activists are the most liberal groups, as well as the groups more concerned with social causes. They are less likely to con-

	Straight Arrows	Due Diligents	Maximizers	Sideliners	Diss/ Contenteds	Re-Activists
Conservative	69.3%	39.1%	30.4%	44.9%	12.0%	6.7%
Moderate	21.8%	37.0%	38.2%	36.3%	30.9%	28.0%
Liberal	8.0%	23.0%	30.5%	17.6%	54.9%	57.0%
Radical	0.9%	1.0%	0.9%	1.1%	2.2%	8.4%
Republican	49.3%	34.9%	25.0%	38.4%	7.9%	10.9%
Strong Republican	34.8%	23.8%	11.5%	28.3%	2.4%	3.4%
Democrat	18.4%	22.4%	44.2%	20.7%	49.8%	47.8%
Strong Democrat	9.5%	11.9%	25.5%	14.6%	44.6%	37.6%
Independent	26.9%	35.6%	24.9%	32.0%	32.7%	35.3%
Lean Republican	22.0%	25.7%	13.1%	22.4%	9.6%	2.0%
Lean Democrat	4.9%	9.9%	11.8%	9.6%	24.1%	33.3%

Source: Yankelovich Boomer Dreams Study, 2006

Figure 9-7: Political Identification

sist of family households. They also tend to be higher income, better educated, and employed.

Political attitudes are just one part of a myriad of values and beliefs shaping the various agendas that these groups will be pursuing in the future. The value of the Yankelovich Boomer Dreams study is in its power to differentiate Boomers in terms of their hopes, dreams, and aspirations, and thus in terms of their priorities for the future.

	Straight Arrows	Due Diligents	Maximizers	Sideliners	Diss/ Contenteds	Re-Activists
Several times a week or more	18.7%	9.8%	9.3%	0.5%	1.1%	3.3%
Several times a month to once a week	45.7%	23.3%	24.7%	6.8%	15.5%	4.2%
Once a month or less	24.0%	47.7%	46.4%	37.0%	36.0%	34.6%
Never	11.6%	19.3%	19.7%	55.8%	47.4%	58.0%

Source: Yankelovich Boomer Dreams Study, 2006

Figure 9-8: Attend Place of Worship

Agenda Item: Traditional Values

A large group of Baby Boomers are guided by traditional values, religion in particular. Straight Arrows are the most committed, as seen in Figure 9-9, but Due Diligents and Maximizers are strongly committed to these values as well. In contrast, Diss/Contenteds and Re-Activists are the least likely to express any attachment to or interest in these values.

A rough calculation of percentages multiplied by numbers of Boomers across all segments yields an estimate somewhere in the neighborhood of 39 to 40 million Boomers who say that religion is a "source of comfort" in their lives and about 35 million, the biggest number of whom are Straight Arrows, who want to spend future time and energy "sharing" their religious beliefs with others.

Straight Arrows see a need for sharing their values. They are the most likely to believe that Baby Boomers today have weaker values than the prior generation at the same age. Over three-quarters of Straight Arrows feel

Straight Arrows	Due Diligents	Maximizers	Sideliners	Diss/ Contenteds	Re-Activists
Focus of time/energy over next 5 to 10 years: Deepening and strengthening your relationship with God					
95.6%	87.2%	90.9%	32.3%	23.1%	26.0%
Agree: More and more I look to religion as a source of comfort in my life					
90.1%	59.9%	63.5%	27.4%	12.6%	8.5%
Focus of time/energy over next 5 to 10 years: Sharing your religious beliefs and convictions with others					
84.1%	62.2%	60.2%	9.6%	8.3%	8.7%
Agree: Casual, premarital sex is morally wrong					
84.9%	54.5%	48.6%	41.7%	16.6%	14.6%
Disagree: Everybody should be free to do his or her own thing					
55.1%	37.6%	37.4%	34.9%	14.9%	17.5%

Top 2 box or bottom 2 box on 4-point scale for agree/disagree questions.
Top 3 box on 7-point scale for focus of time/energy questions.
Source: Yankelovich Boomer Dreams Study, 2006

Figure 9-9: Straight Arrows

this way; all other groups have much lower support for this belief, with only Due Diligents and Sideliners as high as two-thirds.

The devotion of Straight Arrows to traditional values is exemplified by their disproportionately high rejection of premarital sex and of free-spirited nonconformity. This pattern is true for all values—duty, hard work, private property, patriotism, law and order, and the role of government. In every case, this commitment is far stronger among Straight Arrows than any other group.

Straight Arrows have the strongest sense of ethical clarity: 90.5 percent say they have a "clear sense" of the right thing to do "in every situation." While over 70 percent in every segment say they do, too, Maximizers are the only other segment that edges above 80 percent. For almost all Straight Arrows—96.9 percent—living a "clean, moral life" is very important. No other segment is as high as 90 percent, and Re-Activists are the lowest at 74.3 percent—which of course is high, but is quite low in comparison to Straight Arrows.

Given their conservative leaning, it is somewhat surprising that only 52.5 percent of Straight Arrows, the same percentage as Maximizers, think that "working through the system" is the best way to get things done. However, as low as this is, it's the highest of any segment. In no other segment does a majority agree. Most Boomers see a need to work outside the system, including almost half of the most conservative, traditionally oriented group.

This is not to imply that Straight Arrows don't believe in the system— 80.6 percent want to achieve the American Dream and 63.2 percent say they have already done so; in both cases, the highest of any segment. This is because 64.6 percent believe the opportunities they hoped for as young people were available to them when they got older. Similarly, 71.2 percent say they are better off today than their parents were at the same age. Straight Arrows have accomplished this while 64.3 percent, the highest of any segment, say they have maintained balance in their lives.

The Straight Arrow focus on traditional values, and on an active engagement with spreading those values, does not, however, portend a continuation of the same old politics as in the past. As seen in the Yankelovich Boomer Dreams data, political activism is not as high a priority for them as it was for

Evangelical religious leaders like Jerry Falwell, Pat Robertson, or James Dobson. Indeed, the Boomer generation of Evangelical religious leaders includes many like Rick Warren, Jim Wallis, Ronald Sider, and Joel Hunter, who want to transcend politics as usual by expanding the focus of their convictions to include social issues like AIDS, global warming, poverty, and Darfur.[1] In this way, the moralistic style of Straight Arrows will come to intersect with the moralistic style of other Boomers at the opposite end of the spectrum in terms of ideology and religion. Politics and social activism will be transformed as long-antagonistic partisans find themselves in league together, sharing a righteous common cause.

Nor do Straight Arrows need to think just in terms of politics in order to have an impact. In particular, they have economic clout.

The annual market for Christian products of all sorts is $7.5 billion, which doesn't include services like the Faith Guard insurance policy from Guide-One Mutual that insures your car with no deductible as long as you're driving to your place of worship.[2] Books, music, and video are the obvious parts of this market, but other products include toys, kitchen items, clothing, aerobics videos, and more. Growth rates exceed overall retail sales, with Christian products sold through mainstream retailers growing about 30 percent per year.[3] The total market for Christian products is expected to reach at least $9.5 billion by 2010.[4] The size of this market makes it influential, not to mention the guides published by Christian watchdog groups that provide ratings and recommendations about advertising, consumer products, travel, and more.

As big as this market is, though, there is plenty of untapped potential. Generally speaking, the Christian market is driven by specialty niche companies. With only a few exceptions such as Hallmark, Wal-Mart, and HarperCollins, major companies have not pursued values-based targeting of consumers like Straight Arrows, even though over half of Evangelicals (just to highlight one group) spend $50 or more per month on Christian products. Additionally, Christians tend to be geographically clustered in ways that make direct marketing easy and affordable.[5]

The United States is the most religious country—primarily Christian—in the developed world, yet Christian enterprises thrive off the radar, almost as a subculture. Religious activist organizations are the ones in the headlines, but religious charities, philanthropies, nonprofits, and legal services groups abound. Concerned Women for America, founded in 1979 by Beverly LaHaye—wife of Tim LaHaye, co-founder of The Moral Majority Coalition and co-author of the bestselling Left Behind series—has as many members as, if not more than, the National Organization for Women.

Millions of students are educated at every grade by schools with religious affiliations. Religious reasons account for the home schooling of about one-third of the million-plus children who are taught in that way.[6]

Religious media are thriving. There are several press associations, dozens of cable channels, thousands of radio stations and Web sites, and hundreds of TV stations, magazines, newsletters, and publishers serving this community. More than 60 million copies have been sold of the Left Behind series of apocalyptic Christian novels written by Tim LaHaye and Jerry Jenkins and published by Christian publisher Tyndale House. Rick Warren, a leading Evangelical and founder of the 20,000-member Saddleback Church in Lake Forest, California, has sold more than 20 million hardcover copies of his book *The Purpose Driven Life: What On Earth Am I Here For?*, published in 2002 by Evangelical publisher Zondervan. It is the bestselling nonfiction hardcover book in U.S. history. In the few years immediately after 9/11, Christian book sales boomed even as book sales suffered in general.

Traditional values, religion in particular, will be high on the Baby Boomer agenda to come. The largest segment of Boomers is deeply committed to these values as first priorities in their hopes, dreams, and aspirations for the future. Big percentages of Boomers in other segments place high importance on these values, too.

Straight Arrows recognize that their beliefs run counter to the cultural mainstream. Hence, they look for alternatives outside the system, which already exist in many commercial domains. To the extent that Straight Arrows stay within this narrow universe, polarization will grow. Marketers must lead the way in bridging this gap with more inclusive mainstream offerings and appeals. Marketers can do society a service by boosting their bottom lines in this way.

Agenda Item: Luxury

Maximizers are the most enthusiastic Boomer segment. They think Boomers are special, they look forward to the future, they want more of everything, and they want more out of everything.

This Boomer segment has something in common with every strain of Baby Boomer interests and passions. They share traditional values with Straight Arrows and Due Diligents, but they also sympathize with the social concerns of Diss/Contenteds and Re-Activists. Yet personal concerns are their central focus, not spiritual or societal concerns. They want all the gusto they can get from their personal experiences and pastimes, as seen in Figure 9-10.

There is more that Maximizers want to do, accomplish, and attain. Life's luxuries are a big part of this, both material and intangible. Maximizers are the most likely to say that "material things" are important to them, although the 51 percent majority is far from universal. At the same time, they are the most likely to value "once-in-a-lifetime experiences" and the most likely to "feel the need" to be involved with something "meaningful." They want more stuff as well as something more than stuff.

Straight Arrows	Due Diligents	Maximizers	Sideliners	Diss/ Contenteds	Re-Activists
Focus of time/energy over next 5 to 10 years: Buying some of the things you've always wanted to buy					
44.6%	58.5%	72.1%	43.0%	28.3%	42.5%
Identify with most: Driven to achieve more over content with what you have					
33.5%	32.8%	65.3%	45.3%	21.2%	43.7%
Focus of time/energy over next 5 to 10 years: Enjoying more of life's luxuries					
41.1%	58.4%	69.6%	48.9%	28.7%	47.2%
Agree: Baby Boomers are, in some ways, a special generation compared to generations before or after them					
44.6%	35.8%	56.7%	39.0%	31.9%	40.3%

Top 3 box on 7-point scale for agree/disagree question.
Top 3 box on 7-point scale for focus of time/energy questions.
Source: Yankelovich Boomer Dreams Study, 2006

Figure 9-10: Maximizers

Philanthropic Smoothie Leverage ⑤'s *Elgatown Ent R + Roll*

In their disproportionate desire for a blend of meaning and material-ism, Maximizers are the purest incarnation of this element of the genera-tional character of Boomers and their shared history. The iconic transition from the hippies of the 1960s and 1970s to the yuppies of the 1980s and be-yond was a personal path legitimized and mainstreamed by the leading figures of rock'n'roll, long the mainstay of Boomer cultural expression. Musicians who toiled as social visionaries and artistic outsiders were even-tually eclipsed by those who thrived as social butterflies and industry insid-ers, perhaps exemplified no better than by the morphing of Jefferson Airplane, an edgy outsider psychedelic band, into Jefferson Starship, a trea-cly insider pop band. The Who turned their rock opera *Tommy* into a 1975 movie aimed at making a mainstream commercial success out of their sem-inal 1969 concept album. In 1978, a similarly motivated cinematic effort fol-lowed for the Beatles' 1967 masterpiece, *Sgt. Pepper's Lonely Hearts Club Band*. Mega-stars like Fleetwood Mac, the Eagles, Led Zeppelin, Rod Stew-art, and Peter Frampton pioneered a new jet-setting lifestyle for rock'n'roll artists that only Elvis had known to that point. All of this was coun255cul-ture gone big time, and it opened a door for Boomers to conflate meaning and materialism without feeling apologetic. Obviously, Boomers have re-sponded to this in different ways, but Maximizers personify it more than any other segment.

Maximizers expect success. They are the one segment with a majority believing that their financial position will be better in ten years than it is to-day. They are the least likely to see any limits on their future prospects be-cause of their age, with only 28.9 percent doing so. They are the most likely to say that their abilities are above average and that they can succeed if they just work hard enough. They are far and away the most likely to feel that the best years of Baby Boomers are ahead, with 83.1 percent believing so.

Two-thirds of Maximizers want more "excitement and sensation," com-pared to less than half of every other group except for Due Diligents, at barely more than half. Technology is one of the ways Maximizers expect to find their thrills. They are the most open to new technologies of any seg-ment and 87.3 percent, the highest of any segment, believe it is "essential" to keep up with technology.

This interest in excitement and facility with technology is well suited for a self-inventive world. A little over half of Maximizers like to change their persona periodically and keep their looks up to date. Half even think the institution of marriage is becoming obsolete; no other segment breaks 40 percent.

Maximizers are indiscriminate about how to fill up their days. They are the highest or near the top for every future activity included in the Yankelovich Boomer Dreams study. Of course, this goes for worries, too. Maximizers want to do everything, so they worry about everything as well. But they don't worry to the point of timidity. Like Straight Arrows, 80 percent want to achieve the American Dream.

Above all else, Maximizers fear irrelevance, so they test themselves by living vigorously and doing it all. They want the most and, by extension, the best.

Maximizers are more likely than any other segment to believe that the idea of luxury will describe Baby Boomers in the future. This is a common self-evaluation, with seven in ten or so of Boomers in the other segments agreeing. But among Maximizers, it's 84.7 percent. Most Boomers have high tastes; Maximizers especially so.

Boomers have spent their lifetimes cultivating the sophisticated palates that they will carry forward into their older years. They have matured with a marketplace in which "above average" has become the cost of entry. Every car and hotel room should have the look and feel of luxury. Every home should show off a designer's touch, whether it's Martha Stewart or HGTV. The argot of prosperity has become the vernacular. This is the "mainstreaming of affluence"—the presumption that everyone should be able to enjoy the consummate things that were once the exclusive preserve of the rich and elite.[7] Gourmet coffee, sushi, day spas, overnight delivery, wireless phones, cosmetic surgery, golf vacations, adventure trips, boutiques, antilock brakes, and reserve wines—all are now within reach of the average person. Today's bare minimum is yesterday's extra special. There is a new floor in the consumer marketplace and it has a penthouse view.

With affluence as a mainstream expectation, it has become difficult to charge a premium for luxury. Consumers are less willing to accept a trade-off between price and quality. Cheap no longer means shoddy; it just means a great price on the best stuff.

Many factors have made this possible, including greater excellence in design and production from decades of corporate quality initiatives like Six Sigma; steady declines in the costs of technology paralleled by steady increases in power, performance, and speed; the offshoring of manufacturing and service; and the shopping information now available to consumers via the Internet. With nothing to make luxury special, difficult, or costly, Boomers, like all consumers, have grown accustomed to it.

Luxury has become the norm of the middle-class even as middle-income households are under financial pressure. A 2002 pictorial piece for the *New York Times Magazine* profiled seven families with household incomes equal to the national median of $54,400.[8] Each of these families had big financial obligations and little savings, but each had recently splurged on at least one expensive luxury item—a vintage car, a boat, an SUV, a second home, a wide-screen TV, an entertainment center, an expensive vacation, a digital camera, or a swimming pool.

One of the biggest transformations Boomers are bringing to their aging years is a set of higher expectations about quality, service, and indulgence in everything they do. The growth in surfing is at the high end of private lessons, exclusive resorts at obscure breaks, and high-tech gear, for which older consumers are the primary target group.[9] The DIY home-improvement business is seeing big gains from high-end kitchen and bath renovations. Boomers fueled the 20 percent sales growth in bathroom remodeling from 2005 to 2006. This is not restricted to luxury homes; there were twice as many bath renovations in total in 2006 compared to 2003, with people at all income levels three times as likely over that same period to do high-end bath renovations.[10] Boomers are bringing their high-end tastes to many other categories, too, from pet food to travel to cosmetics to wine and more.

This edge of luxury will go beyond nicer stuff. The difference worth the price is no longer the product but the experience. In a marketplace of luxury parity in which high-end product features are taken for granted, only experiences offer a meaningful point of difference, something that Boomers like Maximizers want as much as anything else in their quest to get the most and the best.

Agenda Item: Transparency

Due Diligents and Sideliners want to stay active and influential, but they don't share the interest shown by Maximizers in getting involved in everything. Due Diligents are worried about pushing the edge, and Sideliners don't see the appeal. Prudence, temperance, skepticism, and caution characterize their attitudes.

The caution of Due Diligents is evident in the attitudes shown in Figure 9-11.

Due Diligents are the most concerned about "taking care" of themselves. This is reflected in their unease about everything, from health insurance to mental acuity to aging itself. It carries over to many areas including time, energy, financial security, keeping busy, living independently, having a supportive community, and not being bored. Like Maxi-

Straight Arrows	Due Diligents	Maximizers	Sideliners	Diss/ Contenteds	Re-Activists
Agree: I am concerned about taking care of myself					
75.2%	92.2%	83.6%	71.3%	78.3%	88.4%
Worried about when think of retirement: Having sufficient health care insurance					
62.6%	92.2%	67.5%	64.3%	81.6%	79.0%
Identify with most: Own instincts over listening to experts					
75.9%	91.7%	70.2%	85.3%	78.6%	87.7%
Identify with most: Simplifying over packing more in					
83.4%	90.9%	73.0%	82.6%	84.5%	81.0%
Worried about when think of retirement: Not being mentally sharp					
53.2%	82.5%	77.7%	55.0%	60.7%	66.7%
Identify with most: Heart over head					
44.8%	71.2%	54.7%	42.3%	52.7%	58.4%
Agree: Aging is inevitable so we just have to get used to slowing down and doing less					
50.2%	65.4%	40.6%	54.6%	54.3%	42.5%

Top 2 box on 4-point scale for agree/disagree questions.
Source: Yankelovich Boomer Dreams Study, 2006

Figure 9-11: Due Diligents

mizers, though, Due Diligents are open to the possibility of doing many different things in the years ahead. It's just that their motto is safety first. Safe adventure is the thrill they seek. Safety needs to be easily and simply recognizable, which is to say transparently obvious.

Notwithstanding their watchfulness, Due Diligents are the most likely of any Boomer segment to trust their hearts and go with gut instinct. Perhaps this is because they are looking to deal with uncertainty in a way that gives them more of a feeling of control. They are the most interested in simplifying, but not if it means frugality, sacrifice, or privation. Simplification is about controlling needs and expectations, which is reflective of the watchfulness valued by Due Diligents.

Sideliners approach life with reserve as well, as seen in the attitudes shown in Figure 9-12.

More so than Boomers in any other segment, Sideliners are loners. They want to work out problems by themselves and they prefer time alone. This is reflected in their lower level of interest in nearly all future activities.

Sideliners are the least likely to claim a strong connection to their communities or to want to be engaged in politics. Similarly, when asked whether

Straight Arrows	Due Diligents	Maximizers	Sideliners	Diss/ Contenteds	Re-Activists
Disagree: I have a strong sense of connection with the community where I live					
31.1%	35.0%	36.7%	62.3%	42.1%	38.7%
Agree: If I have a problem, I prefer to work it out alone					
62.5%	68.2%	61.4%	74.0%	63.5%	63.0%
Identify with most: Financial satisfaction over creative satisfaction					
48.4%	30.4%	43.8%	63.7%	40.4%	25.2%
Identify with most: Time with yourself over time with friends					
56.1%	40.9%	47.2%	63.1%	41.9%	46.9%
Disagree: Focus of time/energy over next 5 to 10 years: Getting more involved in politics					
38.4%	38.7%	34.7%	62.3%	23.3%	10.8%

Top 2 box or bottom 2 box on 4-point scale for agree/disagree questions.
Top 3 box or bottom 3 box on 7-point scale for focus of time/energy questions.
Source: Yankelovich Boomer Dreams Study, 2006

Figure 9-12: Sideliners

Ethical Consumers

Activism

194   *Generation Ageless*

Advocate not
Dem just
but Disclose

they preferred friends with similar or different values, Sideliners were the most likely of any Boomer segment to prefer friends with similar values. They want a cocoon of connections that draws them further into themselves.

Sideliners are mistrustful of authority and feel most comfortable with their own judgments and instincts. Folded in upon themselves, they are vigilant about reducing their exposure to disappointment or injury by others. They want the bottom line to be transparent.

Led by Due Diligents and Sideliners, Baby Boomers are going to practice vigilance by demanding complete transparency. Already, as part of the general dynamic of self-invention, a move is afoot to restore trust through greater transparency. Glen Urban, marketing professor and former dean at the MIT Sloan School of Management, trumpets this imperative in his book *Don't Just Relate—Advocate!: A Blueprint for Profit in the Era of Consumer Power* (Upper Saddle River, New Jersey: Wharton School Publishing, 2005). Urban believes that the contemporary distrust of business is so widespread and deep-seated that an entirely new business model of trust-based marketing is needed. This means customer advocacy or putting the interests of consumers first, primarily by empowering them through full disclosure. Urban argues that the only way for companies to advance their own interests is to make them a secondary priority.

In a world of self-invention, this is the only option anyway. Consumers can get whatever information they seek whether companies are willing to provide it themselves or not. The qualms that Boomers like Due Diligents and Sideliners feel about their security and well-being mean a greater interest in vigilance. In a world in which authorities are less trusted than ever, Boomers won't take someone else's word for it. They want to see it all and even do it all for themselves.

Agenda Item: Ethical Consuming

Ethical consuming can reflect any political or ideological persuasion. It is simply the act of shopping to support companies that incorporate certain kinds of ethical practices into the ways in which they do business. The issues that get the most attention are the environment, labor, organics, lending, and trade. But ethical consumption can be guided by any sorts of values or issues.

Ethical consuming is the kind of activism that is attractive and affordable for many aging Boomers, particularly Diss/Contenteds and Re-Activists. Both of these Boomer segments are focused on societal issues as they look ahead. They want to marshal their growing sense of righteousness to support various social causes, albeit within certain parameters.

These Boomer segments want to lend their support as long as they get back what they need and want, too. Diss/Contenteds are dissatisfied with the status quo and willing to do what they can for reform, but only if doing so does not disrupt their lifestyles. Re-Activists are more willing to make sacrifices in order to get reengaged before it's too late, but they do not want to relive the tumult of their youth. Protest is a channel for Re-Activists to continue to discover and reinvent themselves as much as a way of making a difference.

Both Diss/Contenteds and Re-Activists see a need for change and are anxious for progress to be made. Figures 9-13 and 9-14 show the key attitudes that define each segment.

Diss/Contenteds are worried about the future. They, like Re-Activists, are willing to challenge authority to make things better.

Straight Arrows	Due Diligents	Maximizers	Sideliners	Diss/ Contenteds	Re-Activists
Agree: A lot of things we take for granted wouldn't be possible without government policies and guarantees					
39.9%	53.2%	63.9%	42.0%	81.6%	65.5%
Identify with most: Worried about the future over look forward to the future					
28.4%	52.2%	33.9%	48.7%	61.0%	43.0%
Identify with most: Challenge authority over accept authority					
45.8%	40.8%	64.8%	60.1%	90.3%	88.6%
Agree: All I want out of life is enough to be comfortable; more than that is not worth the effort					
33.1%	59.6%	34.2%	38.4%	53.2%	37.7%

Top 2 box on 4-point scale for agree/disagree questions.

Figure 9-13: Diss/Contenteds

	Straight Arrows	Due Diligents	Maximizers	Sideliners	Diss/ Contenteds	Re-Activists
Focus of time/energy over next 5 to 10 years: Getting more involved in politics						
	61.6%	61.3%	65.3%	37.7%	76.7%	89.2%
Focus of time/energy over next 5 to 10 years: Working to fix the inequities in society						
	35.6%	56.0%	73.4%	12.3%	64.7%	89.1%
Focus of time/energy over next 5 to 10 years: Working on behalf of human rights in society						
	28.3%	59.5%	68.0%	7.5%	66.9%	85.7%
Identify with most: Standing out over fitting in						
	54.6%	43.8%	58.5%	65.3%	64.8%	83.7%
Disagree: Focus of time/energy over next 5 to 10 years: Having a quiet retirement						
	42.6%	24.8%	26.3%	38.1%	25.3%	52.1%

Top 2 box on 4-point scale for agree/disagree questions.
Top 3 box or bottom 3 box on 7-point scale for focus of time/energy questions.
Source: Yankelovich Boomer Dreams Study, 2006

Figure 9-14: Re-Activists

Compared to other segments, Diss/Contenteds and Re-Activists are much more willing to defy convention and to think the system should be changed. Over 80 percent of both segments agree that people should be free to do their own thing. Both are much more willing—along with Due Diligents—than other segments to try new things. Over 90 percent of Diss/Contenteds and Re-Activists believe the basic safeguards of privacy are under siege.

Diss/Contenteds and Re-Activists are the most concerned about social "threats and challenges." They are the most disappointed in how society has turned out. Compared to what they thought it would be when they were in their twenties, 92 percent of Diss/Contenteds and 93.1 percent of Re-Activists say it is worse, as opposed to 70-some percent of all other segments. This seems to be rooted in a belief that people have not received enough help from government. The majority of these two segments do not believe that hard work always pays off, whereas the majority of every other segment believe it does. The same pattern is true for the belief that the biggest problems cannot be solved without the help of government. Over 80 percent of Diss/Contenteds and Re-Activists believe that government today "is not doing enough to help those at the bottom."

More than any other segment, Diss/Contenteds and Re-Activists want to get involved in politics. This desire is stronger among Re-Activists, at 89.2 percent, than among Diss/Contenteds, at 76.7 percent. Sideliners are under 40 percent, and it's less than two-thirds of all other segments.

Comfort and quiet are important to them, though. Diss/Contenteds don't want to give up their contentment, and Re-Activists wish for some quiet even as they ratchet up their involvement in social causes.

Re-Activists, in particular, have personal priorities that rival their commitment to social causes. They want to stretch themselves and tackle new things. They are willing to change just for the sake of change. They want experiences more than stuff, and they want to engage with something meaningful. Creative satisfaction is more important than financial satisfaction for 74.8 percent of Re-Activists, by far the highest percentage of any segment. Nearly all Re-Activists, 91.5 percent, agree that "discovering more" about themselves has always been important—again, by far the highest percentage of any segment. Like Maximizers, they have a strong interest in every activity and interest they could take up over the next five to ten years.

Diss/Contenteds and Re-Activists are looking to get more engaged in social causes, but both segments want to do so without lifestyle sacrifices. Ethical consuming as their style of political and social engagement is a good alternative, especially as tracking the ethical performance of companies gets easier and more routine.

A past class project at the MIT Media Lab is a good illustration of what's ahead. For this project, a graduate student at the Media Lab came up with a technology concept he called the Corporate Fallout Detector. To use it, a consumer would scan a product's bar code. The device would then search a database loaded onto the memory chip containing whatever information is of interest to that consumer. For this student's concept, the worse the record of the manufacturer of that product on pollution and ethics, the faster and the louder the device would click with a sound like that of a Geiger counter (hence the name). A research sociologist at Microsoft has invented something similar. His device uses a scanner, a hand-held computer, and a wireless Internet connection. A consumer scans the bar code and the device searches the Internet for information about dangers or hazards.[11]

Imagine a shopping trip once such a device is commercialized. A consumer could check for anything, from ingredients that would trigger an allergy to companies with poor ethical practices. This could be done for any issue—the environment, Third World labor practices, trade with certain nations, product safety, workplace safety, labor relations, contributions to political parties, support of charitable organizations, presence of women or people of color in top management, truth in advertising, and more. Advertising claims could be second-guessed or completely ignored. Criteria never considered before would become central to the decision-making of consumers. The only requirement would an accessible database of pertinent information.

Led by Diss/Contenteds and Maximizers, Boomers are going to transform shopping into a new sort of engagement with social causes. This is the way to recommit without compromising their comfort or self-development. Shopping is something that Boomers have always done well, and now it can become the vehicle by which they make the difference they want to make. Indeed, this is something that all Boomers can do, not just the small percentage who might reprise their roles as youthful protestors.

Ethical issues will become an important product characteristic, and in a marketplace of luxury parity, ethical criteria will often be the deciding factor since all choices will measure up on other tangible criteria. While ethical consuming is of interest to all generations, only Boomer dollars can make it more than a niche fad. Indeed, Diss/Contenteds and Re-Activists have the highest incomes of any Boomer segment.

Information and guidance for ethical consuming are more available than ever before. Co-op America maintains a Web site with research about the ethical practices of hundreds of major corporations and publishes a national directory of green-approved businesses. The Ethical Consumer Research Association makes its ratings of over 50,000 businesses available online. CRO magazine covers business ethics and reports on the activities and initiatives that companies are undertaking.

Green consumption alone is an enormous market. From organic cosmetics to green homes to eco-travel, the so-called LOHAS market (the popular acronym for the estimated 40 million consumers who seek and shop in accordance with Lifestyles of Health and Sustainability) is estimated to be nearly $200 billion.[12]

Ethical travel, which includes ecotourism, is an emerging growth area in the travel market. Web sites like EthicalTraveler.org, ResponsibleTravel .com, Planeta.com, and TourismConcern.org.uk are springing up, offering advice and resources for travelers who want to be more mindful about where their money is going and how they are affecting local culture. Ecotourism by itself represents 20 percent of global tourism and is growing at three times the rate of the travel industry as a whole.[13]

The next battle fought by Boomers will be waged at the cash register. Boomers are more committed than ever to values and causes that are important to them. By channeling that passion through their pocketbooks, Boomers will continue to matter for as long as they can swipe their credit cards and double-click the icon to place their orders.

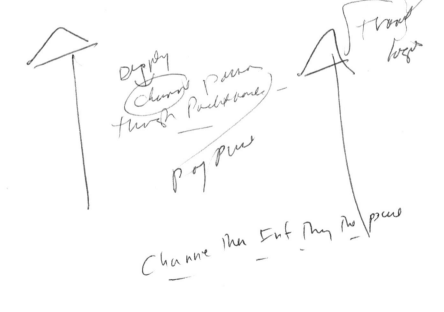

ten

Breaking Every Rule

*A*s far as Boomers are concerned, rules were made to be broken.

At every encounter with tradition and convention, Boomers have challenged and remade the established ways of doing things. This is their generational history—ever more rule-breaking as the next domain of rebelliousness is added to those before it. Boomers have always sought to reinvent their situations to accommodate new approaches and fresh ways of doing things.

Boomers have felt more confidence in themselves than in traditional authorities or established ways of doing things. They have been unwilling to follow along merely for the sake of abiding by the rules. The old rules of work, life, and play, whatever they were, have never been viewed by Boomers as being vested with some inherent presumption of authority and legitimacy. This is not a matter of political or moral conviction; it is a generational view. Rules have been broken left and right. Boomers have demanded that authorities and rules of all sorts prove themselves worthy of being obeyed.

The theme of breaking the rules plays well with Boomer business leaders. Management consultants counsel businesspeople to think differently in order to be more insightful about their offerings and business models. But for Boomers, what resonates is not merely a new perspective but throwing out the rulebook.

Gallup consultants Marcus Buckingham and Curt Coffman had a canny sense about what would capture the imagination of Boomer businesspeople when they came up with the title for their runaway bestseller, *First, Break*

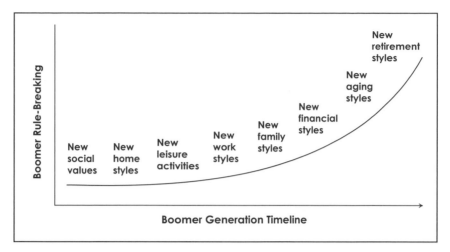

Figure 10-1

Marketing Thought-Starter: Reinvent Their Wheels

The evolution of Boomer taste in cars is a good illustration of Boomer rule-breaking. It used to be that people would trade up from small cars to big cars. In the early 1970s, the Yankelovich MONITOR predicted that in the future, young people would no longer move from small cars to big cars; instead, they would trade up within small cars. This proved to be true, and it was the foothold that Toyota, Nissan (then known as Datsun), and Honda needed to compete with Detroit.

As Boomers got older and settled down, completely new types of vehicles were invented for them. Minivans came first, offering them more room along with greater comfort. SUVs came next, giving Boomers a feeling of more control and greater safety. Now, it's anything sporty, zesty, or youthful, from compact SUVs originally intended for a younger audience but now popular among Boomers to sporty two-seater convertibles with retro designs to luxury sedans that emphasize power and indulgence over status and success.

The mistake has been to assume that Boomers would "mature" as they got older. In fact, Boomers have always tried to age without getting

(continued)

Break the Rules.

(continued)

old. They want to keep their youthful edge no matter what their age. So designing cars for "mature" adults is sure to miss the mark with this generation. Boomers never "matured" into station wagons like their parents. An updated model has never been enough to connect with them; only a completely new design will do.

The Yankelovich MONITOR group uses a particular consulting approach to help clients targeting Boomers that reflects this essential truth: To win the loyalty of Boomers, a brand must break the rules. It is a four-step process of diagnosing the opportunities associated with Boomer rule-breaking.

Step one is an internal brainstorming to specify all of the existing rules that characterize how consumers make decisions today.

Step two is a consulting exercise to identify the ways in which these rules can be broken—three ways in particular: "Antitheticals" represent the complete opposites of existing rules; "Nuances" offer variations on the existing rules; and "Paradoxes" provide new combinations of elements thought to be incompatible under existing rules. These alternatives are used as input for developing products and positionings built around new rules.

Step three is a research project to find the combinations of alternative components with the greatest interest and potential demand among Boomers. Typically, this involves quantitative modeling to identify an optimal set of new rules.

The final step is the application of these new rules to marketing targeting. Usually, segments of Boomers emerge, each with its own way of breaking the rules. Linkage models are calculated to identify these segments by name and address in customer databases, and concepts are created and tested that use these new rules to develop better products and brands.

All the Rules: What the World's Greatest Managers Do Differently (New York: Simon & Schuster, 1999). Their book sold over one million copies in hardcover in its first three years after publication. It catapulted Gallup's management consulting practice into the big time. Gallup now earns only 1 percent of its revenues from its high-profile public-opinion polling; the rest comes from speeches, seminars, training, and consulting.[1] The advice

Gallup offers is solid and valuable, but the packaging to promote it to the Boomers now running American business is genius. Breaking the rules is how Boomers define progress, improvement, and success.

Rule-breaking is a theme that pops up in the titles of lots of books for businesspeople. To name but a few: *Breaking Robert's Rules: The New Way to Run Your Meeting, Build Consensus, and Get Results*, by Lawrence Susskind and Jeffrey Cruikshank (New York: Oxford University Press USA, 2006). *Break the Rules and Get a Great Job*, by William Cohen (New York: Prentice Hall Press, 2001). *How to Think Like Einstein: Simple Ways to Break the Rules and Discover Your Hidden Genius*, by Scott Thorpe (Naperville, Ill.: Sourcebooks, 2000). *Extreme Success: The 7-Part Program That Shows You How to Break the Rules and Succeed Without Struggle*, by Rich Fettke (New York: Fireside/Simon & Schuster, 2002). *10 Golden Rules of Freelance Writing and How I Broke Them to Make It as a Magazine Writer*, by Bob Frieday (Bangor, Me.: Booklocker.com, 2003). *Breaking the Rules: Removing the Obstacles to Effortless High Performance*, by Kurt Wright (Highlands Ranch, Colo.: CPM Publishing, 1998). *Who Cares What You're Supposed to Do: Breaking the Rules to Get What You Want in Love, Life and Work*, by Victoria Dickerson and Carla Fine (New York: Perigree Trade/ Penguin Putnam, 2004). *Breaking the Rules of Project Management* (Oshawa, Ontario, Canada: Multi-Media Publications, Inc., Audiobook, 2005). *The Internet Entrepreneurs: Business Rules Are Good; Break Them*, by Chris Hall (New York: Financial Times/Prentice Hall, 2000).

The last title in this list is a reminder that one of the primary reasons Boomer pundits were so enamored of the dot-com era was that it seemed to be the start of a future in which all the old rules would no longer apply. New rules would run the economy: no more recessions, high productivity forever, globalization as a panacea, unlimited value creation, and an ever-rising Dow. The allure of rule-breaking gave that era much of the interest it held for Boomers. Even after the dot-com crash, the appeal of rule-breaking has lost none of its generational draw. The July 24, 2006 cover of *Fortune* exclaimed, "Sorry, Jack!" and beneath an x'ed-over picture of former General Electric CEO Jack Welch was the proclamation, "Welch's Rules for Winning Don't Work Anymore (But We've Got 7 New Ones That Do)."

Breaking the Old Software Rules

Boomers have pioneered entirely new business propositions grounded in rule-breaking, the free software and open-source software movements chief among them. Boomer Richard Stallman (b. 1953) is the pioneering figure in the free software movement.[2] As a programmer at the MIT Artificial Intelligence Laboratory in the late 1970s and early 1980s, Stallman was part of the early academic hacker culture that focused on exploration and collaboration and that was hostile to secrecy and authority. As the computer industry moved in the early to mid-1980s to software products that could run on different types of computers (so-called portable software), a more restrictive business model was adopted. To preserve and protect revenue opportunities, computer manufacturers adopted restrictions preventing users from modifying or adapting the software that came with one machine to share and use on a competitor's machine. Source code was no longer distributed, and software licenses prohibited copying and redistribution. Or to put it another way, rules were instituted that closed off the free exchange and individual control that had long been a core part of hacker culture.

Stallman objected to these developments on philosophical grounds. Freedom was his highest value, not only as a way to develop software but as a broad ethical and social principle. In the case of software, he felt that restrictions on modifying, copying, and redistributing software were a fundamental breach of basic rights and freedoms, so he undertook a series of programming initiatives to challenge the dominance of proprietary software by offering free software that provided the same functionality and quality while preserving the ability of people to cooperate and share.

Free software is more about control over one's experiences than about getting something for nothing. Stallman's reaction against software restrictions reflected his belief that non-free software is "the basis of an antisocial scheme to dominate people."[3] So, in the Boomer spirit of breaking rules, he set out to undermine restrictions that he felt were closing off priceless freedoms worth far more than the revenue streams or market valuations of computer companies.

In September 1983, Stallman announced the launch of the GNU project. GNU is a so-called recursive acronym for GNU's Not Unix to signal that it is a software alternative to Unix that, while Unix-like, contains no Unix code and, unlike Unix, is free. While Stallman did much of the early work himself (for which he has been recognized with many honorary degrees and awards, including a 1990 MacArthur "Genius" Fellowship), GNU has been shepherded along by the cooperative efforts of thousands of collaborators. The key development in the GNU project was the 1991 development of the so-called Linux kernel by Finnish software engineer Linus Torvalds. The Linux version of GNU is now a mainstream competitor to Unix—an entirely new business proposition arising from a Boomer determination to break the rules. In 1985, Stallman also started the nonprofit Free Software Foundation to serve as an organizing body overseeing and managing licenses, copyrights, directories, definitions, hosting, education, and so forth.

A related yet competing strain of thought is represented by the Open Source Initiative, a nonprofit organization to promote, certify, and license open-source software. The open-source software movement is similar to the free software movement with respect to control over copying, modifying, and redistributing software. The two movements differ, however, in the reasons they believe that users should be given control. The philosophical values of freedom are foremost for Stallman and his articulation of free software, whereas pragmatic values are more important for the promoters of the open-source software movement such as Boomer Eric Raymond (b. 1957).

Open-source software is usually discussed in terms of the practical impact of collaboration. The more people working on a problem, the more likely it is that a good, durable solution will be found. As Raymond once put it in a maxim he calls Linus' Law, in honor of Linus Torvalds, "Given enough eyeballs, all bugs are shallow."[4] For open-source advocates, broader social issues are secondary and in some cases, proprietary software might even be acceptable, especially in terms of the free choice people can exercise in their decisions to use open-source versus proprietary software. Open source is rule-breaking twice over—a reaction against software restrictions as well as a reaction against the strict alternative represented by Stallman's free-software ideas.

A World of Collaboration

Open source is no longer confined to software. It has become a broader cultural phenomenon focused on the general concept of access to a product's sources and the ability to modify and change a product oneself.[5] Open-source filmmaking is in its early stages. The concept is one in which collaborating producers and actors use freely available footage and materials to create the ultimate product. The animated film *Elephant's Dream* is the first open-source movie, and the documentary *The American Revolution* is the first open-source documentary.

The open-source model for media is known as iterative media, which refers to a process involving numerous feedback loops and opportunities for collaboration: collaborative planning, collaborative production, collaborative editing, collaborative distribution, and collaborative remixing of the final content into other new products.[6] Collaborative user participation is the central idea behind the next phase of Internet content development, known popularly as Web 2.0.[7] With blogs, fan fiction sites, social networking sites, instant messaging, chat rooms, digital video recorders, wiki sites, auction sites, swap sites, and more, people now find themselves immersed in a new world of participation, engagement, control, and collaboration. Collaborative engagement is now mainstream, part of the world of self-invention.

The contemporary culture of collaboration and participation is rooted in the generational resistance of Boomers to authority, secrecy, and centralized control. Through these values and priorities, Boomers laid the groundwork for what is occurring today.

When confronted with rules and restrictions during their lives, Boomers have sought to break them, creating in the process a new culture of personal engagement and collaborative production. In keeping with their youthful sensibility, they have always tested limits and challenged established authorities. Patterns that arise organically have been preferred to rules imposed from on high. The contributions of individuals are believed to be more valuable and more trustworthy than the strictures and demands of institutions.

Organic

Left to Do

Boomers are not finished breaking the rules. There is too much left to be accomplished, and thus too many rules still in need of being broken.

When asked in the 2006 Yankelovich Boomer Dreams study how they felt about American society today, only 27.2 percent reported feeling satisfied. Compared to where they thought American society would be right about now when they were in their twenties and just getting started, 77.5 percent of Boomers said it is "worse."

Boomers are happier with their personal positions. Nearly two-thirds —64.7 percent—report being personally satisfied today. Only 38.7 percent say their situations are worse today than where they thought they would be when they were in their twenties, and only 17.4 percent think their personal situations will be worse ten years from now.

Despite feeling good about their personal situations, general concerns about American society lead 51.5 percent of Boomers to feel pessimistic about the future. Only 32.6 percent feel optimistic. Clearly, Boomers feel that more needs to be done, and to a large extent they hold themselves responsible.

When asked in the Boomer Dreams study if they had accomplished all they wanted to by this point in their lives, only 53.7 percent agreed. While this is a majority, there remains a substantial proportion of Boomers who had expected more of themselves by now. This applies not only to themselves but to their generation as a whole. Only 42.8 percent of Boomers agreed that Baby Boomers are a special generation. Even though the accomplishments of their generation were rated as successful by 57.1 percent, over 40 percent feel that it has not lived up to its potential.

Boomers are judging themselves against a tough standard. Figure 10-2 shows the comparisons Boomers made of themselves relative to Matures, GenXers, and Echo Boomers at comparable ages.

In general, Boomers see GenXers and Echo Boomers as being only slightly worse than they were at similar ages. Compared to Matures, though, Boomers see themselves as being much worse.

While Boomers are slightly more likely to say they are more accomplished in their forties and fifties than Matures were at the same age, they are much less likely to see themselves as better in terms of having strong values, being social committed, living up to their potential, and making a difference.

Whatever Boomers have done—and they have done plenty—they don't think they have done as much as Matures or as much as they should have done irrespective of the prior generation. Boomers know that there is more to be done, and so they have to stay involved in order to do it.

How Boomers compare themselves at comparable ages	Vs. Matures	Vs. GenXers	Vs. Echoes
Accomplished			
More	34.4%	38.8%	38.5%
Less	27.0%	28.7%	34.6%
Values			
Stronger	12.6%	39.2%	40.0%
Weaker	64.9%	38.4%	37.3%
Visionary			
More	36.2%	36.3%	40.0%
Less	35.5%	33.2%	34.9%
Socially Committed			
More	30.3%	36.0%	41.0%
Less	46.4%	37.3%	37.0%
Living Up to Potential			
Better	19.3%	36.4%	37.8%
Worse	41.5%	32.2%	35.8%
Making a difference			
More	27.8%	35.9%	38.9%
Less	42.1%	33.0%	34.2%
Source: Yankelovich Boomer Dreams Study 2006			

Figure 10-2: How Boomers Stack Up

Finding a New Way

Boomers universally agree—93.7 percent—that it is "important for all to look for ways to get involved and improve society." But this will take a new approach because, by and large, Boomers don't believe in the system. Both left and right on the political spectrum, they never did, and they still don't today.

Even thought 62.6 percent of Boomers in the Boomer Dreams study said that they wanted to focus more of their time and energy over the next five to ten years on "getting more involved in politics," a mere 44.7 percent agreed that "working through the system is the best way to get things done in life." In only two of the six Boomer segments did a majority think that working through the system is best, and in both of those segments the percentage was under 53 percent. For Boomers, political engagement is likely to entail working around or outside the system. The rules have to be broken to get things done.

There are many institutions that Boomers believe are in need of overhaul. Figure 10-3 shows the percentage of Boomers believing that the institutions listed are in need of "fundamental reform." These results are reported in a way that facilitates a comparison of the 2006 Yankelovich Boomer Dreams study with the work Yankelovich completed in 1973 among Boomers who were then sixteen to twenty-five.

There are a few institutions Boomers regard more highly today, including the military, the penal system, high schools, the FBI, and trade unions. While they think better of political parties today, most Boomers still see a need for reform. Several institutions are viewed as no worse than before, and relatively favorably overall.

However, Congress, the mass media, and, among college-educated Boomers, big business are viewed with a lot less regard than before. Opinions about Congress have especially worsened. It's no surprise, then, that Boomers feel a need to work outside the system. Boomers don't hold favorable views of institutions associated with public policy and politics. This is true as well for other institutions included in the 2006 research that were not asked about in 1973: the presidency, the executive branch, and the federal court system.

	1973		2006	
	Non-College	College	Non-College	College
Penal system	50%	69%	29.3%	55.8%
Political parties	64%	61%	50.3%	58.8%
Big business	45%	54%	53.3%	54.7%
Military	38%	54%	15.2%	23.1%
High schools	38%	52%	23.9%	35.0%
Trade unions	34%	38%	24.8%	28.0%
FBI	27%	37%	16.0%	25.4%
Congress	31%	34%	53.4%	58.0%
Universities and colleges	21%	31%	30.4%	25.0%
Mass media	27%	27%	47.6%	42.8%
Supreme Court	24%	21%	36.3%	28.8%
The Constitution	13%	12%	6.7%	8.0%
Health insurance companies	N/A	N/A	67.8%	66.8%
Pharmaceutical companies	N/A	N/A	49.7%	54.7%
Credit card companies	N/A	N/A	50.4%	50.9%
Social Security	N/A	N/A	48.6%	50.9%
Public schools	N/A	N/A	49.3%	50.7%
Department of Homeland Security	N/A	N/A	37.0%	47.9%
Presidency	N/A	N/A	32.9%	45.1%
Federal Court System	N/A	N/A	39.8%	43.8%
Executive Branch	N/A	N/A	33.8%	43.6%
Legal profession	N/A	N/A	37.1%	38.9%
State government	N/A	N/A	30.4%	34.2%
Medical profession	N/A	N/A	35.6%	33.1%
Organized religion	N/A	N/A	17.7%	30.6%
CIA	N/A	N/A	13.8%	28.5%
Local government	N/A	N/A	31.2%	26.7%
Advertising and marketing	N/A	N/A	16.9%	26.2%
Banks	N/A	N/A	20.7%	25.7%
Police	N/A	N/A	12.3%	21.9%
TSA (Transportation Security Administration)	N/A	N/A	16.9%	21.7%
Airlines	N/A	N/A	21.2%	18.7%
Food companies	N/A	N/A	15.4%	15.4%
The Internet	N/A	N/A	4.5%	7.1%
None	N/A	N/A	5.9%	0.6%

Sources: John D. Rockefeller III Fund Study, 1973, and Yankelovich Boomer Dreams Study, 2006

Figure 10-3: Institutions Needing "Fundamental Reform"

Large percentages of Boomers also see a need for reform of other governmental institutions. Social security is a concern for half of Boomers, as is the Department of Homeland Security and public schools. On the other hand, local and state governments are viewed relatively well. So is organized religion.

Boomers are most concerned about health insurance companies. This is consistent with their other opinions about the quality and affordability of health care in the future. Pharmaceutical companies are a concern to about half of Boomers, too. Boomers are also concerned about credit card companies, perhaps reflecting their general concerns about related issues like privacy and debt.

Interestingly, education is an important determinant of the level of concern expressed by Boomers. With only a handful of exceptions, college-educated Boomers see more need for reform than those without a college education. Moral values and ideology may account for part of the reason why the percentages seeing a need for fundamental reform are higher among non–college educated Boomers for mass media, universities and colleges, and the Supreme Court.

The social issues of interest to Boomers run the gamut, as seen in Figure 10-4.

Only two areas are viewed as important by less than a majority of Boomers. All other areas are mentioned by more than 60 percent of Boomers, and most of those by more than 80 percent.

The number-one issue, mentioned by nearly all Boomers, is the economic competitiveness of America, followed closely by tax reform and a few other economic issues including the price of fuel and the national debt. In short, Boomers see economic issues as most important.

Nearly as important are environmental issues in more traditional areas like air and water pollution. The more contemporary issues of deforestation, overfishing the oceans, and global warming aren't mentioned by quite as many Boomers. Human rights, immigration, and open government are mentioned by almost all Boomers.

Boomers see a plethora of causes worthy of their commitment. There is no shortage of choices for taking on a mission.

America's economic competitiveness	90.0%
Tax reform	89.5%
Human rights	87.8%
Price of fuel	86.8%
Fuel shortages	86.0%
Water pollution	85.2%
Immigration	84.4%
Health of the environment	84.3%
National debt	84.0%
Air pollution	82.2%
More open government	81.5%
Age discrimination	78.4%
Race relations	77.5%
Deforestation	72.0%
Over-fishing the oceans	69.3%
Gender equality	68.8%
Endangered species	68.7%
Globalization	66.2%
Birth control	64.9%
Global warming	64.8%
Abortion	63.4%
Welfare	62.3%
Sexual freedom	47.0%
Gay rights	41.1%

Top 3 box on 7-point scale

Source: Yankelovich Boomer Dreams Study, 2006

Figure 10-4: Importance of Social Issues

No Legacy

Boomers want a mission, but not to leave a legacy. They want to make a difference for themselves today.

In the 2006 Yankelovich Boomer Dreams study, only 22.4 perce
Boomers expressed any interest in being a part of something that leaves
a legacy for future generations. Even for their own families, only 23.7
percent reported any concern about leaving a legacy other than money.

Boomers most interested in leaving a legacy, whether for future generations or for family, are those with the greatest concern about and interest in
causes, community, and charity. They are also the most likely to feel that
government can't get the job done, so nongovernmental agencies and individuals must step up. Hence, even more so than other Boomers, they are focused on remaining active and independent in their older years. But these
Boomers are a small percentage of their generation.

Most Boomers are not thinking about leaving something behind; they
want to get something done today. Taking care of their own immediate interests will be the way in which, without meaning to, they create the legacy
they leave behind. Once again, it is the Boomer focus on self that winds up
spilling over into helping others.

Speaking to Boomers about their legacies won't motivate them as much as
addressing their current needs and priorities. It is often said that Boomers
may be the first generation in American history to leave less for the next generation than they were bequeathed by the prior one. Whether or not this truly
reflects their spending and saving, it accurately expresses Boomer values and
interests. Boomers grew up living for today and not worrying about the future. They continue to ignore the future in favor of the present moment.

Boomers live in the moment. They fix things when they need to. They
spend what they have. They invent what they like themselves. They intend
to stay engaged, even working. They want to have fun, not make sacrifices.
They want to sustain a youthful blitheness forever. Boomers are carrying a
middle age–less mindset into the future.

Winning the Race

In Aesop's classic fable of the tortoise and the hare, perseverance pays off
for the tortoise. Its steady determination to keep going and stay in the

race makes for victory in the end. It is an apt metaphor for Generation Ageless.

Middle age–less Boomers would probably be quite content to live life as turtles, for turtles have the capacity to live for centuries. This stems from the fact that turtles don't grow old. They age, of course, but their organs do not break down over time. If not for disease, predators, and accidents, turtles might literally live forever.[8]

A turtle named Harriet that Charles Darwin took from the Galápagos Islands during the famous voyage that inspired his theory of evolution made international news when she died in 2006 at the age of 171. A 250-year-old turtle in an Indian zoo captured by British sailors during the reign of King George II died that same year. Turtles are the true Methuselahs of the animal kingdom. Boomers should be so lucky.

Boomers are determined to stay involved and continue to matter. Old age is not something that they will accept readily and without complaint. Boomers have always made a difference, and they intend to keep doing so.

	Yesterday...	Today...
Growing old	Slowing down	Keeping pace
Staying active	Walking, shopping, visiting	Running, skiing, traveling
A snooze	An afternoon nap	An Ambien
An adventure	Trying a new restaurant	Trying a new country
The authority	Cronkite	Oprah
Favorite tunes	Bootlegged	Downloaded
Being expressive	Tie dye	A tattoo
Having fun	Supper clubs, bridge	Girls' night out, Texas hold'em
Enjoying a feast	A nice steak	Free-range organic chicken
Job success	Corner office	Home office
Mental health	est, TM, Synanon	Zoloft, Paxil, Prozac
The environment	Ozone hole	Melting Poles

Figure 10-5: Boomer Lives

Not all Boomers will be able to live a middle age–less style of life. But even if only a portion does, their numbers will still be huge. There is no escaping the continued presence and impact of Baby Boomers. Like the tortoise, they are in the race to go the distance, and by the mere fact of their determination they expect to win.

Such ambitions do not come without costs. But they offer new rewards and satisfactions, too. Boomers may not enjoy the golden years of their parents, but they will pioneer the middle age–less years that future generations will experience as well. Boomers want to matter, and if for no other reason than numbers alone, they will do so.

What Boomers want from marketers is a hard shell and a clear path. With protections and opportunities, they feel sure they can win. At the very least, Boomers want to try, and that means an ageless, undiminished presence in the consumer marketplace.

Smart marketers will find a place for Generation Ageless Boomers in their brand franchises. The rewards of doing so will flow both ways. Boomers will matter, both for themselves and for the companies that offer them what they need and want.

Slow and steady wins the race. Boomers can feel it. They know that it's true and they want to make it so in their lives. Perhaps this idea is new to us today, but Aesop knew it millennia ago. For Boomers, it's time now to make it true once more.

Appendix:

Selected Study Data in Total and by Segments

LIFESTYLE ATTITUDES: *Total Agree*
(Top 2 box agreement on a 4-point agree/disagree scale)

	TOTAL BOOMERS	STRAIGHT ARROWS	DUE DILIGENTS	MAXIMIZERS	SIDELINERS	DISS/ CONTENTEDS	RE-ACTIVISTS
People should try to maintain a youthful spirit about life	96.6%	96.6%	95.7%	97.0%	97.6%	96.9%	95.4%
The possibilities afforded to us by technology are only going to continue to grow	96.6%	97.5%	99.4%	94.6%	97.6%	95.3%	94.2%
I trust my instincts	95.2%	95.1%	90.8%	96.3%	95.5%	95.4%	96.5%
I am very passionate about the causes I care about	94.8%	97.2%	86.9%	97.4%	88.6%	100.0%	97.7%
The actions of a single individual can make a big difference in life	94.8%	96.9%	94.5%	96.0%	88.7%	96.7%	96.3%

	TOTAL BOOMERS	STRAIGHT ARROWS	DUE DILIGENTS	MAXIMIZERS	SIDELINERS	DISS/ CONTENTEDS	RE-ACTIVISTS
People have a responsibility to leave the world a better place than they found it	94.2%	95.2%	97.0%	93.5%	86.5%	99.7%	98.1%
We are all responsible to leave the world a better place when we leave it	93.8%	94.3%	96.0%	98.7%	83.4%	99.1%	97.5%
I think it is important for all of us to look for ways in which we can get involved and improve society	93.7%	96.3%	87.8%	95.5%	83.8%	100.0%	100.0%
Young people can learn a lot from my generation	92.6%	93.6%	93.6%	97.2%	92.7%	95.1%	83.5%
There is no reason why young people and older people can't enjoy the same kinds of things	92.2%	92.2%	95.0%	92.8%	87.7%	93.9%	94.8%
I like to keep up with politics and public issues	92.2%	94.8%	82.3%	85.3%	89.6%	99.8%	99.8%
I have been able to make a meaningful contribution in my job	90.8%	91.7%	92.7%	90.4%	90.3%	96.2%	85.9%
I know how to use technology to make my life more interesting and more enjoyable	90.2%	88.8%	93.6%	89.9%	87.8%	96.4%	91.3%

	TOTAL BOOMERS	STRAIGHT ARROWS	DUE DILIGENTS	MAXIMIZERS	SIDELINERS	DISS/ CONTENTEDS	RE-ACTIVISTS
Without passion and zeal by individual people, important social problems won't ever get solved	90.2%	88.5%	90.0%	93.2%	83.4%	99.6%	94.8%
I feel a responsibility to help others out and support the common good	89.9%	93.4%	88.1%	95.1%	73.6%	96.0%	97.1%
The challenges our society faces in the future are formidable and alarming	89.6%	88.3%	83.5%	93.9%	85.9%	94.7%	94.5%
There is no reason that you have to feel less vital and energetic as you get older	89.0%	86.8%	89.2%	92.8%	90.6%	88.4%	87.5%
Businesses have a social responsibility to their employees and to the community	88.9%	86.6%	92.8%	91.4%	80.0%	96.1%	96.9%
In the future, older people will be much more active and engaged than older people in the past	88.7%	87.3%	92.1%	93.2%	84.3%	90.1%	90.4%
I like knowing what young people are doing and creating	87.7%	86.2%	95.2%	86.8%	79.5%	95.3%	94.0%

	TOTAL BOOMERS	STRAIGHT ARROWS	DUE DILIGENTS	MAXIMIZERS	SIDELINERS	DISS/ CONTENTEDS	RE-ACTIVISTS
Living a clean, moral life is a very important value	87.4%	96.9%	88.4%	83.2%	87.4%	80.6%	74.3%
I keep an eye out for new things to try or to learn	87.3%	85.2%	87.1%	91.4%	82.7%	89.9%	93.0%
I believe that life is a set of endless opportuni- ties no matter what your age	87.3%	88.9%	90.2%	90.5%	80.8%	77.9%	92.8%
I like to discover new ways to use things and teach them to others	86.1%	87.0%	86.3%	89.1%	77.0%	88.0%	92.5%
Private property is sacred	86.1%	92.3%	79.7%	86.4%	93.2%	72.5%	74.5%
A woman does not have to have a man to be happy	85.5%	75.9%	89.6%	93.7%	84.5%	85.7%	96.4%
We can solve the social problems we face today if everybody would just do their one small part to help	85.3%	86.0%	85.1%	93.5%	76.8%	85.6%	86.9%
Duty comes before pleasure	85.2%	91.6%	81.9%	89.0%	82.3%	79.3%	76.6%
Our charities, faith-based organizations and families should be playing a greater role in creating stronger communities and to help people in need	84.1%	94.3%	86.6%	93.9%	80.6%	71.8%	61.5%

	TOTAL BOOMERS	STRAIGHT ARROWS	DUE DILIGENTS	MAXIMIZERS	SIDELINERS	DISS/ CONTENTEDS	RE-ACTIVISTS
It is important to learn from the past and to do things in a proven way	83.0%	87.0%	88.7%	84.5%	82.9%	79.6%	70.7%
Government is far too involved in our personal lives	81.8%	82.0%	86.0%	73.6%	87.8%	78.4%	81.0%
Personal enrichment is very important to me	81.8%	79.7%	87.6%	87.9%	77.2%	80.5%	83.0%
In every situation, I have a very clear sense of the right and the wrong thing to do	80.6%	90.5%	71.4%	81.4%	78.4%	70.2%	73.2%
Government isn't the best answer for most of the problems we face	80.5%	91.9%	87.3%	80.2%	85.1%	54.1%	59.5%
I don't take myself too seriously, I laugh at myself all the time	80.3%	80.0%	79.5%	75.8%	82.0%	78.3%	84.9%
I feel the need not to live beyond my means	80.3%	85.7%	79.3%	72.5%	78.9%	85.7%	76.1%
Business is too concerned with profits and not with public responsibility	80.2%	72.3%	82.1%	85.2%	73.0%	92.9%	93.9%
I am concerned about trying to stay in shape	80.0%	76.0%	86.0%	78.8%	77.9%	81.2%	88.1%

	TOTAL BOOMERS	STRAIGHT ARROWS	DUE DILIGENTS	MAXIMIZERS	SIDELINERS	DISS/ CONTENTEDS	RE-ACTIVISTS
Life should be a never-ending series of adventures	79.8%	72.9%	87.6%	87.5%	78.2%	75.7%	85.6%
I am concerned about taking care of myself	79.6%	75.2%	92.2%	83.6%	71.3%	78.3%	88.4%
Discovering more about myself has always been important to me	79.4%	78.6%	83.6%	85.4%	67.0%	75.7%	91.5%
It is important in my personal life today to stretch myself and try new things	78.1%	72.6%	83.6%	81.6%	71.7%	79.8%	90.5%
I have a very clear idea of my objectives and goals in life	78.1%	86.3%	67.0%	77.0%	74.4%	72.8%	76.6%
I am determined to get more out of life than I am currently getting	77.3%	70.6%	89.6%	89.4%	72.6%	67.0%	83.1%
We expect too much from government today; we need individuals to take more responsibility and be more accountable	76.9%	91.2%	79.0%	81.2%	86.5%	41.5%	46.5%
I try to avoid getting stuck in the same old routine in the way I live my life	76.8%	74.7%	69.6%	83.1%	72.4%	71.4%	88.6%

	TOTAL BOOMERS	STRAIGHT ARROWS	DUE DILIGENTS	MAXIMIZERS	SIDELINERS	DISS/ CONTENTEDS	RE-ACTIVISTS
However much I succeed in the future, it will be more than enough as long as I do it on my own terms	76.5%	69.1%	80.7%	81.8%	75.3%	87.1%	80.2%
There are many areas of life in which I would like to see a return to traditional standards	75.9%	94.8%	87.0%	84.9%	80.1%	48.8%	26.8%
Being spiritually fulfilled is extremely important to me	75.8%	99.0%	88.6%	87.2%	50.1%	49.4%	54.0%
The American dream is something I really want to achieve	75.3%	80.6%	76.1%	80.0%	78.7%	67.2%	58.3%
I am very sure that one day I will get to where I want to be in life	75.0%	75.7%	83.0%	83.0%	71.3%	53.3%	76.9%
My job has given me an interesting and worthwhile challenge	74.9%	78.2%	74.6%	68.4%	80.9%	71.0%	68.9%
I am always ready to tackle something new	74.3%	70.0%	71.6%	81.5%	68.9%	70.9%	87.3%
I am always thinking about the threats and challenges we face in our society and the solutions it will take to fix them	73.9%	71.6%	65.8%	76.9%	63.3%	90.4%	86.7%

	TOTAL BOOMERS	STRAIGHT ARROWS	DUE DILIGENTS	MAXIMIZERS	SIDELINERS	DISS/ CONTENTEDS	RE-ACTIVISTS
We will all need to start making more sacrifices today in order for the future to be okay	73.6%	72.3%	81.5%	79.3%	56.4%	79.8%	85.2%
No matter what, duty always comes before pleasure	73.4%	83.8%	69.2%	68.3%	71.4%	69.1%	64.2%
Having children is a very important value	72.8%	86.0%	80.1%	79.0%	66.2%	54.6%	51.4%
Our society has become too dependent on technology and doesn't know how to function without it	72.3%	74.7%	69.1%	76.7%	72.0%	68.0%	67.6%
What we are lacking most in America today is a compelling vision of the future	72.0%	63.9%	75.8%	71.9%	68.9%	83.9%	84.7%
It is essential to keep up with the latest new technology products and services	72.0%	65.6%	70.3%	87.3%	68.8%	75.3%	73.3%
People's privacy is being destroyed	71.9%	56.6%	70.8%	78.6%	69.4%	90.5%	92.2%
Being a good grandparent is my top priority in life	71.6%	76.4%	83.0%	68.8%	55.7%	68.7%	78.1%

	TOTAL BOOMERS	STRAIGHT ARROWS	DUE DILIGENTS	MAXIMIZERS	SIDELINERS	DISS/ CONTENTEDS	RE-ACTIVISTS
I know my neighbors on a first-name basis	71.4%	71.6%	66.6%	75.0%	68.0%	75.6%	73.1%
It is important for people to continually challenge the established way of doing things	70.1%	57.8%	68.2%	81.3%	56.2%	87.5%	96.2%
People should be entitled to the best medical care as a social right	69.3%	50.7%	74.9%	89.4%	57.8%	91.0%	88.9%
I am always trying to think of something new and different to work toward	69.2%	62.7%	71.2%	74.4%	63.1%	67.5%	86.2%
I am sick and tired of hearing people attack patriotism, morality, and other American values	69.0%	86.0%	70.0%	70.5%	76.6%	42.0%	33.9%
There is almost no job that a man can do that a woman cannot do just as well	68.8%	50.6%	75.4%	78.6%	68.8%	77.8%	89.0%
I have begun to slow down and do things at a less hurried pace	68.7%	73.1%	74.5%	66.2%	65.5%	63.9%	64.6%
I am able to do most things better than the average person	68.6%	63.0%	65.3%	79.3%	68.1%	65.8%	74.3%

	TOTAL BOOMERS	STRAIGHT ARROWS	DUE DILIGENTS	MAXIMIZERS	SIDELINERS	DISS/ CONTENTEDS	RE-ACTIVISTS
People my age can learn a lot from young people	68.5%	64.1%	76.3%	74.9%	54.2%	76.3%	81.3%
Many of the best things about life today were pioneered and made possible by the actions and contribu- tions of the Baby Boomer generation	68.2%	63.8%	70.6%	75.5%	72.5%	63.7%	65.3%
I have had a chance to get ahead in my job	68.1%	70.4%	60.0%	59.9%	73.4%	64.8%	71.9%
I feel a growing need to share important occasions with others	67.0%	71.6%	80.8%	79.0%	52.7%	53.3%	62.0%
Once I get some- thing estab- lished and working in my life, I don't like to change it	66.4%	70.6%	77.1%	63.5%	68.4%	69.5%	48.2%
Whenever life closes in on me, I just pick up and start over	66.0%	65.2%	68.1%	67.1%	69.4%	66.7%	60.2%
I am very concerned about my ability to live indepen- dently and on my own in the years ahead	65.8%	60.6%	76.3%	73.4%	61.2%	68.6%	66.6%

	TOTAL BOOMERS	STRAIGHT ARROWS	DUE DILIGENTS	MAXIMIZERS	SIDELINERS	DISS/ CONTENTEDS	RE-ACTIVISTS
Periodically, it is fun to change things about myself just for the sake of changing	65.7%	63.4%	79.4%	79.4%	49.0%	61.4%	72.6%
No matter how hard I try, I never seem to have enough time to do everything I need to do	65.6%	58.7%	77.6%	67.4%	59.9%	71.1%	75.4%
If I have a problem I prefer to work it out alone	65.4%	62.5%	68.2%	61.4%	74.0%	63.5%	63.0%
I would rather have too much to do and risk being stressed than too little to do and be bored	65.3%	66.4%	66.0%	54.8%	71.6%	54.2%	70.7%
My job has given me the ability to express myself	65.2%	68.1%	58.6%	58.9%	66.7%	71.0%	64.4%
My sex life is satisfactory	65.1%	70.0%	52.7%	63.6%	64.6%	63.4%	65.8%
Even though there are many things I would like to own, I prefer spending my money on experiences that will enrich my life—like travel, vacations, theater, good restaurants, etc.	65.1%	56.0%	67.8%	68.9%	61.2%	75.5%	78.5%

	TOTAL BOOMERS	STRAIGHT ARROWS	DUE DILIGENTS	MAXIMIZERS	SIDELINERS	DISS/ CONTENTEDS	RE-ACTIVISTS
I am better off now than my parents were at my age	65.1%	71.2%	61.5%	57.8%	58.2%	71.0%	67.5%
Hard work always pays off	65.0%	79.9%	66.9%	65.1%	67.0%	43.5%	39.9%
Everybody should be free to do his or her own thing	64.7%	44.9%	72.4%	72.6%	65.1%	85.1%	82.5%
To achieve the American dream, you pretty much have to go your own way and do it on your own terms	64.5%	59.8%	78.5%	61.1%	72.9%	62.8%	58.3%
People should be entitled to a secure retirement as a social right	64.3%	45.8%	72.0%	78.3%	60.5%	83.2%	79.7%
If I had the chance to start over in life I would do things much differently	63.7%	57.0%	78.4%	79.0%	63.4%	48.5%	61.4%
Unless the media embraces a social problem, it will never get the money and attention it needs to get solved	63.6%	50.9%	64.5%	78.5%	50.8%	79.5%	84.0%
If I just work hard enough, eventually I will achieve what I want	62.8%	69.8%	59.9%	74.3%	62.2%	46.8%	47.1%

	TOTAL BOOMERS	STRAIGHT ARROWS	DUE DILIGENTS	MAXIMIZERS	SIDELINERS	DISS/ CONTENTEDS	RE-ACTIVISTS
My job has left me enough free time to pursue my outside interests	62.3%	70.0%	61.7%	54.6%	67.2%	48.6%	56.5%
Lately, I have had to admit to myself that like it or not I am getting to be an old person	62.0%	62.1%	65.4%	63.4%	59.9%	66.6%	58.0%
In the future, I intend to focus less on myself and more on others	61.6%	67.0%	61.1%	73.9%	34.2%	55.1%	78.4%
All the new consumer electronics in music and video make my life more enjoyable	61.5%	54.7%	65.1%	78.2%	57.2%	59.1%	63.6%
The best way to get social problems solved is to work through non-governmental organizations that have dedicated budgets and a single purpose	61.4%	71.4%	66.6%	65.8%	69.1%	30.2%	38.0%
Economic well-being in this country is unfairly distributed	61.3%	41.4%	58.7%	77.1%	49.6%	86.4%	91.8%
The best years of Baby Boomers are yet to come	60.8%	59.1%	70.6%	83.1%	48.6%	49.4%	57.8%

	TOTAL BOOMERS	STRAIGHT ARROWS	DUE DILIGENTS	MAXIMIZERS	SIDELINERS	DISS/ CONTENTEDS	RE-ACTIVISTS
There is too much concern with equality and not enough with law and order	59.7%	79.4%	61.5%	50.0%	83.1%	29.2%	10.3%
I like to seek out and try once-in-a-lifetime experiences	59.6%	51.1%	62.0%	73.7%	52.6%	60.7%	70.9%
I feel the need for something more meaningful to work toward in my life	59.5%	49.8%	71.7%	82.6%	40.6%	58.8%	74.3%
I have a strong connection with the community where I live	59.4%	68.9%	65.0%	63.3%	37.7%	57.9%	61.3%
I feel that my personal values and point of view are shared by most Americans today	59.0%	66.4%	65.3%	66.2%	59.8%	48.4%	35.3%
I like the idea of starting a new career or job if and when I retire	58.3%	53.1%	67.4%	65.9%	54.4%	43.6%	68.2%
I feel that I have achieved the right balance of time in my life for all the things that are important to me	58.2%	64.3%	57.4%	54.1%	57.6%	45.0%	58.0%

	TOTAL BOOMERS	STRAIGHT ARROWS	DUE DILIGENTS	MAXIMIZERS	SIDELINERS	DISS/ CONTENTEDS	RE-ACTIVISTS
My job has offered me security	57.4%	62.8%	41.9%	55.6%	62.6%	62.7%	47.7%
I enjoy keeping up with the new trends and the latest happenings	57.2%	48.1%	61.3%	68.4%	54.7%	64.7%	61.7%
I do not see myself as facing any limits whatsoever because of my age	56.9%	49.7%	54.4%	71.1%	64.2%	52.3%	51.7%
I am interested in spending at least some time in a rural or agricultural living situation	56.7%	50.5%	69.2%	68.2%	54.3%	48.2%	57.9%
I have never felt trapped by a lack of training	56.5%	52.9%	61.2%	47.0%	62.9%	62.9%	58.8%
I feel that I have achieved the American dream	55.5%	63.2%	46.4%	46.3%	53.4%	53.6%	58.4%
Government isn't doing enough to help those at the bottom	54.4%	35.1%	64.0%	62.6%	38.3%	81.2%	88.6%
I need to feel more comfortable with all the new technologies that are around us	54.2%	49.4%	65.3%	66.3%	48.5%	52.9%	53.4%

	TOTAL BOOMERS	STRAIGHT ARROWS	DUE DILIGENTS	MAXIMIZERS	SIDELINERS	DISS/ CONTENTEDS	RE-ACTIVISTS
The good opportunities I saw as a young person were there for me when I got older	53.6%	64.6%	68.4%	45.1%	46.5%	46.1%	42.1%
I like to compete—it makes me perform better and whatever I can get at the end is more rewarding	53.6%	53.9%	58.0%	59.0%	48.9%	54.8%	59.9%
Most people will never achieve the American dream	53.5%	38.2%	54.0%	53.2%	59.5%	65.9%	72.2%
Lots of things we take for granted wouldn't be possible without government policies and guar–antees	52.4%	39.9%	53.2%	63.9%	42.0%	81.6%	65.5%
More and more, I look to religion as a source of comfort in my life	52.3%	90.1%	59.9%	63.5%	27.4%	12.6%	8.5%
Casual, premarital sexual relations are morally wrong	51.8%	84.9%	54.5%	48.6%	41.7%	16.6%	14.6%
Men and women are born with the same human nature, it's the way they're brought up that makes them different	51.2%	47.5%	47.7%	59.4%	53.9%	40.8%	55.1%

	TOTAL BOOMERS	STRAIGHT ARROWS	DUE DILIGENTS	MAXIMIZERS	SIDELINERS	DISS/ CONTENTEDS	RE-ACTIVISTS
Going online makes me feel more connected to other people	50.9%	45.7%	50.5%	56.8%	47.2%	54.9%	59.5%
Aging is inevitable so we just have to get used to slowing down and doing less	50.3%	50.2%	65.4%	40.6%	54.6%	54.3%	42.5%
I like being the first to know about new technologies	50.3%	45.8%	54.2%	62.1%	44.7%	47.7%	54.2%
I have been able to be as successful as I desired	49.7%	54.9%	48.8%	38.0%	47.6%	58.2%	48.9%
Many of the social problems facing us today are rooted in the mistakes or failures of Baby Boomers	48.6%	51.7%	50.7%	54.3%	44.8%	35.5%	47.2%
I work hard at coming out on top in every situation— from the least important to the most important	48.6%	53.8%	53.2%	55.4%	47.7%	34.4%	36.1%
These days I have less and less time for myself	48.0%	41.0%	55.6%	54.2%	47.0%	45.7%	53.9%
Police should not hesitate to use force to maintain order	47.7%	62.0%	52.9%	42.3%	62.4%	20.2%	13.6%

	TOTAL BOOMERS	STRAIGHT ARROWS	DUE DILIGENTS	MAXIMIZERS	SIDELINERS	DISS/ CONTENTEDS	RE-ACTIVISTS
After my children have left home, I will have more time and energy in the years ahead to do something important	47.7%	40.4%	56.9%	55.3%	48.2%	41.6%	52.0%
I don't want to be reminded that I am getting older	47.5%	41.1%	51.5%	56.6%	49.4%	46.3%	47.8%
In my job, I have been able to earn the kind of money I wanted to earn	47.5%	54.0%	43.6%	33.7%	47.5%	56.7%	46.4%
Basically we are a racist nation	47.2%	26.3%	54.7%	70.4%	32.8%	58.3%	77.3%
I often feel that something is missing from my life	46.8%	37.0%	50.8%	62.2%	47.1%	44.8%	50.1%
The best ideas for solving social problems usually come from those who are older, with more experience	46.2%	56.5%	52.6%	44.6%	47.3%	34.3%	26.2%
Working through the system is the best way to get things done in life	44.7%	52.5%	45.9%	52.5%	38.3%	36.1%	31.9%
I never look back, I always look forward	43.3%	43.6%	43.7%	49.9%	41.1%	43.6%	37.9%

	TOTAL BOOMERS	STRAIGHT ARROWS	DUE DILIGENTS	MAXIMIZERS	SIDELINERS	DISS/ CONTENTEDS	RE-ACTIVISTS
I need to find more excitement and sensation to my life	42.1%	28.6%	52.2%	65.2%	41.3%	39.5%	42.9%
It bothers me that advertisers don't care as much about my generation as they did when we were younger	41.0%	41.5%	53.4%	48.4%	35.5%	36.7%	33.7%
I believe that my health over the next 10 years will restrict my abilities and capabilities	40.8%	39.8%	51.9%	30.7%	45.9%	42.8%	38.3%
We cannot solve our biggest problems without govern-ment's help	40.6%	22.0%	46.6%	43.3%	35.3%	72.9%	63.6%
I am concerned about buying products that express my own style and personality	40.5%	39.4%	41.1%	49.3%	37.0%	34.5%	41.2%
Americans should get used to the fact that our wealth is limited and most of us are not likely to become better off than we are now	40.3%	29.7%	41.8%	54.5%	38.3%	51.7%	43.7%

	TOTAL BOOMERS	STRAIGHT ARROWS	DUE DILIGENTS	MAXIMIZERS	SIDELINERS	DISS/ CONTENTEDS	RE-ACTIVISTS
When I was younger, I never thought I would feel as old as I do today	40.0%	36.6%	52.3%	37.4%	41.1%	52.0%	33.4%
I always try to act my age	39.8%	49.9%	35.2%	39.6%	34.3%	28.7%	34.5%
All I want out of life is enough to be comfortable; more than that is not worth the effort	39.2%	33.1%	59.6%	34.2%	38.4%	53.2%	37.7%
The institution of marriage is becoming obsolete	38.0%	37.2%	38.9%	50.3%	39.5%	37.2%	24.7%
Material things like the car I drive and the house I live in are really important to me	37.4%	36.7%	40.7%	51.0%	38.3%	37.1%	21.4%
I'd be willing to work at a boring job as long as the pay is good	37.2%	37.1%	40.8%	37.3%	42.8%	45.1%	22.8%
Even when there is a new and better way to do things, I prefer to stick with what I know as long as it's working for me	36.5%	41.9%	39.0%	44.7%	35.9%	28.0%	19.9%

	TOTAL BOOMERS	STRAIGHT ARROWS	DUE DILIGENTS	MAXIMIZERS	SIDELINERS	DISS/ CONTENTEDS	RE-ACTIVISTS
It is extremely important for me to be seen as someone willing to defy convention	35.9%	21.1%	32.7%	42.5%	27.1%	57.9%	63.3%
It is important to me to keep my look current and fashionable	35.8%	32.2%	41.4%	50.8%	30.0%	26.6%	36.9%
I am concerned about doing whatever I can to make myself look attractive	35.1%	34.4%	42.8%	41.4%	32.1%	27.2%	33.3%
I like to change the kind of person I am every so often	34.3%	23.3%	41.3%	53.7%	28.7%	32.7%	42.1%
I don't think I'll have to do anything extraordinary to reach my goals; eventually, I'll just get there	34.1%	34.8%	37.6%	26.6%	39.0%	38.7%	28.8%
I am looking forward to the day when my children are out of the house	32.4%	26.0%	37.2%	44.1%	29.7%	39.3%	30.6%
In this world, sometimes you have to compromise your principles	31.6%	21.7%	35.9%	37.4%	36.5%	37.4%	34.4%

	TOTAL BOOMERS	STRAIGHT ARROWS	DUE DILIGENTS	MAXIMIZERS	SIDELINERS	DISS/ CONTENTEDS	RE-ACTIVISTS
I have not been able to make as much money as I desired	31.1%	36.3%	29.3%	21.0%	29.7%	25.6%	36.7%
I am more concerned than ever about protecting myself and not taking any risks at all	29.5%	28.0%	25.0%	37.7%	36.8%	26.4%	19.2%
A woman has the right to put her own self-fulfillment ahead of her obligations to her husband and children	28.0%	11.4%	40.7%	34.3%	23.9%	32.6%	52.5%
My best years are behind me	25.9%	24.8%	22.0%	16.4%	35.8%	31.5%	24.2%
I don't expect to get much pleasure from my work; work is just what you do to earn a living	23.2%	16.9%	26.8%	21.6%	24.6%	40.3%	23.5%
In the future, I intend to focus more on myself and less on others	22.7%	11.8%	30.6%	25.7%	32.4%	25.7%	23.0%
I'm more concerned with myself than with the world	22.7%	16.9%	20.7%	25.3%	44.7%	14.3%	8.4%

	TOTAL BOOMERS	STRAIGHT ARROWS	DUE DILIGENTS	MAXIMIZERS	SIDELINERS	DISS/ CONTENTEDS	RE-ACTIVISTS
The American dream is more about the things I have than the way I live my life	22.1%	16.5%	28.6%	35.9%	15.9%	21.2%	24.2%
I want to do everything I possibly can to look 10 or 15 years younger	21.2%	18.7%	27.5%	32.6%	17.8%	19.7%	16.3%
The future belongs to the next generation my gen-eration won't have much to do with it	16.8%	15.9%	18.3%	15.0%	18.5%	22.2%	13.9%
I worry all the time about getting older	15.5%	11.6%	17.3%	15.9%	19.6%	22.2%	12.9%
There is little for people my age to look forward to besides getting older and coping with old age	14.4%	12.7%	12.7%	11.0%	19.3%	18.8%	13.5%
Taking care of a home and raising children is not as fulfill-ing for a woman as having a job or a career	12.8%	7.2%	6.6%	14.9%	12.7%	12.6%	27.1%
People who accept things are better off than those who try to change them	12.5%	11.6%	29.2%	20.4%	8.9%	3.8%	4.9%

	TOTAL BOOMERS	STRAIGHT ARROWS	DUE DILIGENTS	MAXIMIZERS	SIDELINERS	DISS/ CONTENTEDS	RE-ACTIVISTS
I am interested in spending at least some time in a communal or collective living situation	11.8%	7.9%	12.5%	14.6%	8.6%	9.1%	23.2%
You can usually rely on big institutions to do the right thing	9.3%	10.4%	8.1%	16.3%	9.2%	3.0%	3.9%

IDENTIFY WITH MOST: *Integrity over Success*

	TOTAL BOOMERS	STRAIGHT ARROWS	DUE DILIGENTS	MAXIMIZERS	SIDELINERS	DISS/ CONTENTEDS	RE-ACTIVISTS
Integrity	94.0%	95.7%	89.5%	97.3%	86.3%	99.3%	97.7%
Success	6.0%	4.3%	10.5%	2.7%	13.7%	0.7%	2.3%

IDENTIFY WITH MOST: *Learning to live with the lines over Getting plastic surgery to get rid of the lines*

	TOTAL BOOMERS	STRAIGHT ARROWS	DUE DILIGENTS	MAXIMIZERS	SIDELINERS	DISS/ CONTENTEDS	RE-ACTIVISTS
Learning to live with the lines	93.7%	96.7%	91.2%	91.9%	93.6%	94.0%	91.1%
Getting plastic surgery to get rid of the lines	6.3%	3.3%	8.8%	8.1%	6.4%	6.0%	8.9%

IDENTIFY WITH MOST: *Individuality over Conformity*

	TOTAL BOOMERS	STRAIGHT ARROWS	DUE DILIGENTS	MAXIMIZERS	SIDELINERS	DISS/ CONTENTEDS	RE-ACTIVISTS
Individuality	88.7%	81.1%	89.2%	87.1%	90.9%	95.6%	100.0%
Conformity	11.3%	18.9%	10.8%	12.9%	9.1%	4.4%	0%

IDENTIFY WITH MOST: *Hungry for information over Overwhelmed by information*

	TOTAL BOOMERS	STRAIGHT ARROWS	DUE DILIGENTS	MAXIMIZERS	SIDELINERS	DISS/ CONTENTEDS	RE-ACTIVISTS
Hungry for information	84.0%	80.3%	78.9%	87.4%	80.5%	89.9%	93.6%
Over-whelmed by information	16.0%	19.7%	21.1%	12.6%	19.5%	10.1%	6.4%

IDENTIFY WITH MOST: *Simplifying over Packing more in*

	TOTAL BOOMERS	STRAIGHT ARROWS	DUE DILIGENTS	MAXIMIZERS	SIDELINERS	DISS/ CONTENTEDS	RE-ACTIVISTS
Simplifying	82.1%	83.4%	90.9%	73.0%	82.6%	84.5%	81.0%
Packing more in	17.9%	16.6%	9.1%	27.0%	17.4%	15.5%	19.0%

IDENTIFY WITH MOST: *Following your own instincts over Listening to experts*

	TOTAL BOOMERS	STRAIGHT ARROWS	DUE DILIGENTS	MAXIMIZERS	SIDELINERS	DISS/ CONTENTEDS	RE-ACTIVISTS
Following your own instincts	80.4%	75.9%	91.7%	70.2%	85.3%	78.6%	87.7%
Listening to experts	19.6%	24.1%	8.3%	29.8%	14.7%	21.4%	12.3%

IDENTIFY WITH MOST: *Friends who share your values over Friends who have different values*

	TOTAL BOOMERS	STRAIGHT ARROWS	DUE DILIGENTS	MAXIMIZERS	SIDELINERS	DISS/ CONTENTEDS	RE-ACTIVISTS
Friends who share your values	80.3%	86.9%	83.6%	68.6%	90.4%	78.8%	62.9%
Friends who have different values	19.7%	13.1%	16.4%	31.4%	9.6%	21.2%	37.1%

IDENTIFY WITH MOST: *Comfortable with change over Resistant to change*

	TOTAL BOOMERS	STRAIGHT ARROWS	DUE DILIGENTS	MAXIMIZERS	SIDELINERS	DISS/ CONTENTEDS	RE-ACTIVISTS
Comfortable with change	76.7%	74.5%	65.5%	87.7%	68.0%	78.5%	88.8%
Resistant to change	23.3%	25.5%	34.5%	12.3%	32.0%	21.5%	11.2%

IDENTIFY WITH MOST: *Leader over Follower*

	TOTAL BOOMERS	STRAIGHT ARROWS	DUE DILIGENTS	MAXIMIZERS	SIDELINERS	DISS/ CONTENTEDS	RE-ACTIVISTS
Leader	75.1%	73.6%	72.7%	70.4%	72.7%	85.4%	82.4%
Follower	24.9%	26.4%	27.3%	29.6%	27.3%	14.6%	17.6%

IDENTIFY WITH MOST: *Getting a knee replacement over Getting a scooter to get around*

	TOTAL BOOMERS	STRAIGHT ARROWS	DUE DILIGENTS	MAXIMIZERS	SIDELINERS	DISS/ CONTENTEDS	RE-ACTIVISTS
Getting a knee replacement	72.6%	67.5%	63.5%	78.7%	75.3%	76.3%	78.1%
Getting a scooter to get around	27.4%	32.5%	36.5%	21.3%	24.7%	23.7%	21.9%

IDENTIFY WITH MOST: *Idealistic over Cynical*

	TOTAL BOOMERS	STRAIGHT ARROWS	DUE DILIGENTS	MAXIMIZERS	SIDELINERS	DISS/ CONTENTEDS	RE-ACTIVISTS
Idealistic	71.5%	81.5%	67.0%	88.1%	57.4%	54.1%	64.3%
Cynical	28.5%	18.5%	33.0%	11.9%	42.6%	45.9%	35.7%

IDENTIFY WITH MOST: *Looking for answers over Knowing the answers*

	TOTAL BOOMERS	STRAIGHT ARROWS	DUE DILIGENTS	MAXIMIZERS	SIDELINERS	DISS/ CONTENTEDS	RE-ACTIVISTS
Looking for answers	70.4%	66.6%	68.4%	72.6%	55.9%	82.6%	91.0%
Knowing the answers	29.6%	33.4%	31.6%	27.4%	44.1%	17.4%	9.0%

IDENTIFY WITH MOST: *Paring down over Accumulating more*

	TOTAL BOOMERS	STRAIGHT ARROWS	DUE DILIGENTS	MAXIMIZERS	SIDELINERS	DISS/ CONTENTEDS	RE-ACTIVISTS
Paring down	65.7%	69.5%	66.7%	48.4%	59.8%	75.4%	77.9%
Accumulating more	34.3%	30.5%	33.3%	51.6%	40.2%	24.6%	22.1%

IDENTIFY WITH MOST: *Standing out over Fitting in*

	TOTAL BOOMERS	STRAIGHT ARROWS	DUE DILIGENTS	MAXIMIZERS	SIDELINERS	DISS/ CONTENTEDS	RE-ACTIVISTS
Standing out	61.3%	54.6%	43.8%	58.5%	65.3%	64.8%	83.7%
Fitting in	38.7%	45.4%	56.2%	41.5%	34.7%	35.2%	16.3%

IDENTIFY WITH MOST: *Challenge authority over Accept authority*

	TOTAL BOOMERS	STRAIGHT ARROWS	DUE DILIGENTS	MAXIMIZERS	SIDELINERS	DISS/ CONTENTEDS	RE-ACTIVISTS
Challenge authority	61.0%	45.8%	40.8%	64.8%	60.1%	90.3%	88.6%
Accept authority	39.0%	54.2%	59.2%	35.2%	39.9%	9.7%	11.4%

IDENTIFY WITH MOST: *Doing something completely new over Settling down to a routine*

	TOTAL BOOMERS	STRAIGHT ARROWS	DUE DILIGENTS	MAXIMIZERS	SIDELINERS	DISS/ CONTENTEDS	RE-ACTIVISTS
Doing something completely new	60.2%	50.6%	60.3%	66.2%	54.6%	70.0%	77.3%
Settling down to a routine	39.8%	49.4%	39.7%	33.8%	45.4%	30.0%	22.7%

IDENTIFY WITH MOST: *Looking forward to the future over Worried about the future*

	TOTAL BOOMERS	STRAIGHT ARROWS	DUE DILIGENTS	MAXIMIZERS	SIDELINERS	DISS/ CONTENTEDS	RE-ACTIVISTS
Looking forward to the future	59.5%	71.6%	47.8%	66.1%	51.3%	39.0%	57.0%
Worried about the future	40.5%	28.4%	52.2%	33.9%	48.7%	61.0%	43.0%

IDENTIFY WITH MOST: *Content with what you have over Driven to achieve more*

	TOTAL BOOMERS	STRAIGHT ARROWS	DUE DILIGENTS	MAXIMIZERS	SIDELINERS	DISS/ CONTENTEDS	RE-ACTIVISTS
Content with what you have	58.8%	66.5%	67.2%	34.7%	54.7%	78.8%	56.3%
Driven to achieve more	41.2%	33.5%	32.8%	65.3%	45.3%	21.2%	43.7%

IDENTIFY WITH MOST: *Special over Average*

	TOTAL BOOMERS	STRAIGHT ARROWS	DUE DILIGENTS	MAXIMIZERS	SIDELINERS	DISS/ CONTENTEDS	RE-ACTIVISTS
Special	57.7%	56.6%	58.6%	61.4%	51.7%	50.6%	68.1%
Average	42.3%	43.4%	41.4%	38.6%	48.3%	49.4%	31.9%

IDENTIFY WITH MOST: *Making do with less over Finding ways to get more*

	TOTAL BOOMERS	STRAIGHT ARROWS	DUE DILIGENTS	MAXIMIZERS	SIDELINERS	DISS/ CONTENTEDS	RE-ACTIVISTS
Making do with less	56.6%	57.4%	53.7%	51.1%	48.8%	70.2%	65.5%
Finding ways to get more	43.4%	42.6%	46.3%	48.9%	51.2%	29.8%	34.5%

IDENTIFY WITH MOST: *Creative satisfaction over Financial satisfaction*

	TOTAL BOOMERS	STRAIGHT ARROWS	DUE DILIGENTS	MAXIMIZERS	SIDELINERS	DISS/ CONTENTEDS	RE-ACTIVISTS
Creative satisfaction	55.1%	51.6%	69.6%	56.2%	36.3%	59.6%	74.8%
Financial satisfaction	44.9%	48.4%	30.4%	43.8%	63.7%	40.4%	25.2%

IDENTIFY WITH MOST: *Time with yourself over Time with friends*

	TOTAL BOOMERS	STRAIGHT ARROWS	DUE DILIGENTS	MAXIMIZERS	SIDELINERS	DISS/ CONTENTEDS	RE-ACTIVISTS
Time with yourself	52.1%	56.1%	40.9%	47.2%	63.1%	41.9%	46.9%
Time with friends	47.9%	43.9%	59.1%	52.8%	36.9%	58.1%	53.1%

IDENTIFY WITH MOST: *Laid-back over Earnest*

	TOTAL BOOMERS	STRAIGHT ARROWS	DUE DILIGENTS	MAXIMIZERS	SIDELINERS	DISS/ CONTENTEDS	RE-ACTIVISTS
Laid-back	51.5%	44.6%	63.3%	50.7%	49.2%	64.6%	55.2%
Earnest	48.5%	55.4%	36.7%	49.3%	50.8%	35.4%	44.8%

IDENTIFY WITH MOST: *Adjusting to the future as it unfolds over Taking care of the future*

	TOTAL BOOMERS	STRAIGHT ARROWS	DUE DILIGENTS	MAXIMIZERS	SIDELINERS	DISS/ CONTENTEDS	RE-ACTIVISTS
Adjusting to the future as it unfolds	51.3%	53.5%	59.6%	40.5%	58.0%	49.3%	43.9%
Taking care of the future	48.7%	46.5%	40.4%	59.5%	42.0%	50.7%	56.1%

IDENTIFY WITH MOST: *Following your heart over Following your head*

	TOTAL BOOMERS	STRAIGHT ARROWS	DUE DILIGENTS	MAXIMIZERS	SIDELINERS	DISS/ CONTENTEDS	RE-ACTIVISTS
Following your heart	51.0%	44.8%	71.2%	54.7%	42.3%	52.7%	58.3%
Following your head	49.0%	55.2%	28.8%	45.3%	57.7%	47.3%	41.7%

How well each of the following described Baby Boomers in the past
(Top 3 box agreement on a 7-point describes completely/not at all scale)

	TOTAL BOOMERS	STRAIGHT ARROWS	DUE DILIGENTS	MAXIMIZERS	SIDELINERS	DISS/ CONTENTEDS	RE-ACTIVISTS
Rock'n'roll	92.8%	94.7%	96.0%	89.9%	93.2%	89.1%	91.1%
Women's rights	90.4%	91.8%	92.0%	91.9%	86.9%	90.1%	89.7%
Sexual freedom	88.4%	84.5%	93.8%	89.2%	87.3%	90.8%	92.5%
Experimentation	87.9%	86.5%	88.7%	89.5%	86.9%	83.4%	92.6%
Challenging the status quo	87.7%	89.5%	95.7%	83.4%	88.9%	77.7%	87.1%
Youthfulness	87.6%	89.6%	92.6%	88.7%	89.4%	69.9%	86.4%
Having an active lifestyle	86.9%	86.7%	90.9%	88.5%	86.9%	81.3%	86.1%

	TOTAL BOOMERS	STRAIGHT ARROWS	DUE DILIGENTS	MAXIMIZERS	SIDELINERS	DISS/ CONTENTEDS	RE-ACTIVISTS
Risk-taking	85.7%	86.3%	92.6%	92.4%	85.8%	74.9%	78.8%
Playing hard	84.7%	85.3%	91.4%	89.2%	80.8%	76.4%	83.8%
Making a difference	84.5%	82.8%	88.1%	87.2%	83.5%	79.0%	87.2%
Taking on new challenges	84.1%	83.4%	85.7%	90.3%	79.8%	80.9%	85.6%
Social justice	83.6%	87.5%	87.8%	84.5%	78.0%	79.7%	80.2%
Equality	83.3%	86.9%	86.5%	87.3%	78.3%	72.3%	81.7%
Social causes	82.7%	84.9%	85.0%	83.0%	81.6%	73.3%	82.9%
Political activism	82.5%	85.0%	74.8%	88.3%	83.6%	71.0%	80.8%
Shaping the future	81.7%	84.3%	86.5%	83.0%	80.1%	72.0%	79.2%
Protesting	80.6%	78.2%	85.4%	84.9%	80.4%	77.7%	80.1%
Fashion and style	79.7%	81.4%	90.7%	86.7%	73.4%	64.6%	78.4%
Making money	79.5%	80.3%	80.8%	81.8%	80.8%	73.8%	75.7%
Liberalism	78.6%	79.7%	74.6%	77.8%	78.1%	76.1%	81.5%
Environ- mentalism	78.0%	77.8%	88.6%	81.2%	71.3%	68.8%	82.2%
Drugs	77.0%	80.1%	82.7%	79.4%	73.9%	65.7%	74.8%
Making a contribution	76.3%	75.4%	76.1%	79.8%	72.9%	75.9%	79.2%
Spending	76.0%	76.9%	80.5%	79.3%	80.9%	68.2%	65.1%
Luxury	74.2%	78.1%	81.1%	78.5%	76.1%	69.7%	56.5%
Being self- absorbed	70.3%	76.0%	73.0%	71.9%	69.0%	62.3%	60.6%
Radicalism	70.3%	73.9%	71.7%	72.7%	68.9%	61.5%	65.4%
The underdog	68.6%	68.6%	75.2%	75.2%	67.2%	53.6%	67.7%
Celebrity	68.3%	75.9%	71.8%	73.8%	62.5%	58.5%	56.7%
Selfishness	67.7%	73.5%	69.4%	68.0%	68.8%	52.9%	59.8%
Working hard	67.4%	65.8%	73.5%	73.4%	65.6%	65.7%	63.8%
Home and family	65.5%	60.3%	72.6%	78.0%	56.9%	65.5%	70.9%
Charity	62.6%	57.1%	71.6%	74.5%	60.4%	50.2%	66.2%
Selflessness	58.0%	53.8%	59.0%	67.0%	57.9%	59.9%	56.1%
Marriage	55.5%	52.6%	68.0%	66.0%	49.7%	53.3%	51.7%

	TOTAL BOOMERS	STRAIGHT ARROWS	DUE DILIGENTS	MAXIMIZERS	SIDELINERS	DISS/ CONTENTEDS	RE-ACTIVISTS
Debt	48.2%	43.5%	56.9%	60.9%	50.3%	36.0%	43.4%
Conserva-tism	45.6%	44.4%	52.2%	53.5%	49.2%	37.8%	35.0%
A quiet lifestyle	38.8%	30.7%	46.3%	56.1%	36.9%	41.8%	33.9%
Acting their age	37.0%	34.1%	48.8%	47.2%	33.2%	35.6%	30.8%

How well each of the following will describe Baby Boomers in the future
(Top 3 box agreement on a 7-point describes completely/not at all scale)

	TOTAL BOOMERS	STRAIGHT ARROWS	DUE DILIGENTS	MAXIMIZERS	SIDELINERS	DISS/ CONTENTEDS	RE-ACTIVISTS
Having an active lifestyle	85.0%	86.9%	92.5%	88.4%	81.5%	76.0%	81.7%
Making money	83.2%	85.2%	85.9%	86.2%	77.1%	75.3%	86.7%
Home and family	80.1%	79.1%	78.1%	86.7%	80.5%	79.1%	76.6%
Spending	77.2%	77.0%	82.9%	81.8%	78.5%	61.3%	75.7%
Luxury	75.8%	77.1%	70.7%	84.7%	77.2%	67.1%	70.1%
Social causes	74.3%	77.9%	91.0%	81.6%	67.9%	53.5%	68.0%
Debt	74.3%	73.6%	65.7%	76.5%	78.8%	61.1%	80.6%
Youthful-ness	73.3%	75.1%	86.0%	78.4%	62.4%	70.7%	71.4%
Political activism	73.1%	74.1%	79.6%	82.9%	67.4%	59.8%	71.2%
Equality	72.4%	72.7%	81.2%	83.6%	67.3%	56.8%	70.1%
Environ-mentalism	72.4%	70.7%	78.1%	74.6%	67.7%	63.4%	81.3%
Making a contribution	72.3%	73.5%	83.6%	84.3%	66.0%	55.9%	67.0%
Social justice	71.4%	76.1%	83.1%	77.9%	63.6%	51.2%	68.5%
Making a difference	70.6%	70.5%	82.3%	82.7%	62.7%	63.0%	65.1%
Shaping the future	69.3%	74.0%	77.2%	78.5%	61.0%	56.2%	62.7%
Charity	68.4%	69.6%	82.6%	72.8%	60.4%	52.5%	71.7%
A quiet lifestyle	67.0%	65.0%	79.8%	68.9%	68.4%	58.5%	63.8%

	TOTAL BOOMERS	STRAIGHT ARROWS	DUE DILIGENTS	MAXIMIZERS	SIDELINERS	DISS/ CONTENTEDS	RE-ACTIVISTS
Marriage	66.9%	66.4%	69.8%	77.5%	64.3%	57.6%	63.8%
Women's rights	66.6%	64.7%	72.8%	77.0%	59.8%	63.5%	67.0%
Taking on new challenges	66.3%	65.4%	86.3%	80.6%	58.6%	44.8%	62.5%
Working hard	66.2%	67.6%	70.5%	80.5%	59.2%	55.3%	60.7%
Playing hard	61.6%	60.9%	71.6%	76.1%	54.0%	45.4%	60.7%
Conservatism	60.8%	65.6%	61.9%	67.1%	61.7%	40.9%	53.0%
Fashion and style	59.7%	63.8%	66.1%	75.8%	49.0%	41.4%	54.6%
Rock'n'roll	59.4%	58.4%	72.1%	59.8%	59.9%	46.4%	59.2%
Selflessness	59.1%	61.6%	62.7%	68.2%	52.5%	45.2%	58.0%
Challenging the status quo	57.4%	61.6%	62.7%	71.4%	44.8%	50.6%	51.8%
Liberalism	56.3%	53.2%	68.0%	62.4%	47.4%	55.7%	61.4%
Selfishness	55.0%	56.7%	60.6%	54.9%	53.2%	45.0%	55.4%
The underdog	54.8%	54.5%	61.2%	62.5%	47.2%	49.6%	56.4%
Being self-absorbed	54.7%	56.5%	53.8%	56.1%	55.4%	48.9%	52.4%
Risk-taking	54.1%	51.2%	64.0%	84.6%	50.8%	22.8%	43.9%
Sexual freedom	50.4%	42.0%	60.9%	56.7%	51.2%	45.9%	56.6%
Celebrity	48.6%	49.7%	60.7%	57.3%	40.0%	44.1%	42.9%
Experimentation	48.5%	45.9%	56.0%	64.8%	39.5%	36.3%	50.9%
Protesting	45.2%	41.4%	49.2%	66.4%	39.6%	30.4%	45.1%
Drugs	44.3%	45.8%	41.3%	49.4%	44.7%	46.6%	35.5%
Radicalism	42.9%	43.5%	43.0%	61.6%	36.4%	27.8%	39.2%
Acting their age	40.5%	37.4%	49.1%	54.2%	39.3%	33.0%	32.8%

How worried you are about each of the following as you think about your retirement? (*Top 3 box agreement on a 7-point describes completely/not at all scale*)

	TOTAL BOOMERS	STRAIGHT ARROWS	DUE DILIGENTS	MAXIMIZERS	SIDELINERS	DISS/ CONTENTEDS	RE-ACTIVISTS
Having sufficient health-care insurance coverage	70.4%	62.6%	92.2%	67.5%	64.3%	81.6%	79.0%
Getting sick and frail	66.5%	55.7%	75.9%	76.9%	62.6%	71.0%	74.3%
Having enough money to get by on	63.9%	58.2%	78.4%	74.9%	57.0%	62.4%	65.9%
Being able to live independently	62.8%	50.2%	76.9%	76.6%	60.2%	59.0%	71.6%
Not being mentally sharp	62.8%	53.2%	82.5%	77.7%	55.0%	60.7%	66.7%
Being short of energy and vitality	59.4%	51.2%	78.7%	75.3%	50.9%	46.6%	66.8%
No longer being able to live life to the fullest	51.8%	39.4%	67.0%	70.9%	42.4%	56.7%	57.6%
Being in charge of your affairs	50.1%	34.2%	63.2%	73.9%	48.3%	50.9%	51.6%
Not being able to live in your current home	39.6%	24.9%	51.2%	70.4%	37.3%	41.5%	32.2%
Being treated as an old person	37.9%	26.1%	46.4%	61.8%	29.8%	41.1%	40.4%
Not being taken seriously	37.7%	27.2%	46.2%	58.9%	32.8%	20.4%	48.1%
Being bored with your life	35.4%	19.4%	54.2%	59.2%	33.1%	40.9%	31.5%
Being relegated to the sidelines	33.9%	21.5%	41.9%	61.7%	24.9%	27.5%	40.4%
Having enough to do and keep busy	33.8%	15.3%	57.5%	54.9%	32.8%	27.7%	40.4%

	TOTAL BOOMERS	STRAIGHT ARROWS	DUE DILIGENTS	MAXIMIZERS	SIDELINERS	DISS/ CONTENTEDS	RE-ACTIVISTS
Being stuck doing the same old things every day	33.7%	19.6%	51.5%	50.7%	35.2%	29.1%	34.9%
Living some-where that is not vibrant and exciting	29.4%	14.1%	40.5%	51.6%	27.5%	24.4%	35.8%
Being taken advantage of in some scam	28.5%	15.8%	36.6%	57.3%	21.0%	24.4%	31.7%
Not having the opportunity to be in charge of something	26.3%	10.3%	35.3%	52.7%	16.0%	29.4%	37.6%
Finding a community of other people to be with	26.2%	13.1%	41.1%	43.6%	23.8%	27.0%	28.6%
Not being involved in social causes	25.4%	13.3%	29.2%	36.3%	10.9%	35.9%	49.9%
Not being current on what's going on	8.7%	2.8%	9.8%	21.7%	11.3%	1.5%	6.8%

How likely you are to focus your energies and invest your time over the next five to ten years on each of the following?
(Top 3 box agreement on a 7-point describes completely/not at all scale)

	TOTAL BOOMERS	STRAIGHT ARROWS	DUE DILIGENTS	MAXIMIZERS	SIDELINERS	DISS/ CONTENTEDS	RE-ACTIVISTS
Focusing more time and energy on your grand children	80.0%	86.3%	89.5%	73.8%	56.8%	89.2%	95.5%
Spending more time with family	77.2%	78.3%	88.2%	87.9%	66.0%	67.2%	77.0%
Reading more books	76.3%	78.6%	75.3%	82.5%	61.6%	62.7%	93.0%
Getting more out of life	75.4%	69.4%	84.2%	87.3%	63.3%	61.1%	94.8%

	TOTAL BOOMERS	STRAIGHT ARROWS	DUE DILIGENTS	MAXIMIZERS	SIDELINERS	DISS/ CONTENTEDS	RE-ACTIVISTS
Taking more control over your future	73.6%	67.6%	83.8%	87.1%	66.4%	62.1%	82.2%
Doing things I've always wanted to do	73.5%	67.6%	83.6%	86.8%	57.8%	67.1%	91.1%
Having enough money to get by	72.6%	67.5%	76.8%	76.3%	70.0%	76.1%	78.8%
Learning a new skill or hobby	71.0%	68.6%	73.5%	80.7%	60.8%	54.6%	87.4%
Having new adventures that are exciting and fun	70.7%	61.4%	85.0%	85.0%	58.5%	59.5%	89.3%
Planning your retirement	68.1%	63.6%	73.6%	75.8%	62.0%	65.1%	76.6%
Making new friends	67.4%	65.6%	76.7%	86.7%	44.4%	57.6%	82.1%
Saving for/ spending money on my grandchildren	67.4%	70.4%	78.5%	67.8%	56.6%	69.1%	69.5%
Forgiving yourself more	66.7%	69.5%	78.9%	77.4%	45.0%	57.5%	76.1%
Getting more involved in social causes that matter to you	66.1%	65.6%	67.2%	84.3%	25.3%	78.3%	96.4%
Deepening and strengthening your relationship with God	65.3%	95.6%	87.2%	90.9%	32.3%	23.1%	26.0%
Developing new skills and expertise	64.8%	56.9%	82.7%	77.9%	51.6%	34.3%	91.4%
Working to make your community a better place	64.3%	63.8%	67.7%	76.5%	25.9%	81.6%	93.2%

	TOTAL BOOMERS	STRAIGHT ARROWS	DUE DILIGENTS	MAXIMIZERS	SIDELINERS	DISS/ CONTENTEDS	RE-ACTIVISTS
Expressing yourself in more creative ways	63.6%	54.7%	81.4%	79.7%	45.5%	45.5%	88.9%
Unleashing your personal potential	63.1%	53.1%	75.9%	82.8%	49.3%	37.0%	89.0%
Taking courses to learn something new	62.8%	56.7%	77.4%	76.4%	50.3%	33.1%	85.6%
Getting more involved in politics	62.6%	61.6%	61.3%	65.3%	37.7%	76.7%	89.2%
Exploring your potential in new and innovative ways	62.0%	52.5%	76.4%	83.5%	43.7%	38.6%	88.6%
Fulfilling your lifelong dreams and ambitions	61.1%	54.9%	78.5%	82.8%	45.1%	43.8%	71.6%
Traveling and seeing the world	60.3%	53.8%	63.7%	76.9%	43.4%	61.3%	77.5%
Mentoring and helping young people	60.1%	63.6%	61.6%	81.0%	31.3%	47.9%	75.9%
Fighting against feeling old	57.8%	47.0%	73.5%	76.4%	53.5%	43.9%	64.7%
Cutting back on spending, shopping, and buying	57.5%	56.1%	65.3%	63.0%	52.8%	50.0%	60.5%
Excelling in your job	55.0%	47.9%	66.0%	68.7%	47.8%	46.8%	63.5%
Making more money	55.0%	50.0%	74.0%	67.6%	54.0%	40.1%	49.3%
Contributing more time to charity	54.3%	56.7%	66.0%	74.1%	9.9%	49.8%	83.7%
Testing yourself in new ways to prove yourself	54.0%	42.9%	71.0%	77.5%	43.2%	23.9%	73.7%

	TOTAL BOOMERS	STRAIGHT ARROWS	DUE DILIGENTS	MAXIMIZERS	SIDELINERS	DISS/ CONTENTEDS	RE-ACTIVISTS
Helping out my children financially	52.7%	48.0%	68.3%	68.1%	42.8%	42.4%	55.7%
Finding something totally different to do in my life	52.4%	36.1%	73.8%	78.0%	44.2%	26.3%	72.8%
Working to help protect the environment	50.5%	33.1%	64.2%	68.5%	25.7%	68.6%	84.2%
Redefining the purpose of your life	49.4%	35.5%	68.8%	75.9%	42.0%	22.1%	64.2%
Working to fix the inequities in society	48.9%	35.6%	56.0%	73.4%	12.3%	64.7%	89.1%
Focusing more time and energy on your grandchildren	48.9%	55.4%	56.5%	62.1%	33.6%	35.9%	43.8%
Enjoying more of life's luxuries more often	48.6%	41.1%	58.4%	69.6%	48.9%	28.7%	47.2%
Contributing more money to charity	48.6%	53.0%	64.5%	70.5%	6.4%	30.1%	73.2%
Buying some of the things you've always wanted	48.2%	44.6%	58.5%	72.1%	43.0%	28.3%	42.5%
Playing by fewer rules	48.1%	29.8%	54.8%	62.6%	46.3%	48.0%	71.2%
Moving to a new place to live	47.8%	41.1%	58.4%	62.9%	39.4%	32.9%	59.3%
Sharing your religious beliefs and convictions with others	46.1%	84.1%	62.2%	60.2%	9.6%	8.3%	8.7%
Saving for/ spending money on my grandchildren	45.9%	50.3%	57.9%	57.1%	33.8%	35.1%	39.1%

	TOTAL BOOMERS	STRAIGHT ARROWS	DUE DILIGENTS	MAXIMIZERS	SIDELINERS	DISS/ CONTENTEDS	RE-ACTIVISTS
Becoming more physically active or more involved in sports	45.4%	30.0%	63.0%	63.6%	37.9%	35.0%	64.4%
Putting yourself first more often	45.0%	33.3%	58.9%	61.8%	44.8%	40.8%	46.2%
Working on behalf of human rights in society	44.8%	28.3%	59.5%	68.0%	7.5%	66.9%	85.7%
Doing more writing	44.2%	40.5%	48.0%	61.5%	27.2%	25.5%	65.7%
Finding the real you	43.3%	31.5%	73.3%	71.3%	24.9%	18.9%	58.7%
Having a quiet retirement	42.4%	43.4%	49.3%	51.0%	43.3%	32.7%	31.0%
Giving into your impulses more	41.0%	30.7%	51.1%	54.8%	34.1%	29.9%	57.6%
Becoming more involved with people and Web sites on the internet	40.8%	31.6%	55.3%	61.8%	23.8%	36.7%	54.9%
Avoiding big changes in your life	37.4%	35.4%	45.1%	45.5%	38.5%	35.6%	27.4%
Getting more involved with art	36.1%	22.4%	50.0%	55.7%	20.9%	25.0%	63.3%
Getting as disconnected from work as possible	36.1%	23.5%	40.4%	60.0%	39.1%	29.1%	35.3%
Creating things online	35.3%	28.0%	55.0%	48.7%	20.4%	27.1%	48.8%
Starting a new career	34.1%	23.1%	49.4%	55.0%	23.5%	12.3%	52.9%
Buying or building the home of your dreams	33.9%	25.7%	50.2%	62.3%	24.6%	11.8%	36.1%

	TOTAL BOOMERS	STRAIGHT ARROWS	DUE DILIGENTS	MAXIMIZERS	SIDELINERS	DISS/ CONTENTEDS	RE-ACTIVISTS
Settling down to a routine	33.2%	33.1%	46.7%	34.5%	32.1%	25.5%	28.9%
Learning another language	32.2%	20.1%	44.4%	59.3%	16.7%	13.5%	53.5%
Acting your age	32.0%	32.8%	34.2%	37.6%	31.0%	25.1%	28.1%
Starting your own company	25.3%	18.8%	37.3%	46.9%	16.0%	14.0%	28.3%
Creating more music	23.5%	16.6%	44.5%	40.4%	6.7%	21.7%	30.7%

Notes

Introduction

1. Allison Hope Weiner, "Yo, Rocky, Or Rambo, Gonna Fly Now at 60," *New York Times*, November 21, 2006.

2. Mary Elizabeth Hughes and Angela M. O'Rand, *The American People, Census 2000: The Lives and Times of Baby Boomers*, Population Reference Bureau (New York: Russell Sage Foundation, 2004).

3. U.S. Census Bureau, Historical Census of Housing Tables, *Census of Housing*, accessed at http://www.census.gov/hhes/www/housing/census/historic/owner.html on January 18, 2007.

4. James Patterson, *Grand Expectations: The United States, 1945–1974* (New York: Oxford University Press, 1996).

5. Dan Yankelovich interview, "The First Measured Century," PBS program hosted by Ben Wattenberg, transcript accessed at http://www.pbs.org/fmc/interviews/yankelovich.htm on January 12, 2007.

6. Jules Witcover, *The Year the Dream Died: Revisiting 1968 in America* (New York: Warner Books, 1998).

7. Robert D. Kaplan, "Looking the World in the Eye," *The Atlantic Monthly*, December 2001.

8. "American Experience: Jimmy Carter," PBS program produced by WGBH, transcript accessed at http://www.pbs.org/wgbh/amex/carter/peopleevents/e_malaise.html on January 18, 2007.

9. Eugene Cullen Kennedy, "Even in Religion, Boomers Call the Shots," *Atlanta-Journal Constitution*, Op-Ed, February 16, 2007.

Chapter 1

1. U.S. Census Bureau, *Statistical Abstract of the U.S.*, Table 12: Resident Population Projections by Age and Sex: 2005 to 2050, accessed at http://www.census.gov/prod/2005pubs/06statab/pop.pdf on February 18, 2007.

2. CNBC, "American Boomers Now a $2 Trillion Market," accessed at http://www.msnbc.msn.com/id/12288534/ on December 31, 2006.

3. Liz Szabo, "Cancer Burden Expected to Soar," *USA Today*, March 14, 2007.

4. Clese Erikson, Edward Salsberg, Gaetano Forte, Suanna Bruinooge, and Michael Goldstein, "Future Supply and Demand for Oncologists : Challenges to Assuring Access to Oncology Services," *Journal of Oncology Practice*, March 2007.

5. George Gaberlavage, *Beyond 50.04: A Report to the Nation on Consumers in the Marketplace: Executive Summary*, May 2004, accessed at http://www.aarp.org/research/reference/agingtrends/aresearch-import-861.html on February 18, 2007.

6. "Taking Stock of Baby Boomers," *Women's Wear Daily*, November 3, 2004.

7. David B. Wolfe and Robert Snyder, *Ageless Marketing: Strategies for Reaching the Hearts and Minds of the New Majority* (Chicago: Dearborn Trade Publishing, 2003).

8. Melinda Beck with Deborah Witherspoon, Donna Foote, Jody Brott, Jerry Buckley, Kim Rogal, and Joe Contreras, "The Baby Boomers Come of Age," *Newsweek*, March 30, 1981.

9. "Population: Babies Mean Business," *Newsweek*, August 9, 1948.

10. Kathleen Fackelmann, " 'Rough Time' Ahead for Boomers as They Age," *USA Today*, September 26, 2007.

11. American Pet Products Manufacturers Association, "Industry Statistics & Trends," n.d., accessed at http://www.appma.org/press_industrytrends.asp on February 20, 2007.

12. ReportBuyer.com, accessed at http://www.reportbuyer.com/consumer_goods_retail/pet_products/brand_building_u_s_pet_products_market.html on February 20, 2007.

13. Congressional Research Service, *Membership of the 109th Congress: A Profile*, November 19, 2006, accessed at http://www.senate.gov/reference/resources/pdf/RS22007.pdf on January 23, 2007.

14. Kelly Greene, "Golden Years—Marketing Surprise: Older Consumers Buy Stuff, Too," *Wall Street Journal*, April 6, 2004.

15. United States Government Accountability Office, *Report to Congressional Committees: Baby Boom Generation: Retirement of Boomers Is Unlikely to Precipitate Dramatic Decline in Market Returns, But Broader Risks Threaten Retirement Security*, GAO-06-718, July 2006.

16. Maxwell McCombs and Donald L. Shaw, "The Agenda Setting Function of the Mass Media," *Public Opinion Quarterly*, 1972 (vol. 73), pp. 176–187.

17. The Yankelovich MONITOR was begun in 1971 and is the longest-running, most highly regarded tracking of consumer value and lifestyle trends.

18. There are lots of claims on being the first to study and name Baby Boomers. The work at Yankelovich was the earliest, and Skelly has been recognized for being among the first to call this generation by the name Baby Boomers. See her obituary: Kenneth N. Gilpin, "Florence Skelly Altman, 73, Market Research Pioneer, Dies," *New York Times*, April 30, 1998.

19. Dan Yankelovich provides a comprehensive review of this early research in an interesting and informative speech he gave in May 1997 entitled "Lurch & Learn," accessed at http://www.danyankelovich.com/lurchandlearn.html on January 24, 2007.

20. "A Special Kind of Rebellion," *Fortune*, January 1968.

21. Columbia Broadcasting System, *Generations Apart*, a documentary broadcast in three parts on May 20, May 27, and June 3, 1969.

22. The first two are *Youth and the Establishment* (New York: JDR 3rd Fund, Inc., 1971) and *The Changing Values on Campus* (New York: Washington Square Press, 1973).

Chapter 2

1. CQ Transcripts Wire, "President Bush's State of the Union Address," January 31, 2006, accessed at http://www.washingtonpost.com/wpdyn/content/article/2006/01/31/AR2006013101468.html on July 16, 2006.

2. Landon Jones, "Swinging 60s?" *Smithsonian Magazine*, January 2006, accessed at http://www.smithsonianmagazine.com/issues/2006/january/presence.php on July 4, 2006.

3. Sheryl Gay Stolberg, "A Touchy Topic: Boomer in Chief Hits the Big 6–0," *New York Times*, July 6, 2006, national edition, p. A1; Johanna Neuman, "Bush, a Charter Member of the Boomer Generation, Prepares to Turn 60," *Los Angeles Times*, July 4, 2006, p. A-17; Jennifer Loven, "Bush Faces 60th Birthday with Wisecracks," Associated Press Online, July 1, 2006.

4. Shalanda Gordon, Carol Keegan, and Linda Fisher, *Boomers Turning 60*, National Member Research, Knowledge Management Group, AARP, June 2006, p. 1.

5. Kathleen O'Brien, "Young-at-Heart Boomers Put a New Face on 'Aging,'" *The Star-Ledger*, December 10, 2006, accessed at http://www.nj.com/news/ledger/index.ssf?/base/news-10/1165728976320830.xml&coll=1 on December 31, 2006.

6. Rob Stein, "Baby Boomers Less Healthy Than Parents?" *Washington Post*, April 20, 2007.

7. Rick Lyman, "Census Report Foresees No Crisis Over Aging Generation's Health," *New York Times*, March 10, 2006.

8. John W. Rowe and Robert L. Kahn, *Successful Aging* (New York: Pantheon, 1998).

9. Quoted in Leila Shotton, "The Role of Older People in Our Communities," *Nursing Ethics*, vol. 10, no. 1 (2003).

10. Rance Crain, "Boomer Boon: 'Crazy Aunts and Uncles' Spend $1.7 Trillion," *AdAge*, April 2, 2007.

11. Crain, ibid.

Chapter 3

1. Lifespan figures from www.infoplease.com, accessed at http://www.infoplease.com/ipa/A0005148.html and http://www.infoplease.com/ipa/A0005148.html on December 22, 2006. Workforce figures from Joanna Short, "Economic History of Retirement in the United States," E H.net Encyclopedia, accessed at http://eh.net/encyclopedia/article/short.retirement.history.us on December 4, 2006.

2. Federal Interagency Forum on Aging-Related Statistics, *Older Americans: Key Indicators of Well-Being*, Appendix A: Detailed Tables, Table 1B, accessed at http://www.aoa.gov/agingstats/tables%202001/tables-population.html on January 24, 2007.

3. Social Security Online, History, *1994–96 Advisory Council Report*, accessed at http://www.socialsecurity.gov/history/reports/adcouncil/report/table1d.htm on February 16, 2007; and Rick Montgomery, "U.S. Growing Older—At a Slower Rate," *Deseret News*, December 13, 2006.

4. Steve Lohr, "The Late, Great 'Golden Years,'" *New York Times*, March 6, 2005.

5. Frank Litsky, "Cowher Resigns, Not Retires, as Steelers' Coach," *New York Times*, January 6, 2007.

6. American Association of Retired People, *Staying Ahead of the Curve: The AARP Work and Career Study*, September 2002.

7. SeniorJournal.com, "Thirteen Million Baby Boomers Care for Ailing Parents, 25% Live with Parents," accessed at http://www.seniorjournal.com/NEWS/Boomers/5-10-19BoomersCare4Parents.htm on December 22, 2006.

8. MedicalNewsToday.com, "Baby Boomers Value Caring for Aging Parents More Than Earlier Generation," accessed at http://www.medicalnews

today.com/medicalnews.php?newsid=58056&nfid=rssfeeds on December 22, 2006.

9. American Association of Retired People, *Planning for Tomorrow's Talent Needs in Today's Competitive Environment*, a Report Prepared for AARP by Towers Perrin, December 2005, p. 20.

10. Towers Perrin HR Services, *Working Today: Understanding What Drives Employee Engagement*, The 2003 Towers Perrin Talent Report.

11. Associated Press, "Poll: Boomers May Delay Social Security," *Houston Chronicle*, January 3, 2007, accessed at http://www.chron.com/disp/story.mpl/ap/fn/4441893.html on January 4, 2007.

12. American Association for Retired Persons, "Boomers Envision Retirement II," May 2004.

13. Merrill Lynch, "'The New Retirement Survey' from Merrill Lynch Reveals How Baby Boomers Will Transform Retirement," press release, February 22, 2005, accessed at http://www.ml.com/index.asp?id=7695_7696_8149_46028_46503_46635 on July 9, 2006.

14. Referenced in National Tour Association Research and Development Council, *Current Assessment Report for the Baby Boomer Market*, January 2002.

15. Scott Reynolds, Neil Ridley, and Carl E. Van Horn, *A Work-Filled Retirement: Workers' Changing View on Employment and Leisure*, a publication of John J. Heldrich Center for Workforce Development, Edward J. Bloustein School of Planning and Public Policy, Rutgers University, August 2005.

16. National Commission on Social Security, *A Nationwide Survey of Attitudes Toward Social Security*, May 14, 1981, accessed through National Archives and Records Service, Record Group 220, Item No. 3-220-81-1, Records of Presidential Committees, Commissions and Boards.

17. Marc Reynolds, "The Selling of Retirement, and How We Bought It," *Washington Post*, February 6, 2005, accessed at http://www.civicventures.org/publications/articles/selling_of_retirement.cfm on February 21, 2007.

18. Stephen E. Snyder and William N. Evans, *The Impact of Income on Mortality: Evidence from the Social Security Notch*, September 21, 2004, accessed at http://www.bsos.umd.edu/econ/evans/wpapers/snyder_evans_notch.pdf on February 8, 2007.

19. Amy Joyce, "AARP Pitches for Older Workers," *Washington Post*, March 1, 2005, p. E03.

20. Federal Interagency Forum on Aging-Related Statistics, *Older Americans 2004: Key Indicators of Well-Being*, accessed at http://agingstats.gov/chartbook2004/economics.html#Indicator 11 on February 20, 2007.

21. Lohr, "The Late, Great 'Golden Years.'"

22. Elizabeth Olson, "Some Web Job Sites Put Out 'Gray Hair Welcome' Signs," *New York Times*, January 14, 2007.

23. Lohr, "The Late, Great 'Golden Years.'"

24. Paul Taylor, Cary Funk, and Peyton Craighill, *Working After Retirement: The Gap Between Expectations and Reality*, Pew Research Center, A Social Trends Report, 2006.

25. American Association of Retired People Knowledge Management Group National Member Research, "Boomers Turning 60," June 2006.

26. Christopher Conte, "Expert Exodus," Governing.com, February 2006, accessed at http://www.governing.com/articles/2know.htm on July 13, 2006.

27. Dave Lefkow, "The Future Labor Shortage," ere.net, August 23, 2005, accessed at http://www.ere.net/ARTICLES/DEFAULT.ASP?CID=%7B328A6F 88-8180-4CDD-A809-862FFEF5D565%7D on December 5, 2006.

28. Sidney Taurel, "The Future of Aging: The Consequences of the Biomedical Revolution," Speech to Town Hall Los Angeles, March 2, 2004, accessed at http://www.lilly.com/news/speeches/040302_speech_st_futureofaging.html on July 12, 2006.

29. Ernst & Young, LLP, "Putting It Off Until Tomorrow: Ernst & Young LLP Aging Workforce Survey Shows Corporate America Foresees a Looming Wisdom Withdrawal but Delays Addressing the Issue," press release, January 26, 2006, accessed at http://www.ey.com/global/Content.nsf/US/Media_-_Release_-_01-26-06DC on July 13, 2006.

30. Knowledge@Wharton, "What Labor Shortage? Debunking a Popular Myth," August 27, 2003, accessed at http://knowledge.wharton.upenn.edu/article.cfm?articleid=837 on December 5, 2006.

31. Lefkow, "The Future Labor Shortage."

32. Peter Francese, "Working Women," *American Demographics*, March 1, 2003.

33. Olson, "Some Web Job Sites"; and Laura Raines, "Companies Increasingly Value Experience, Dedication of Boomers," *Atlanta Journal-Constitution*, May 28, 2006.

34. Ibid.

35. Janis Hines and Laurel Kennedy, "How to Avoid the 'Big One,'" *NetAssets*, a newsletter published by HR Management Services, Inc., May 23, 2006, accessed at http://www.hrms-netassets.net/templates/template.asp?articleid =1809&zoneid=63 on July 9, 2006.

36. Martin Crutsinger, "Savings Rate at Lowest Since 1933," Associated Press, January 30, 2006; and Associated Press, "Savings Tumble Poses Risk to Boomers," *New York Times*, February 1, 2007.

37. Daniel Radner, "The Retirement Prospects of the Baby Boom Generation," *Social Security Bulletin*, Spring 1998.

38. John Gist, *Comparing Boomers' and Their Elders' Wealth at Midlife*, AARP Public Policy Institute Data Digest, September 2005.

39. Damon Darlin, "A Contrarian View: Save Less, Retire with Enough," *New York Times*, January 27, 2007.

40. Abraham Mosisa and Steven Hipple, "Trends in Labor Force Participation in the United States," *Monthly Labor Review*, October 2006.

41. Margot Hornblower, "Learning to Learn," *Time*, February 24, 1997; and U.S. Census Bureau, *The 2007 Statistical Abstract: The National Data Book*, Table 272.

42. Marilyn Moats Kennedy, "Are You Ready for Post-Retirement Life?" *Kennedy's Career Strategist*, June 2004, accessed at http://www.moatskennedy .com/newsletter_june04.html on March 10, 2007.

43. Ken Dychtwald and Sheila Forsberg, "Interview: 'Rehirement' Before Retirement," *WorldatWork Journal*, Fourth Quarter 2001, accessed at http://www .agewave.com/media_files/EJ10N4_1.pdf on March 11, 2007; and Ken Dychtwald, "Ageless Aging," *The Futurist*, July 1, 2005, accessed at http://209.85.165.104/ search?q=cache:DTKpJoR_1roJ:www.dychtwald.com/media_files/futurist.ht ml+%22ken+dychtwald%22+rehirement+%22age+wave%22+education&hl =en&ct=clnk&cd=13&gl=us&ie=UTF-8 on March 11, 2007.

44. Marcie Pitt-Catsouphes and Michael A. Smyer, *Older Workers: What Keeps Them Working?*, The Center on Aging & Work/Workplace Flexibility at Boston College, Issue Brief 01, July 18, 2005.

45. Deborah Parkinson, *Voices of Experience: Mature Workers in the Future Workforce*, The Conference Board report R-1319-02-RR, November 2002.

Chapter 4

1. For additional perspective on this topic, see chapters 4 and 10 of *Coming to Concurrence: Addressable Attitudes and the New Model for Marketing Productivity* (Chicago: Racom Communications, 2005), by J. Walker Smith, Ann Clurman, and Craig Wood.

2. Matthew Creamer, "A. G. Lafley Tells Marketers to Cede Control to Consumers to Be 'In Touch,'" AdAge.com, October 6, 2006.

3. Jim Stengel, "The Future of Marketing," Speech Presented to AAAA Media Conference, February 12, 2004.

4. *Time*, December 25, 2006.

5. Elizabeth M. Grieco and Rachel C. Cassidy, *Census 200 Brief: Overview of Race and Origin*, March 2001; and Rachel Swarms, "Hispanics Resist Racial Grouping by Census," *New York Times*, October 24, 2004.

6. Sam Roberts, "It's Official: To Be Married Means to Be Outnumbered," *New York Times*, October 15, 2006.

7. Leanne Abdnor, *Social Security Choices for the 21st Century Woman*,

CATO Project on Social Security Choice, SSP No. 33, February 24, 2004, accessed at http://www.cato.org/pubs/ssps/ssp33.pdf on April 2, 2007.

8. James Gleick, "The Way We Nest Now: When the House Starts Talking to Itself," *New York Times Magazine*, November 16, 2003.

9. Clint Eastwood, January 10, 2007 interview on *Fresh Air*, produced by WHYY, accessed at http://www.npr.org/templates/story/story.php?storyId =6781357 on January 24, 2007.

10. Stephen Dubner, "Choosing My Religion," *New York Times Magazine*, March 31, 1996.

11. Bill Bishop, "The Great Divide: Church, Political Beliefs Align; People Decide Where to Worship Based on the Congregation's Culture," *Austin American-Statesman*, July 25, 2004.

12. Damien Cave, "New York Plans to Make Gender Personal Choice," *New York Times*, November 7, 2006.

13. Damien Cave, "City Drops Plan to Change Definition of Gender," *New York Times*, December 6, 2006.

14. John Robinson, "The Irrelevance of Time," *College Park: The University of Maryland Magazine*, Fall 1999.

15. Mohanbir Sawhney, "Rethinking Marketing in a Connected World," January 2003, accessed at http://www.mohansawhney.com/registered/content /presentations/RethinkingMarketing.pdf on May 6, 2004.

16. Caren Osten Gerszberg, "At Your Request, A Bespoke Adventure," *New York Times*, June 24, 2005.

17. Fancesco Galli Zugaro, "Frequent Flier: A Professional Vacationer Goes on Safari," *New York Times*, July 18, 2006.

18. Wade Clark Roof, *A Generation of Seekers: The Spiritual Journeys of the Baby Boom Generation* (New York: HarperSanFrancisco, a division of Harper-Collins, 1993).

19. Many domesticated animals are described in terms of neoteny. The juvenile characteristics, or babyish looks, that make them so endearing persist for life. Human evolution is even thought to have benefited from neoteny. The human brain is much less developed at birth than the brains of other primates and thus takes longer to develop and mature relative to sexual maturation, a growth process said to confer adaptive advantages to humans.

20. B. G. Charlton, "The Rise of the Boy-Genius: Psychological Neoteny, Science and Modern Life," *Medical Hypotheses*, vol. 67 (2006).

21. Ron Alsop, "Is Earning an Executive M.B.A. Past 50 Worth It?" *Wall Street Journal*, March 27, 2007.

22. Jennifer Vlegas, "Serious Study: Immaturity Levels Rising," Discovery News, June 23, 2006, accessed at http://dsc.discovery.com/news/2006/06/23/ immature_hum.html?category=human on January 4, 2007.

Chapter 5

1. Elizabeth Pope, "Older, Wiser, Fitter," *Boston Globe Magazine*, April 16, 2006, p. 28.

2. Rebecca R. Kahlenberg, "Wellness Industry Is Looking Strong," *Washington Post*, March 5, 2006, p. K01; and Jack Kelly, "Personal Best," *Pittsburgh Post-Gazette*, June 14, 2006, p. C-2.

3. Duff Wilson, "Aging: Disease or Business Opportunity?" *New York Times*, April 15, 2007.

4. ABCnews.com, "Injuries Sending Boomers to Doctors in Droves," June 6, 2006, accessed at http://abcnews.go.com/GMA/Diet/story?id=2044217 on July 18, 2006.

5. Stephanie Smith, " 'Boomeritis': A Generation of Sports Injuries," CNN .com, accessed at http://www.cnn.com/2003/HEALTH/05/15/boomeritis/index.html on July 18, 2006.

6. Maggie Fox, "Drug Use Falls Except Among Older Adults," *MaconDaily .com*, September 7, 2006, accessed at http://maconareaonline.com/news .asp?id=15057 on September 7, 2006.

7. J. Walker Smith, *2004 Marketing Resistance Survey: A Yankelovich MONITOR® OmniPlus Study Topline Report*, April 15, 2004.

8. Charles Schewe, "How to Communicate with Older Adults," *American Demographics*, August 1991.

9. James Gorman, "The Altered Human Is Already Here," *New York Times*, April 6, 2004.

10. American Academy of Orthopaedic Surgeons, "Total Knee and Hip Replacement Surgery Projections Show Meteoric Rise by 2030," press release, March 24, 2006, accessed at http://www6.aaos.org/pemr/news/press_release .cfm?PRNumber=442 on July 19, 2006.

11. American Society for Aesthetic Plastic Surgery, press release, "11.5 Million Cosmetic Procedures in 2005," February 26, 2006, accessed at http://www .surgery.org/press/news-release.php?iid=429 on July 7, 2006. See also "Cosmetic Surgery Trends," accessed at http://www.surgery.org/download/2005 trends.pdf on July 7, 2006.

12. ABC News, "Great-Grandmother Gives Birth at 62," February 19, 2006, accessed at http://abcnews.go.com/GMA/Health/story?id=1637601&page=1 on July 7, 2006.

13. Denise Grady, "Second Drop in Cancer Deaths Could Point to a Trend, Researchers Say," *New York Times*, January 18, 2007.

14. Duke University News & Communication, "No Natural Limit to Life Expectancy, Says Duke Researcher," May 9, 2002, accessed at http://www.dukenews .duke.edu/2002/05/vaupelage0502.html on January 2, 2007.

15. The bumper sticker that reads "I may be fat but you're ugly and I can diet" will no longer be much of an insult in a world where both size and looks can be readily changed and perfected.

16. Ramez Naam, "Bulletproof," *Fast Company*, March 2006.

17. Melinda West Seifert, "Appearances Count—To the Point of Bias?" *Austin Business Chronicle*, July 20, 2001.

18. Ibid.

19. Eryn Brown, "Sometimes, Nips and Tucks Can Be Career Moves," *New York Times*, February 12, 2006, and Seifert, "Appearances Count."

20. American Society for Aesthetic Plastic Surgery, *Cosmetic Surgery Quick Facts: 2005 ASAPS Statistics*, accessed at http://www.surgery.org/press/procedurefacts-asqf.php on February 27, 2007.

21. Miranda Hitti, "Weight Loss Surgery Soars in U.S.," *WebMDHealth*, January 11, 2007, accessed at http://www.medscape.com/viewarticle/550685 on February 27, 2007.

22. Jacqueline Mitchell, "Baby Boomers Help Stoke the Demand for Cars Aimed at Youth," Detnews.com, March 9, 2005, accessed at http://www.detnews.com/2005/autosconsumer/0503/16/F01-111735.htm on July 14, 2006.

23. George P. Blumberg, "The Car Is for Kids, but Gramps Is Driving," *New York Times*, July 3, 2005.

24. Associated Press, "Baby Boomers Push RV Ownership to Record," *New York Times*, May 22, 2006.

25. Jennifer Alsever, "A Place to Park Your R.V. (Golf Privileges Included)," *New York Times*, April 16, 2006.

26. Robin Hindery, "You're Never Too Old for Dodgeball," ABCnews.com, February 19, 2006, accessed at http://abcnews.go.com/Health/wireStory?id=1638246 on July 14, 2006.

27. Dierdre Donahue, " '*Rejuvenile*' Toys with the Idea of Adulthood," *USA Today*, June 20, 2006, p. 1D.

28. Entertainment Software Association, *2006 Sales, Demographic and Usage Data*, 2006, p. 2.

29. Chris Morris, "Whither the Gray Gamer?" *CNN/Money.com*, February 10, 2006, accessed at http://money.cnn.com/2006/02/09/commentary/game_over/column_gaming/index.htm on July 14, 2006.

30. Jack Cox, "Barbie Embraces Her Inner Sexpot," *Denver Post*, May 15, 2006, p. F-01.

31. Mattel, "Top Fashion Designers Partner with Barbie™ Brand to Launch Adult Collection Barbie™ Luxe," press release, October 18, 2005, accessed at http://www.shareholder.com/mattel/news/20051018-176951.cfm on July 14, 2006.

32. Wikipedia.com, "AFOL," accessed at http://en.wikipedia.org/wiki/AFOL on July 15, 2006.

33. Scott Craven, "Lego Fans Have Chance to Turn Passion into Job," *The Arizona Republic*, March 16, 2006, accessed at http://www.azcentral.com/arizonarepublic/arizonaliving/articles/0316lego0316.html on July 15, 2006.

34. Jeff Leeds, "Uncool but True: The AARP Demographic Leads the Music Market. But Who Will Lead It?" *New York Times*, November 26, 2006, Section 2, pp. 1, 22.

35. Stephen Farber, "Hollywood Awakens to the Geriatric Demographic," *New York Times*, July 2, 2006.

36. David Bauder, "Study: TV's Youth Obsession Backfiring," WashingtonPost.com, November 19, 2006, accessed at http://www.washingtonpost.com/wp-dyn/content/article/2006/11/19/AR2006111900359.html on December 7, 2006.

37. Brent Herrington, "Baby Boomers: Home, Neighborhood, Community," Presentation at PCBC Vision of Home Breakfast, June 18, 2004.

38. "Boomers Wanted," *The Post and Courier* (Charleston, S.C.), July 7, 2006.

39. Alan Finder, "Rural Colleges Going Urban to Stay Vital," *New York Times*, February 7, 2007.

40. Traci Purdum, "The Age of Design," *Industry Week*, August 1, 2002.

41. Keith Bradsher, "As U.S. Buyers Age, Designers of Autos Make Subtle Shifts," *New York Times*, March 1, 1999.

42. Wikipedia entry on "Universal Design," accessed at http://en.wikipedia.org/wiki/Universal_design on March 13, 2007.

43. Teri Agins, "Reshaping Boomer Fashion," *Wall Street Journal*, April 15, 2005.

44. Freedonia Group, "U.S. Demand to Grow 11% Annually Through 2008," online brochure for *Cosmeceuticals to 2008*, November 1, 2004, accessed at http://www.freedoniagroup.com/pdf/1872smwe.pdf on February 25, 2007.

45. Packaged Facts, *Market Trends: The U.S. Cosmeceuticals and Anti-Aging Products Market*, January 1, 2005, Table of Contents Summary, accessed at http://www.packagedfacts.com/prod-toc/ Trends-Cosmeceuticals-Anti-1037623/ on February 25, 2007.

46. Anne D'Innocenzio, "Revlon Wants to Be the New 50," *The Raleigh News & Observer*, April 15, 2006, accessed at http://www.newsobserver.com/104/story/428925.html on February 25, 2007.

47. Anne D'Innocenzio, "Revlon's Vital Leads Charge into New Territory: Over-50 Crowd," *The Honolulu Advertiser*, April 16, 2006, accessed at http://the.honoluluadvertiser.com/article/2006/Apr/16/bz/FP604160315.html on February 25, 2007.

48. Liesi E. Hebert, Paul A. Scherr, Julia L. Bienas, David A. Bennett, and Denis A. Evans, "Alzheimer Disease in the U.S. Population," *Archives of Neurology*, August 2003.

49. Joe Verghese, Richard B. Lipton, Mindy J. Katz, Charles B. Hall, Carol A. Derby, Gail Kuslansky, Anne F. Ambrose, Martin Sliwinski, and Herman Buschke, "Leisure Activites and the Risk of Dementia in the Elderly," *The New England Journal of Medicine*, June 19, 2003.

50. Institute of Medicine of the National Academies, online summary of report entitled *Dietary Supplements: A Framework for Evaluating Safety*, April 1, 2004, accessed at http://www.iom.edu/CMS/3788/4605/19578.aspx on February 27, 2007.

51. Agriculture and Agri-Food Canada, *Functional Foods and Nutraceuticals, Annex C—World Market Data on Functional Food Sales*, n.d., accessed at http://www.agr.gc.ca/misb/fb-ba/nutra/index_e.php?s1=bmi&page=annexc on February 27, 2007.

52. Stephanie Thompson, "Dark Chocolate Sales Soar 40%," *AdAge*, August 27, 2006.

53. Jennifer Barrett, "The 100-Calorie Snack Attack," *Newsweek*, August 14, 2006.

54. A. Elizabeth Sloan, "Bringing Back Boomers," *Flavor & the Menu*, Spring 2006.

55. Andrew B. Geier, Paul Rozin, and Gheorghe Doros, "Unit Bias: A New Heuristic That Helps Explain the Effect of Portion Size on Food Intake," *Psychological Science*, June 2006.

56. Bharat Book Bureau, online summary of *In Vitro Diagnostics to 2009—Market Size, Market Share, Market Leaders, Demand Forecast, Sales, Company Profiles, Market Research, Industry Trends*, 2005, accessed at http://www.bharatbook.com/bookdetail.asp?bookid=8047&publisher= on March 1, 2007.

57. Parks Associates, "Revenues from Digital Home Health Services to Top $2.1 Billion in 2010," press release, March 2, 2006, accessed at http://www.parksassociates.com/press/press_releases/2006/health_pr2.html on March 3, 2007.

58. Institute for the Future, *2006 Map of the Decade*, accessed at http://www.iftf.org/features/map_of_the_decade.html on March 3, 2007.

59. Parija Bhatnagar, "Baby Boomers: Do-It-For-Me Generation," CNNMoney.com, May 11, 2005, accessed at http://money.cnn.com/2005/05/11/news/fortune500/boomers_difm/ on March 1, 2007.

60. Parija Bhatnagar, "Best Buy's 'Geek Squad' to the Rescue," CNNMoney.com, June 16, 2004, accessed at http://money.cnn.com/2004/06/16/news/fortune500/best_buy/ on March 1, 2007.

61. University of Phoenix, "Facts About the University of Phoenix," n.d., accessed at http://phoenix.edu/about_us/the_facts/the_facts.aspx on March 1, 2007.

62. Alex Wright, "From Ivory Tower to Academic Sweatshop," Salon.com, January 26, 2005, accessed at http://dir.salon.com/story/tech/feature/2005/01/26/distance_learning/index.html on March 1, 2007.

63. Harry H. Brakeley and Jeanne C. Meister, "Greater Expectations: How Corporate Education Can Boost Company Performance," *Outlook*, February 2005, accessed at http://www.accenture.com/Global/Research_and_Insights/Outlook/By_Issue/Y2005/ToAdvantage.htm on March 1, 2007.

64. Brian Kelley, "Online Corporate Education and Online Training: What's the Difference?" *HR Management*, April 2006.

65. Patricia Leigh Brown, "Growing Old Together, in a New Kind of Commune," *New York Times*, February 27, 2006.

66. The Elder Cohousing Network, Home Page, accessed at http://www.abrahampaiss.com/ElderCohousing/index.htm on March 3, 2007.

67. Andrew Jacobs, "Extreme Makeover, Commune Edition," *New York Times*, June 11, 2006.

68. Patricia Leigh Brown, "Retirees Discover a Place to Foster Their Inner Artist," *New York Times*, September 19, 2006.

69. Barbara A. Ormond, Kirsten J. Black, Jane Tilly, and Seema Thomas, *Support Services Programs in Naturally Occurring Retirement Communities*, U.S. Department of Health and Human Services, November 2004, accessed at http://aspe.hhs.gov/daltcp/Reports/NORCssp.htm#findings on March 3, 2007.

70. Perry Garfinkel, "Easing the Inward Journey, with Modern Amenities," *New York Times*, December 24, 2006.

71. Scott Goetz, "Wanderluxe: Extreme Adventure Meets High Luxury," *Elite Traveler*, May 2006.

Chapter 6

1. A. O. Scott, "In Search of the Best," *New York Times Book Review*, May 21, 2006.

2. Quoted in Ed McClanahan, editor, "The Day the Lampshades Breathed," *Spit in the Ocean #7: All About Ken Kesey* (New York: Penguin Books, 2003).

3. See the photo at http://www.snopes.com/photos/people/microsoft.asp, accessed on December 14, 2006.

4. Stewart Brand, "We Owe It All to the Hippies," *Time*, Special Issue, Spring 1995, accessed at http://technohippie.com/archives/stewartbrand.html on December 14, 2006.

5. Sharon Waxman, "The Graying of Naughty," *New York Times*, December 31, 2006.

6. See the articles published in the 2004 series *The Great Divide* in the *Austin American-Statesman* on April 4, April 8, May 2, May 30, July 25, and December 4 by Bill Bishop. These particular statistics come from the articles published on April 4, "The Schism in U.S. Politics Begins at Home"; and December 4, "An Utterly Polarizing U.S. Election."

7. The Pew Center for People and the Press, *Broad Support for Political Compromise in Washington*, January 22, 2007, accessed at http://people-press.org/reports/pdf/302.pdf on January 23, 2007.

8. Thanks to Bill Bishop for noting this.

9. Patrick J. Buchanan, "1992 Republican National Convention Speech," August 17, 1992, accessed at http://www.buchanan.org/pa-92-0817-rnc.html on January 28, 2007.

10. Carol Hanisch, "The Personal Is Political," dated February 1969 as published in *Notes from the Second Year: Women's Liberation* (New York: Radical Feminism, 1970), Shulamith Firestone and Anne Koedt, eds., accessed at http://scholar.alexanderstreet.com/download/attachments/2259/Personal+Is+Pol.pdf?version=1 on January 28, 2007.

11. Peter Wallsten and Tom Hamburger, "The GOP Knows You Don't Like Anchovies," *Los Angeles Times*, June 25, 2006.

12. Thomas B. Edsall, "Democrats' Data Mining Stirs an Intraparty Debate," *Washington Post*, March 8, 2006; and Dan Balz, "Democrats Aim to Regain Edge in Getting Voters to the Polls," *Washington Post*, October 8, 2006.

13. Spotlight Analysis is a client of Yankelovich.

14. Milton Friedman, "The Social Responsibility of Business Is to Increase Its Profits," *New York Times Magazine*, September 13, 1970.

15. Richard Todd, "The Green 50: The Industrialist," *Inc. Magazine*, November 2006.

16. From http://www.firmsofendearment.com, accessed on January 29, 2007.

17. For additional perspective on this topic, see chapter 3 of *Coming to Concurrence: Addressable Attitudes and the New Model for Marketing Productivity* (Chicago: Racom Communications, 2005), by J. Walker Smith, Ann Clurman, and Craig Wood.

18. Ronald Inglehart, *Modernization and Postmodernization: Cultural, Economic, and Political Change in Societies* (Princeton, N.J.: Princeton University Press: 1997).

19. Ed Kerschner, "The All American Shopping List," UBS Warburg, April 1, 2001. This report and these themes in particular were developed in large part from data and analysis in the Yankelovich MONITOR.

Chapter 7

1. USA Today On Deadline, "FAA: Pilots Should Be Able to Retire at 65, Not 60," January 30, 2007, accessed at http://blogs.usatoday.com/ondeadline/travel/index.html on March 28, 2007.

2. Rob Stein, "Scientists Finding Out What Losing Sleep Does to the Body," *Washington Post*, October 9, 2005.

3. Robert D. Peters, Esther Wagner, Elizabeth Alicandri, Jean E. Fox, Maria L. Thomas, David R. Thorne, Helen C. Sing, and Sharon M. Balwinski, "Effects of Partial and Total Sleep Deprivation on Driving Performance," *Public Roads*, January/February 1999.

4. NCSDR/NHTSA Expert Panel on Driver Fatigue and Sleepiness, *Drowsy Driving and Automobile Crashes*, n.d., accessed at http://www.nhtsa.dot.gov/people/injury/drowsy_driving1/drowsy.html on March 28, 2007.

5. Laura Petrecca, "We Should Be Feeling Very Sleepy, Considering Flood of Sleep Aids," *USA Today*, March 12, 2007; and Melinda Fulmer, "The Price of a Good Night's Sleep," MSN.com, Money, n.d., accessed at http://moneycentral.msn.com/content/Savinganddebt/Savemoney/P150429.asp on March 28, 2007.

6. Associated Press, "Sleepy Boomers Fluffing Up Mattress Sales," MSNBC.com, March 8, 2007, accessed at http://www.msnbc.msn.com/id/17518809/ on March 28, 2007.

7. Allison Van Dusen, "Boomers' Biggest Health Mistakes," Forbes.com, January 19, 2007, accessed at http://www.forbes.com/2007/01/18/boomer-health-mistakes-forbeslife-cx_avd_0119boomermistakes.html on January 30, 2007.

8. Rick Lyman, "Census Report Foresees No Crisis Over Aging Generation's Health," *New York Times*, March 10, 2006, quoting Richard Suzman, head of the Behavioral and Social Research Program for the National Institute on Aging.

9. David Leonhardt, "What's a Pound of Prevention Really Worth?" *New York Times*, January 24, 2007.

10. William J. Holstein and Mike Tharp, "Boomers, Start Your Engines," *U.S. News & World Report*, June 26, 2000.

11. Helene Stapinski, "Let's Talk Dirty: We Won't Clean, Don't Ask Us," *American Demographics*, November 1998.

12. Krysten Crawford, "Medical Tourism Agencies Take Operations Overseas," *Business 2.0 Magazine*, August 3, 2006, accessed at http://money.cnn.com/2006/08/02/magazines/business2/medicaltourism.biz2/index.htm on March 12, 2007.

13. Amelia Gentleman, "Controversy in India Over Medical Tourism," *International Herald Tribune*, December 2, 2005.

14. Arnold Milstein and Mark Smith, "America's New Refugees—Seeking Affordable Surgery Offshore," *New England Journal of Medicine*, October 19, 2006.

15. Oxford Analytica, "'Medical Tourism' Industry Grows Rapidly," Forbes .com, October 26, 2006, accessed at http://www.forbes.com/business/2006/10/25/health-medical-tourism-biz-cx_1026oxford.html on March 12, 2007.

16. Ichiro Kawachi, Bruce P. Kennedy, and Kimberly Lochner, "Long Live Community: Social Capital as Public Health," *The American Prospect*, No. 35 (November/December 1997).

17. Richard G. Wilkinson, *Unhealthy Societies: The Afflictions of Inequality* (London: Routledge, 1996).

18. The New Standard, "Health Care Costs Main Cause of Personal Bankruptcy, Study Finds," February 4, 2005, accessed at http://newstandardnews .net/content/?action=show_item&itemid=1439 on February 8, 2007. See also National Coalition on Health Care, "Health Insurance Cost," accessed at http://www.nchc.org/facts/cost.shtml on February 8, 2007.

19. For a good introductory overview of these alternative approaches, see Malcolm Gladwell, "The Moral Hazard Myth," *The New Yorker*, August 29, 2005.

Chapter 8

1. For a discussion of the role of 9/11 with respect to these trends, see J. Walker Smith, "Trying to Get Back to Business as Usual in Trying Times," September 26, 2001, available upon request from Yankelovich, Inc.

2. Anabel Quan-Hase and Barry Wellman, "How Does the Internet Affect Social Capital," Draft 4, dated November 12, 2002. See also Jeffrey Boase, John B. Horrigan, Barry Wellman, and Lee Rainie, "The Strength of Internet Ties," Pew Internet & American Life Project, January 25, 2006. Both sources accessed at http://www.chass.utoronto.ca/~wellman/publications/index.html on February 6, 2007.

3. See Robert Cialdini, *Influence: Science and Practice* (New York: Allyn & Bacon, 2000).

4. J. Walker Smith, "100-Point Type: Imagining the Banner Headlines of Tomorrow's Newspaper," Keynote Speech for CEOs for Cities National Meeting, December 1, 2005.

5. Lisa Berkman and Lester Breslow, *Health and Ways of Living: The Alameda County Study* (New York: Oxford University Press, 1983).

6. Stephanie Brown, Randolph Nesse, Amiram Vinokur, and Dylan Smith, "Providing Social Support May Be More Beneficial Than Receiving It: Results from a Prospective Study of Mortality," *Psychological Science*, no. 14 (2003).

7. Tejac Advertising, press release, "The Over-45 Generation," May 24, 2004, accessed at http://www.tejacadv.com/TEJAC_business_presence/press-releases/pressrel_2.htm on February 6, 2007; and KGRR.FM Broadcast Transcript, n.d., accessed at http://www.kgrr.com/broadcasts.cfm on February 6, 2007.

Chapter 9

1. Michael Luo and Laurie Goodstein, "Emphasis Shifts for New Breed of Evangelicals," *New York Times*, May 21, 2007.

2. Barrie McKenna, "The Prophet Motive: U.S. Faithful Form Rich Market," GlobeandMail.com, September 25, 2006, accessed at http://www.theglobe andmail.com/servlet/story/LAC.20060925.RFAITH25/TPStory/Business on February 10, 2007.

3. Chris Bagley, "The Reason for the Season: Companies Aim Christian Toys at the Mainstream," *The Californian*, an edition of the *North County Times*, December 23, 2006, accessed at http://www.nctimes.com/articles/2006/12/24/news/californian/21_16_1712_23_06.txt on February 10, 2007.

4. Troy Lyndon, "The New God Game," BusinessWeek.com, December 1, 2006, accessed at http://www.businessweek.com/innovate/content/dec2006/id20061201_680266.htm?chan=innovation_game+room_industry+trends on February 10, 2007.

5. McKenna, "The Prophet Motive."

6. National Center for Education Statistics, "1.1 Million Homeschooled Students in the United States in 2003," n.d., Figure 2, accessed at http://nces.ed.gov/nhes/homeschool/figures.asp?PopUp=true&FigureNumber=fig02 on February 10, 2007.

7. David Brooks featured this Yankelovich idea of the "affluent attitude" as one of the most important yet underrated ideas of 2002. See David Brooks, "On Target and Off; . . . and In With the Underrated," *New York Times*, December 28, 2002.

8. Camille Sweeney, "The Middle of the Middle Class," *New York Times Magazine*, June 9, 2002.

9. Matt Higgins, "Surf's Upscale as Sport Reverses Beach Bum Image," *New York Times*, February 11, 2007.

10. Emily Fredrix, "Generation Lets Luxury Flow in Bath," *Chicago Tribune*, January 25, 2007.

11. Will Wade, "A Good Corporate Citizen? This Scanner Can Tell," *New York Times*, August 28, 2003.

12. Jerry Adler, "Going Green," *Newsweek*, July 17, 2006.

13. Susan Llewelyn Leach, "Travelers Who Strive to Do No Harm," *Christian Science Monitor*, December 22, 2004.

Chapter 10

1. Anne Fisher, "Break All the Rules," *Fortune*, July 2005.

2. Wikipedia.com, "Richard Stallman," accessed at http://en.wikipedia .org/wiki/Richard_Stallman on July 12, 2006.

3. Jeremy Andrews, "Interview: Richard Stallman," Kerneltrap.org, January 4, 2005, accessed at http://kerneltrap.org/node/4484 on July 12, 2006.

4. Wikipedia.com, "Eric S. Raymond," accessed at http://en.wikipedia.org/ wiki/Eric_S._Raymond on July 12, 2006.

5. Wikipedia.com, "Open Source," accessed at http://en.wikipedia.org/ wiki/Open_source on July 12, 2006.

6. Kenbyte's blog, "Iterative Media: Treating Collaborative Media Like Open Source Code," Echochamberproject.com, accessed at http://www .echochamberproject.com/node/798#iterativemedia on July 23, 2006.

7. Tim O'Reilly, "What Is Web 2.0," September 20, 2005, accessed at http:// www.oreillynet.com/pub/a/oreilly/tim/news/2005/09/30/what-is-web-20 .html on July 23, 2006.

8. Natalie Angier, "Slow Is Beautiful," *New York Times*, December 12, 2006.

Index

About the Authors

J. Walker Smith

J. Walker Smith, Ph.D., is president of Yankelovich, Inc. He is co-author of *Rocking the Ages: The Yankelovich Report on Generational Marketing* (New York: HarperBusiness, 1997), a highly regarded assessment of generational marketing strategies; *Life Is Not Work, Work Is Not Life: Simple Reminders for Finding Balance in a 24/7 World* (Berkeley, Calif.: Wildcat Canyon Press, 2001), a collection of short essays and personal reflections on work/life balance picked by the *Wall Street Journal* as one of the ten best work-life books of 2001; and *Coming to Concurrence: Addressable Attitudes and the New Model for Marketing Productivity* (Chicago: Racom Communications, 2005). Described by *Fortune* magazine as "one of America's leading analysts on consumer trends," Walker is a much sought-after speaker and authority on social trends in America whose quotable insights appear regularly in the national media and business press. He does a weekly commentary called "City Views" for *Smart City*, a public radio show about cities and community life, as well as regular columns in *Restaurants & Institutions*, *Marketing Management*, and *Media* magazines. Walker's insights have been prominently featured and profiled in many publications, including *American Demographics*, which had a cover story about him in May 1998.

Prior to Yankelovich, Walker was director of research for DowBrands, Inc. He was a summer lecturer at the annual School of Marketing Research at the University of Notre Dame for fourteen years and is a past vice president of the marketing research division of the American Marketing Association. Walker is a director of Premiere Global Services, a member of the Board of Advisors for the School of Journalism and Mass Communications at the University of North Carolina at Chapel Hill, and a director of the American Marketing Association Foundation. He holds three degrees from the University of North Carolina at Chapel Hill, including a doctorate in Mass Communication. He was the commencement speaker for the U.N.C.–Chapel Hill 2005 Graduate School Doctoral Hooding Ceremony. Walker and his wife, Joy, live in Atlanta, Georgia.

Ann Clurman

Ann Clurman is senior partner at Yankelovich, Inc. Her primary responsibilities are focused on the Yankelovich MONITOR®, the firm's unparalleled study of consumer attitudes that forecasts lifestyles and behaviors. She has in-depth experience translating MONITOR research into growth opportunities for a wide range of client industries, including personal care, health, retail, telecommunications, advertising, and media. Described by *U.S. News and World Report* magazine as "one of the best researchers and generation-watchers," Ann is a nationally recognized authority and lecturer on American consumers. A knowledgeable and spirited speaker, she speaks before diverse client, industry, and government groups and is often quoted in the media. She is the co-author of two acclaimed and ground-breaking books, *Rocking the Ages, The Yankelovich Report on Generational Marketing* (New York: HarperBusiness, 1997) and *Coming to Concurrence: Addressable Attitudes and the New Model for Marketing Productivity* (Chicago: Racom Communications, 2005).

Ann holds a bachelor's degree with Phi Beta Kappa honors from New York University and a master's degree from Brown University. She resides in New York City.